Conversations with Robert Penn Warren

Literary Conversations Series

Peggy Whitman Prenshaw
General Editor

D1252011

Photo credit: © 2005 Nancy Crampton

Conversations with Robert Penn Warren

Edited by
Gloria L. Cronin and Ben Siegel

University Press of Mississippi
Jackson

www.upress.state.ms.us

The University Press of Mississippi is a member of the Association of American University Presses.

Copyright © 2005 by University Press of Mississippi
All rights reserved
Manufactured in the United States of America

13 12 11 10 09 08 07 06 05   4 3 2 1

∞

Library of Congress Cataloging-in-Publication Data

Conversations with Robert Penn Warren / edited by Gloria L. Cronin and Ben Siegel.
   p. cm. — (Literary conversations series)
Includes index.
ISBN 1-57806-733-2 (cloth : alk. paper)—ISBN 1-57806-734-0 (pbk. : alk. paper)
   1. Warren, Robert Penn, 1905– —Interviews. 2. Authors, American—20th century—
Interviews. 3. Southern States—Intellectual life—1865–. I. Cronin, Gloria L., 1947–.
II. Siegel, Ben, 1925– . III. Series.

   PS3545.A748Z656   2005
   813'.52—dc22   2004053642

British Library Cataloging-in-Publication Data available

Books by Robert Penn Warren

Novels

Night Rider. Houghton, 1939.

At Heaven's Gate. Harcourt, 1943.

All the King's Men. Harcourt, 1946.

World Enough and Time: A Romantic Novel. Random House, 1950.

Band of Angels. Random House, 1955.

The Cave. Random House, 1959.

Wilderness: A Tale of the Civil War. Random House, 1961.

Flood: A Romance of Our Time. Random House, 1964.

Meet Me in the Green Glen. Random House, 1971.

A Place to Come To. Random House, 1977.

Poetry

Thirty-six Poems. Alcestis Press, 1936.

Eleven Poems on the Same Theme. New Directions, 1942.

Selected Poems: 1923–1943. Harcourt, 1944.

Brother to Dragons: A Tale in Verse and Voices. Random House, 1953.

To A Little Girl, One Year Old, In a Ruined Fortress, illustrated by Jane Daggett.
    Yale University, 1956.

Promises: Poems 1954–1956. Random House, 1957.

You, Emperors, and Others: Poems 1957–1960. Random House, 1960.

Selected Poems: New and Old, 1923–1966. Random House, 1966.

Incarnations: Poems 1966–1968. Random House, 1968.

Audubon: A Vision. Random House, 1969.

Or Else: Poem/Poems 1968–1974. Random House, 1974.

Selected Poems: 1923–1976. Random House, 1977.

Now and Then: Poems 1976–1978. Random House, 1978.

Being Here: Poetry 1977–1980. Random House, 1980.

Rumor Verified: Poems 1979–1980. Random House, 1981.

Have You Ever Eaten Stars?: Poems 1979–1980. Random House, 1981.

*Chief Joseph of the Nez Perce, who called themselves the Nimipu, "the real people":
    a poem*. Random House, 1983.

New & Selected Poems: 1923–1985. Random House, 1985.

The Collected Poems of Robert Penn Warren. Edited by John Burt. Louisiana
   State University Press, 1998.

Selected Poems of Robert Penn Warren. Edited by John Burt. Louisiana State
   University Press, 2001.

Short stories

The Circus in the Attic and Other Stories. Harcourt, 1947.

Blackberry Winter. Cummington Press, 1946.

Novellas

Prime Leaf. American Caravan IV, 1931.

Literary criticism

Understanding Poetry: An Anthology for College Students, with Cleanth
   Brooks. Holt, 1938.

Understanding Fiction, with Cleanth Brooks. Crofts, 1943.

Fundamentals of Good Writing–A Handbook of Modern Rhetoric, with Cleanth
   Brooks. Harcourt, 1950.

A Plea in Mitigation: Modern Poetry and the End of an Era. Wesleyan
   College, 1966.

American Literature: The Makers and the Making, with Cleanth Brooks and
   R. W. B. Lewis. St. Martin's, 1974.

Cleanth Brooks and Robert Penn Warren: A Literary Correspondance. Edited by
   James A. Grimshaw. University of Missouri Press, 1998.

Children's books

Remember the Alamo. Random House, 1958.

The Gods of Mount Olympus, Random House, 1959.

*How Texas Won Her Freedom: The Story of Sam Houston and the Battle of
   San Jacinto.* San Jacinto Museum of History, 1959.

Plays

All the King's Men: A Play. Random House, 1960.

Essays

I'll Take My Stand, The South, and the Agrarian Tradition. Harper, 1930.

Selected Essays. Random House, 1958.

A Time to Hear and Answer: Essays for the Bicentennial Season. University of
Alabama Press, 1976.

Portrait of a Father. University Press of Kentucky, 1988.

Jefferson Davis Gets His Citizenship Back. University Press of Kentucky, 1980.

New and Selected Essays. Random House, 1989.

Historical works

Segregation: The Inner Conflict in the South. Random House, 1956.

The Legacy of the Civil War: Meditations on the Centennial. Random
House, 1961.

Who Speaks for the Negro. Random House, 1965.

Biography

John Brown: The Making of a Martyr, Payson & Clarke. 1929.

As editor

A Southern Harvest: Short Stories by Southern Writers. Houghton
Mifflin, 1937.

An Approach to Literature: A Collection of Prose and Verse, with Cleanth
Brooks. F. S. Crofts and Company, 1939.

An Anthology of Stories from the Southern Review, with Cleanth Brooks.
Louisiana State University Press, 1953.

Short Story Masterpieces, with Albert Erskine. Dell Books, 1954.

Six Centuries of Great Poetry: From Chaucer to Yeats, with Albert Erskine. Dell
Publishing Company, 1955.

A New Southern Harvest: An Anthology, with Albert Erskine. Bantam
Books, 1957.

The Scope of Fiction, with Cleanth Brooks. Appleton-Century-Crofts, 1965.

Selected Poems by Dennis Devlin, with Allen Tate. Holt, Rinehart, and
Winston, 1963.

Faulkner: A Collection of Critical Essays. Prentice Hall, 1966.

Randall Jarrell, 1914–1965, with Robert Lowell and Peter Taylor. Farrar, Straus and
Giroux, 1967.

Selected Poems of Herman Melville: A Reader's Edition. Random House, 1970.

John Greenleaf Whittier's Poetry: An Appraisal and a Selection. University of
   Minnesota Press, 1971.
Homage to Theodore Dreiser, On the Centennial of His Birth. Random
   House, 1971.
Katherine Anne Porter: A Collection of Critical Essays. Prentice-Hall, 1979.
The Essential Melville. Ecco Press, 1987.

Other

William Faulkner and His South. Schools of English University of Virginia, 1951.
A Robert Penn Warren Reader. Random House, 1987.
Selected Letters of Robert Penn Warren: The Apprentice Years, 1924–1934.
   Edited by William Bedford Clark. Louisiana State University Press, 2000.
Selected Letters of Robert Penn Warren: The Southern Review *Years, 1935–1942.*
   Edited by William Bedford Clark. Louisiana State University Press, 2001.

Contents

Introduction

For several decades following World War II, the most admired and respected literary figure in academe was Robert Penn Warren. Those were exciting years for American letters. Saul Bellow, Norman Mailer, Bernard Malamud, Philip Roth, Ralph Ellison, James Baldwin, John Updike, Thomas Pynchon, William Styron, and Flannery O'Connor, among others, were publishing the early novels and short stories that established their reputations. John Crowe Ransom, Robert Lowell, Randall Jarrell, Theodore Roethke, John Berryman, Richard Wilbur, and Denise Levertov were among those doing the same with their poetry. But no writer other than Warren was by critical and academic consensus recognized as a major novelist and poet, as well as a major critic and innovative teacher.

In 1986 Warren was appointed the first Poet Laureate of the United States. He was the only writer to have received three Pulitzer Prizes—and for both fiction and poetry. He also won, for his poetry, a National Book Award, the Bollingen Prize, the National Medal for Literature, and the National Humanities Foundation's Thomas Jefferson Award. His writings about literature and his literary criticism placed him in the top rank of the twentieth century's most influential critics. Best known for his novel *All the King's Men*, Warren published ten other novels, fifteen volumes of poetry, two plays, a biography of John Brown, and numerous books and essays on cultural and literary criticism. In addition, he edited—with Cleanth Brooks—three anthologies (*Understanding Poetry, Understanding Fiction,* and *Modern Rhetoric*) that literally changed the way literature was taught in the university classroom.

While Warren awaited acceptance to the U.S. Naval Academy during the summer of 1920, a stone thrown carelessly by his younger brother, Thomas, cost him the vision in one eye. His potential naval career was gone, but all was hardly lost. Young Robert had very early developed a taste for nature and for reading, especially fiction and history. His arrival at Vanderbilt University in 1921 coincided with a gathering of talented writers in Nashville. These young men were drawn together by an interest in writing poetry and discussing philosophy, as well as nurturing a nostalgia for the culture of the agrarian South. Although they seem never to have aspired to be an intellectual movement, they have been linked since by the title of the magazine they published, *The Fugitive*. Warren's older classmate, Allen Tate, and one of his teachers, John Crowe Ransom, were at the beginnings of their distinguished literary careers. Indeed, his teachers, especially Ransom and Donald Davidson, quickly recognized Warren's writing ability. Prominent among the Fugitives, they exerted a strong influence upon the impressionable newcomer and found a place in their magazine for his first efforts at verse. He also became involved in the campus debates about the South's role in a rapidly industrializing America, and about literature's function and role in a modern society. These subjects, as his interviews make clear, figure prominently in both his fiction and nonfiction. By the time he graduated (*summa cum laude*) from Vanderbilt in 1925, "Red" Warren had decided on a writing career.

But he had also set his sights on an academic career to support his literary ambitions, as had his Vanderbilt mentors. Earning his master's in English at the University of California, Berkeley, Warren headed briefly for doctoral studies at Yale, and then to Oxford as a Rhodes Scholar. At twenty-five, he received his B. Litt. from Oxford and returned to the United States. He began his teaching career that same year (1930) at Southwestern College, and a year later joined the Vanderbilt faculty. But in 1934 he accepted a position at Louisiana State University at Baton Rouge. There he collaborated with Cleanth Brooks, who had also been a part of the Vanderbilt Fugitives and had studied with him at Oxford. Both men had been attracted to the ideas on literature of a new generation of critics. These scholar-critics were reacting to the accusation that only nonserious students majored in English literature. Wishing to introduce "greater rigor" into their teaching, these young critics insisted on a literary text's organic nature and emphasized such interpretive modes as irony, paradox, and structure to explicate a work. Described as "close readers," they quickly found themselves labeled the "New Critics." In 1938 Brooks and Warren published their groundbreaking textbook, *Understanding Poetry*, which organized many of the New Critical ideas into a coherent method of literary study. Five years later, the pair published a companion volume, *Understanding Fiction*, and the two texts transformed the reading and teaching of literature in the universities and inspired a generation of followers who dominated English departments during the 1950s and 60s.

In addition, the duo founded and directed the *Southern Review*, a quarterly that proved tremendously influential in literary and cultural circles. But Warren's first poetry collections (*Thirty-Six Poems*, 1935; *Eleven Poems on the Same Theme*, 1942; *Selected Poems, 1923–1943*, 1944) and first novels (*Night Rider*, 1939; *At Heaven's Gate*, 1943) attracted little notice. When, in 1942, the LSU administration suspended publication of his journal, Warren accepted a position as director of creative writing at the University of Minnesota, where he remained until 1951. He was never again to take up residence in the South. It was during this time that Warren not only consolidated his reputation as a literary critic, but also became successful as a novelist. In 1946 he published *All the King's Men*, a novel based upon the career of the Louisiana demagogue, Huey Long, and suddenly he found himself famous. The novel garnered great popularity and critical praise, even winning its young author his first Pulitzer Prize.

Interestingly enough, Warren maintained that none of his characters speaks for him and that the reader cannot know the real Robert Penn Warren through his writings. Taking Mr. Warren at his word, the reader here might well expect to derive a clearer image of him from his interviews than from his novels and poems. Still, despite Warren's prolific output and literary success, interviewers were relatively slow in seeking him out. In 1939, *Partisan Review* did include him among a second group of seven writers to deal by mail with seven questions on "The Situation in American Writing." Responding with a candor that would soon become familiar, he dismissed several questions out of hand and made short work of the others. Surprisingly, Warren did not sit for his first interview with a major publication until 1950, after the huge success of *All the King's Men*, when he agreed to talk with Harvey Breit, assistant editor of the *New York Times Book Review*.

Around this time Warren made several major changes in his life. In 1951 he left the University of Minnesota to accept a professorship of playwriting at Yale, and he ended his first marriage to Emma Brescia. Then in 1952 he married Eleanor Clark, with whom he would have two children. Shortly after the appearance of *Brother to Dragons* (1953), Warren published an autobiographical sketch in the *New York Herald Tribune Book Review* titled "Robert Penn Warren (A Self-Interview)." Quickly recounting some of the external data of his life and schooling, Warren concluded with a brief glimpse into his daily writing habits. "I like to write in the morning," he confided. "I try never to depend on later revision: don't leave a page until you have it as near what you want as you can make it that day. I like to write in foreign countries, where the language is not your own, and you are forced into yourself in a special way."

He also liked good conversation. In May 1956, he joined some of his old Vanderbilt friends for a three-day freewheeling discussion of, among other subjects, college teaching, creativity, poetry, the individual, and democracy. Warren had thoughts on each of the panel's subjects—especially on the importance of good teachers, but he quickly moved on to his favorite subject: poetry. He viewed the process of writing poetry as "an exploration." More specifically, he explained, "the poem is a way of knowing what kind of a person you can be, getting your reality shaped a little bit better. And it's a way of living." In the early 1950s Warren had returned to the writing of poetry after a dry period of nine years. His second Pulitzer Prize (but first for poetry) came with *Promises: Poems, 1954–1956*.

In subsequent interviews, Warren was quick to take issue with several other then-current labels. When a participant at the Vanderbilt Literary Symposium used the term "young writer," Warren expressed his disapproval. "Let's don't say 'the young writer,' " he flared. "Any writer who is not young had better shut up shop. . . . Once he thinks he's an old writer who knows, he's finished." Warren also expressed discomfort with the label of "Southern writers." The important thing here, as he saw it, was not to "equate them. Some clearly are synthetic, and write by imitating, trying to pose as another writer; some are purely imitators and have no personality except a synthetic one they're attached to. They use the group label as a way of trying to achieve some identity, of trying to be writers at all." Anyone writing about these writers should discern the differences. (Ironically, Warren would himself use the labels "young writer" and "Southern writers" in later interviews.)

It was seven years before Warren sat for his next interview. In 1966, he engaged in an extended exchange with faculty members and students at Union College, in Schenectady, New York. Here Warren did manage to add a few insights to several familiar topics. Criticism was one. An interviewer suggested that critics write to "to explain away the confusion" caused by literary works. Warren whimsically replied that he "would welcome some clarity, or some help towards clarity. He then added: "What we want, I think, is not added confusion but a mental experience that gives a sense of moving from disorder to order, to a moment of poise."

The next year (1967) Warren sat with Chicago book columnist Roy Newquist to discuss his early life, the South and its writers, and race relations, and to reflect on his own thought processes when writing. Asked about the genesis of *All the King's Men*, Warren replied that "I was writing novels and living in Louisiana . . . all of my novels have come out of the same sort of thing, out of a world I knew something about." Perhaps his most surprising comments were in reply to the familiar request to evaluate current literary criticism and reviews. Obviously, Newquist had in mind the New Criticism, of which Warren was a recognized leader. "On the academic side," said Warren, "I think that 'high-brow academic criticism' as opposed to straight reviewing has passed through a very strange phase where exegesis of a certain sort has become the order of the day, and this is a necessary phase, but it's about run its course. They're moving to something else." If Warren harbored any regrets at the fading of formalist criticism, he gave no indication.

In his second visit to Union College, Warren stressed the poet's need to strive for truth. "Lying doesn't come naturally to the poet. You're uncomfortable about it. And usually someone will tell you when you're faking it." The element of truth was also central at the 1968 Southern Historical Association meeting in New Orleans, when Warren sat with novelists Ralph Ellison and William Styron and historian C. Vann Woodward for a panel discussion, "The Uses of History in Fiction." Getting quickly to the core of the subject, Warren declared that the major "difference here between history and fiction is that the historian does not know his imagined world; he knows *about* it, and he must know all he can about it, because he wants to find the facts *behind* that world. But the fiction writer must claim to *know* the *inside* of his world for better or for worse. He mostly fails, but he claims to know the inside of his characters, the undocumentable inside."

Central to Warren's evolving philosophy of life is the concept of the South as a cultural entity. He was asked by television interviewer Edwin Newman why the South produced so many "celebrated writers." Warren, who apparently never stopped thinking about such questions, pointed out that the South, boasting such native sons as Jefferson and Washington, was the true "home of our republic." But it had been isolated by the "deep, very deep moral ambiguities" stemming from slavery. In effect, the region had been "carrying on a tradition outside of the American tradition." This caused "an internal struggle" that resulted in "a very frozen world, cut off from modernity up until the First World War." The war brought on the great cultural shock "of meeting the outside world, really meeting it."

Two years later, in 1973, Warren invited into his home novelist William Kennedy to talk about the novel. Not surprisingly, Kennedy, the Pulitzer Prize-winning novelist of political and general human chicanery in Albany, New York, began with questions about the "political novel" and about *All the King's Men*. Warren recalled that he had not found his structure for the novel until he decided to make Jack Burden the story's narrator. The conversation then moved on to the interplay of fact and fiction (or journalism and the imagination) in the contemporary "nonfiction novel." Warren pointed out that such a blending was hardly new and could be found in Daniel Defoe's *A Journal of the Plague Year* (1722) or Stephen Crane's *The Red Badge of Courage* (1895), as well as in Truman Capote's *In Cold Blood* (1965). But the imagination, he insisted, is what truly matters. "The fact novel is fine for décor, the milieu. When the real crisis comes it's always the thing seen from the inside that sticks."

The centenary year of 1976, as well as promptings by television interviewer Bill Moyers, moved Warren to take stock of contemporary attitudes. He attributed the "vast disenchantment" of the modern age to "some deep change" being experienced by "the whole Western world," much of it brought on by technology. But what especially troubled him was the decline of history departments and the "sense of the past . . . passing out of the consciousness of the generation." He did not know how people "can have a future without a sense of the past." The sad truth was that "the past is dead for a great number of young people; it just doesn't exist." In addition, in the past the individual was valuable because his "hands were valuable, there were things for hands to do." Now most work is being done by machines, and the individual is devalued. Also, people, especially Americans, believe that everything can be fixed by the expert. The result is that "our faith has gone from God to experts," who often prove unreliable. But at bottom, technology is not the problem: "it's how we use it, that's important."

In the last decade of his life, Warren generously granted many more interviews. In them, he patiently fielded questions very similar to those he had responded to repeatedly through the years. But he managed on each occasion to offer fresh insights or new perspectives. In a conversation with Peter Stitt, of the University of Houston, Warren attempted to explain his lack of formal religious belief. "I am a creature of this world," he stated, "but I am also a yearner, I suppose. I would call this temperament rather than theology—I haven't got any gospel." After a brief discussion of writers that have interested him (Melville, Whittier, Coleridge, Dreiser), Warren admitted that he still considered himself a Southern writer. "I can't be anything else. You are what you are. I was born and grew up in Kentucky, and I think your early images survive. Images mean a lot of things besides pictures."

`In 1980 Warren and William Styron sat with Louis D. Rubin for a joint interview. Rubin pointed out that both writers were Southerners who had been away from the South for many years, but their fiction was generally set there. "Actually, it seems to me that though your basic images and attitudes may change in many ways," Warren responded, "they are always fundamentally conditioned by what you knew in small and large ways very early in life." He had not wanted to leave the South, but he had lost his Vanderbilt job and had felt pressured to leave Louisiana State University, and so he had gone to Minnesota. The moving away was, Warren suggested, "a part of the Southern experience—the moving out from and looking back at the past."

Several of the most intimate and revealing of his many discussions were held with David Farrell at the onset of the 1980s. Warren recalled that at Vanderbilt he had turned to literature, philosophy, and poetry, but had not studied writing as such there. "The only thing approaching 'creative writing,'" recalled Warren, "was this three months, one term, course in advanced writing; thank God there was no other creative writing course." Also, there were "poetry societies," on and off campus. Here Warren revealed, for the first time to an interviewer, his severe depression during his first college years and his attempt at suicide because of his fear of going blind. His loss of his eye had left him "*feeling* maimed." Poetry had in some ways proved his salvation. It is "a way of being open to the world . . . open to experience," he felt. "Poetry is a way of thinking or a way of feeling; a way of exploring."

Three years later, in 1985, Tom Vitale interviewed Warren, honoring him for his eightieth birthday and for the publication of *New and Selected Poems, 1923–1985*. After brief comments on time and nature, Warren recalled his tangential relations to the Nashville Agrarians and his views, both early and late, on the race question. As so often in the past, Warren rounded off the discussion by emphasizing the need for students to memorize and recite poems. As for poets, they should avoid repeating or imitating themselves.

These interviews make clear that Robert Penn Warren thought long and hard about every thing he wrote. Indeed, few writers have been able to pinpoint as precisely the exact source and inspiration for virtually every poem, novel, and, essay. Interviewers tend to ask the same questions, and writers are forced to repeat themselves. Yet this repetition is not without value for both writer and reader. For the bringing together of a writer's ideas and words expressed on varied occasions over many years inevitably provides important insights into that individual's character and work. In fact, such a cumulative index should enable not only the interested reader but also the sensitized writer to look back and discern patterns in his or her own life and thought not realized at the time. Warren admitted repeatedly to making such discoveries when prompted by the questions of his interviewers. Let it be conceded then that in a gathering of interviews granted over five decades, even by an artist as gifted as Warren, some repetition was inevitable. Indeed, a basic consistency of thought and outlook is always to be welcomed. Still, present readers should avoid the temptation to skip over subjects discussed in more than one conversation. Warren offered new details and insights each time he returned to the most familiar ideas or events.

Following Literary Conversations Series procedures, we have arranged the interviews by the date the interview was given. We have silently corrected typographical errors, supplied omitted words, added in italics the full titles of works, and provided needed punctuation marks. Several interviews collected here were reprinted earlier in two companion books, *Robert Penn Warren Talking: Interviews, 1950–1978* (Random House, 1980) and *Talking with Robert Penn Warren* (University of Georgia Press, 1990). Our task in preparing this volume was made much easier by the excellent editorial work of Warren's previous interview editors: Floyd C. Watkins, John T. Hiers, and Mary Louise Weaks. We wish to acknowledge our huge debt to them.

We wish to recognize also the excellent assistance of Korri Roach and Sarah Bylund in all aspects of putting together this volume.

GLC

BS

Chronology

1905 Born on 24 April in Guthrie, Kentucky, to Robert Franklin Warren (1869–1955) and Anna Ruth Penn Warren (1875–1931).

1908 Sister, Mary Cecilia Warren, born on 20 February.

1911 Brother, William Thomas Penn, born on 8 April.

1921 An accident seriously damages one eye, causing Warren to fear sympathetic blindness in his other eye. Spends six weeks in Citizens Military Training Corps at Fort Knox; publishes first poem, "Prophecy," in *The Messkit*. Enrolls at Vanderbilt University.

1923 Contributes poems to *Driftwood Flames* and *The Fugitive*.

1924 Becomes a member of The Fugitives. Attempts suicide on 19 May.

1925 B.A. summa cum laude, Phi Beta Kappa, and Founder's Medalist from Vanderbilt University. Begins graduate studies at the University of California at Berkeley. Meets Emma "Cinina" Brescia.

1927 M.A. from University of California at Berkeley.

1927–1928 Postgraduate work at Yale.

1928 Begins at New College as a Rhodes Scholar.

1929 Secretly marries Emma Brescia in Sacramento, California.

1930 Graduates with Bachelor of Letters, Oxford, as Rhodes scholar. Openly remarries his wife in Marion, Arkansas.

1930–1931 Teaches at Southwestern College of Memphis.

1931 "The Briar Patch" is published in *I'll Take My Stand: The South and the Agrarian Tradition* by Twelve Southerners. Mother, Anna Ruth Penn Warren, dies.

1931–1934 Teaches at Vanderbilt University.

1934–1942 Teaches at Louisiana State University.

1935 Partners with Cleanth Brooks, Jr., to produce *Southern Review*.

1936   Houghton Mifflin Literary Fellowship Award for *Night Rider.*
              Levinson Prize from *Poetry Magazine.* Carolina Sinkler Prize
              from the Poetry Society of South Carolina (would also win in
              1937 and 1938).
1939–1940   Guggenheim Fellowship.
1941   Visiting professor at University of Iowa.
1942   Visiting professor at University of Iowa. *Eleven Poems* receives
              the Shelley Memorial Award.
1942–1950   Professor of English, University of Minnesota.
1944–1945   Chair of Poetry, Library of Congress.
1947   Pulitzer Prize in fiction and National Book Award for *All the
              King's Men.*
1947–1948   Guggenheim Fellowship.
1949   Honorary D. Litt from University of Louisville. Travels to
              California to work on film version of *All the King's Men.* Robert
              Meltzer Award from Screen Writers Guild. Columbia Pictures
              Corporation releases film version of *All the King's Men*, with
              direction and script by Robert Rossen and with Broderick
              Crawford as Willie Stark.
1950   Elected to National Institute of Arts and Letters.
1951   Turns down offer from University of California because of its
              insistence on loyalty oath. Elected to American Academy of Arts
              and Sciences. Divorced from Emma Brescia Warren.
1951–1956   Professor of playwriting at Yale University.
1952   Honorary L.H.D. from Kenyon College. Elected to American
              Philosophical Society. Marries Eleanor Clark on 7 December.
1953   Daughter Rosanna Phelps Warren born on 27 July. Family
              moves into new home in Fairfield, Connecticut.
1955   Father, Robert Franklin Warren, dies. Honorary D. Litt from
              University of Kentucky. Son Gabriel Penn Warren born on 19 July.
1956   Honorary D. Litt from Colby College.
1958   *Promises: Poems 1954–1956* wins the Pulitzer Prize and National
              Book Award. Edna St. Vincent Millay Prize, the Poetry Society
              of America.
1959   Honorary D. Litt from Yale University. Elected to American
              Academy of Arts and Letters. Buys cottage in West Wardsboro,
              Vermont.

1962–1973	Professor of English at Yale University.
1963	Builds vacation home in West Wardsboro, Vermont.
1965	Honorary LL.D. from the University of Bridgeport
1967	Bollingen Prize for poetry from Yale University for *Selected Poems: New and Old 1923–1966.*
1969	Honorary D. Litt from Fairfield University
1970	Honorary D. Litt from Wesleyan University; National Medal for literature for *Audubon: A Vision*. Van Wyck Brooks Award for poetry for *Audubon: A Vision*
1973	Honorary D. Litt from Harvard University. Award for literature, University of South Carolina Professor Emeritus.
1974	Honorary D. Litt from Southwestern College at Memphis, the University of the South, and the University of New Haven. Chosen by National Endowment for the Humanities to deliver the third annual Jefferson Lecture in the Humanities. Distinguished professor at Hunter College.
1975	Honorary D. Litt from Johns Hopkins University. Emerson-Thoreau Award from American Academy of Arts and Sciences.
1976	Copernicus Award from the Academy of American Poets.
1977	Harriet Monroe Prize for poetry.
1979	Pulitzer Prize in poetry for *Now and Then.*
1981	"Willie Stark," a musical based on *All the King's Men* premieres at Houston's Jones Hall and Washington's Kennedy Center: Harold Prince, director; Carlisle Floyd, musical score; baritone Timothy Nolen as Stark. Receives MacArthur Prize Fellowship.
1985	Receives American Academy and Institute of Arts and Letters Gold Medal for Poetry.
1986	Appointed Poet Laureate Consultant in Poetry to the Library of Congress.
1989	Dies in West Wardsboro, Vermont, at the age of eighty-four on 15 September.

Conversations with Robert Penn Warren

The Situation in American Writing

Partisan Review / 1939

From the *Partisan Review*, 6.5 (Fall 1939): 103–13. Reprinted by permission of the publisher.

Seven Questions:

1. Are you conscious, in your own writing, of the existence of a "usable past"? Is this mostly American? What figures would you designate as elements in it? Would you say, for example, that Henry James's work is more relevant to the present and future of American writing than Walt Whitman's?

2. Do you think of yourself as writing for a definite audience? If so, how would you describe this audience? Would you say that the audience for serious American writing has grown or contracted in the last ten years?

3. Do you place much value on the criticism your work has received? Would you agree that the corruption of the literary supplements by advertising— in the case of the newspapers—and political pressures—in the case of the liberal weeklies—has made serious literary criticism an isolated cult?

4. Have you found it possible to make a living by writing the sort of thing you want to, and without the aid of such crutches as teaching and editorial work? Do you think there is any place in our present economic system for literature as a profession?

5. Do you find, in retrospect, that your writing reveals any allegiance to any group, class, organization, region, religion, or system of thought, or do you conceive of it as mainly the expression of yourself as an individual?

6. How would you describe the political tendency of American writing as a whole since 1930? How do you feel about it yourself? Are you sympathetic to the current tendency towards what may be called "literary nationalism"— a renewed emphasis, largely uncritical, on the specifically "American" elements in our culture?

7. Have you considered the question of your attitude towards the possible entry of the United States into the next world war? What do you think the responsibilities of writers in general are when and if war comes?

Robert Penn Warren:

I simply haven't had the time to do a proper set of answers to your questions. They are good questions, I think, and being good, they are not questions which can be answered in an hour or so. But I may give you a few jottings now, which, possibly, may have some statistical interest for you.

1. Yes, Or rather, after a thing is done, I can see its relation to a "usable past." In poetry, this "usable past" is not American, for I feel that American poetry has very little to offer the modern writer—except some of Emily Dickinson and a very little of Emerson. But in fiction the picture appears very different. Certainly, I feel that the work of James is much more relevant to the present and future of American writing than the work of Walt Whitman. On the technical side, the work of Whitman has, it seems to me, been exercising a very destructive influence.

2. I suppose that every writer wants an audience, but I could not undertake to describe the audience which I want at the time when I am actually engaged in writing a poem or a story. The nature of the poem or story is conditioned by many much more immediate concerns.

3. In general, no. I would agree with your statement about the newspapers and liberal weeklies, but I think that your diagnosis is not quite complete. There is a great deal of reviewing which is just stupid without reference to advertising or political pressure; it is probably the result of careless editing, of throwing books out to any reviewer who happens along. The reviewing of poetry is in a worse state than the reviewing of fiction, it seems to me; probably because the reviewers of poetry put on more airs.

4. I haven't tried, but I am sure that I would not have been very successful at it. As for the second part of the question: is there a place in our present economic system for literature as a profession? A lot of money is spent for writing; the trouble is that most of the money which is spent is spent to encourage bad writing.

5. God knows, I don't.

6. The political tendency of American writing since 1930 has been, I suppose, in the direction of social protest. As for my own feelings, I have been in sympathy with the protests, but have not liked most of the literature which the protests have produced. A lot of writers seem to have felt that if the protest was all right the writing would automatically be all right. And there has been, of course, a lot of faddishness; for instance, if you will call the roll, you will find names of people who have been on every band-wagon from flaming youth to communism, through humanism and dada. But this is inevitable.

7. I think that if we get into the next war we are suckers.

A Self-Interview

Robert Penn Warren / 1953

From *New York Herald Tribune Book Review*, 11 October 1953. © 1953 by the *New York Herald Tribune*. Reprinted with permission.

To begin at the beginning, I was born at 7 A.M., April 24, 1905, in Guthrie, in southern Kentucky, a town which has had about the same number of inhabitants—1,500, more or less—ever since I can remember.

The country around, part of the Cumberland Valley, is a mixed country, fine rolling farmland breaking here and there into barrens, but with nice woodlands and plenty of water, a country well adapted to the proper pursuits of boyhood. The streams seem somewhat shrunken now and the woodlands denuded of their shadowy romance, but certain spots there and farther west, where I used to spend my summers on my grandfather's farm, are among my most vivid recollections.

I recollect that grandfather very vividly, too—already an old man when I knew him, a Confederate veteran, a captain of cavalry who had ridden with Forrest, given to discussing the campaigns of Napoleon and, as well, of the immortal Nathan Bedford and to quoting bits of Byron and Scott and compositions like "The Turk Lay in the Guarded Tent." His daughters used to say that he was "visionary," by which they meant he was not practical. No doubt, in their sense, they were right. But in quite another sense, he was, I suppose, "visionary" to me, too, looming much larger than life, the living symbol of the wild action and romance of the past. He was, whatever his own small part in great events may have been, "history." And I liked history. That was what my own father usually selected when he read aloud to his children.

I went to school in Guthrie and at Clarksville, Tennessee, and then, by great good fortune, to Vanderbilt University. For this was the time of the Fugitives at Vanderbilt, a group of poets and arguers—including John Crowe Ransom, Donald Davidson, Allen Tate, Merrill Moore—and I imagine that more of my education came from those sessions than from the classroom. But aside from the Fugitives, writing poetry was almost epidemic at the university, and even an all-Southern center on the football team did some very creditable lyrics of a Housmanesque wistfulness.

After Vanderbilt, graduate work at the University of California, Yale and Oxford (Rhodes Scholar). During those years I had been publishing a good deal of poetry in *The New Republic* and similar magazines, and in my last year at Oxford, at the invitation of Paul Rosenfeld, I did a novelette for *The American Caravan*. It is called *Prime Leaf.*

It is now some six and a half novels (two unpublished and one unfinished) and a collection of short stories later. But the poetry has gone along with the fiction, and I suppose that my last book, *Brother to Dragons*, is a kind of hybrid. It even started out to be a novel, and though it is in verse and is a poem, it has a complicated narrative and involves many fictional problems.

I like to write in the morning. I try never to depend on later revision: don't leave a page until you have it as near what you want as you can make it that day. I like to write in foreign countries, where the language is not your own, and you are forced into yourself in a special way. I like to travel and especially like Italy. I like swimming, walking in the country, arguing, and admiring my six-week-old daughter.

Fugitives' Reunion:
Conversations at Vanderbilt

Fugitive Poets / 1956

From *Fugitives' Reunion: Conversations at Vanderbilt, May 3–5, 1956*, edited by Rob Roy Purdy (Nashville: Vanderbilt University Press, 1959). © 1956 Vanderbilt University Press. Reprinted by permission.

John Crowe Ransom: Well, I would think Mr. Warren ought to speak to that question. Now I know that . . . before he published the long poem *Brother to Dragons* he spoke of why he found that that was not to be represented best in the form of prose fiction, that it would take the poem. I don't think he quite conceived it as an epic, but I would like very much to hear what went through his mind, what he thought of.
Warren: It never crossed my mind I was trying to write an epic, I'll say that. [*Laughter and murmurs*]

William Y. Elliott: And he didn't write one.
Warren: Well, if I had, it would have been by inadvertence.

Elliott: And this is the point I am really trying to make: the poets are really diagnosticians and not creators. And is it possible that our times are so completely out of joint that that's the case?
Warren: Bill, I don't accept your distinction.

Elliott: Well, let's see why not.
Warren: I think you're just making it awfully easy for yourself, the way I look at it.

Elliott: Well, I'm making it hard for you. [*Laughter*] It would have been by inadvertence, I believe, your handling—
Warren: I feel no compulsion. It just doesn't interest me. [*Murmurs*] Definitely, I don't feel any compulsion to try to write a poem. [*Amidst general*

murmur] And you don't worry about whether you're going to call it an epic or "X."

Elliott: What we started out—
Warren: You try to say something in the best way you can.

Elliott: Let me put it this way—
Warren: Your concern isn't there, I think, with trying to write. And what I was quarreling about was the distinction between diagnostics and creation, because *The Waste Land* as a diagnostic poem is as much a creation to me as, well, say, a poem like—what? *Lycidas*? Is that one of the better creative poems?

Elliott: That's right; it's a creative poem.
Allen Tate: You don't think *The Waste Land* is—
Elliott: I don't think *Samson Agonistes* is a creative poem.
Warren: I don't see the distinction, you see. I think they are both at the same level, not in value, necessarily. Though I would be willing to argue that on another occasion, perhaps. But they belong to the same kind of— *Lycidas* is as much a diagnostic poem, a critical poem, as it is a creative poem.

Elliott: Well, I'm just trying to untangle something—
Warren: And it's a real wrangle with the world at large. And more of a wrangle—more explicitly a wrangle than any of this is.

Tate: . . . It was through Baudelaire that I began to investigate the Symbolists under the suggestion of some of the early writings of Ezra Pound rather than T. S. Eliot.
Warren: That was in '23, wasn't it?

Tate: Yes.
Warren: If I remember correctly, that's when I began to read them. Because you and Bill started me reading them—

Louis D. Rubin: How did you get on to Pound?
Tate: Well, I don't know. I had seen him in *The Little Review* and in *Poetry* magazine and various others—the *Dial*, which began about 1920.
Warren: I don't remember a time when Pound wasn't read around here.

Tate: The first time we knew each other, which was in 1921—
Warren: Yes, fall of '21.

Tate: —well, you'd already read Pound, and so had I.
Warren: Well, I read Pound as a freshman, didn't I? That's '21–'22. And I guess it was the next year, it was '22 or '23, I guess, Baudelaire and some other French poets.

Tate: When we were rooming together, particularly, we used to talk about him.
Warren: That was in '22–'23.

Tate: But, Red, I wouldn't think that the Symbolist influence accounted for very much in anything that this group wrote. It was somewhere in the background; we were certainly not Symbolist poets. And I think that some of the critics who have tried to place us in that historical perspective are wrong about it.
Warren: Well, I think you are right about that. I don't think it counted in that sense—

Tate: No.
Warren: —I mean I remember—I think in a very indirect way you'd count it.

Tate: Yes.
Warren: At least for some people. As far as state of mind was concerned about poetry, it was not in terms of direct use of a method. I mean Baudelaire had a very definite effect on some people, say, the line, anyway—

Tate: Yes, on me, too.
Warren: Two or three of us, anyway. I think John passed by without—

Tate: John by-passed those, yes. [*Laughter*]
Ransom: Well, I was two years in France fighting the battle in a rear area, instructing in French matériel, and several nice young ladies introduced me to the poetry of the nineteenth century of France, and I came back—
Warren: I was saying something quite different from that. [*Laughter*]

Ransom: —and I came back with a lot of volumes, and I know that the French Symbolists attracted and perplexed me a great deal. I may not have talked about them, but they were in my consciousness after 1919. Very decidedly.
Warren: Well, I wasn't thinking of your knowledge of them, or awareness of them. I was thinking simply, well, something in relation to your own poetry.

Ransom: Well, I think the—
Warren: And your own state of mind, temperament, as I read it.

Ransom: They had a great gift of phrasing, and they had a great boldness of metaphor. And I felt sure that that belonged some way or other in verse; I don't remember any talk of it, but—
Warren: I remember your talking about it, not only once but on several occasions. But I wasn't thinking of awareness of it in that sense, but something quite different: just a temperamental affinity which I never detected between your work—

Tate: Same time, Red, you know what Edmund Wilson has called the "conversational ironic" thing—
Warren: Yes.

Tate: Now, it seems to me that John developed something of his own which was similar to that but not in the least influenced by it.
Warren: It was similar, but it's not based on it; it's not influenced by it.

Tate: No, not at all. No.
Warren: And I remember at that time that John introduced me to Hardy. And I was struck very early with an affinity there—

Tate: Yes.
Warren: —again no imitation, no modeling, but an affinity of some kind there which I sensed right away. This has no reference to the topic, but I happen to have an anecdote about John's first book of poems. I encountered in California some years ago a man named McClure, who edits the paper at Santa Monica. He owns and edits that paper. Well, he was in France at the

same time that John was as a soldier. And when I was living out there, he wrote me a note—I had never met him or knew anything about him—and said, "I am a friend of an old friend of yours. Won't you come to dinner?" So I went to dinner at his house and had a very pleasant evening. And he said that he was walking down the street with John Ransom, who was a good soldierly companion of his during that period, and they went to get the mail at the battery mail distribution. And they got a few letters, and John got a little package. And he opened the little package, and there were two copies of *Poems About God* in it. And he said John hadn't seen the book before, and he opened it and inspected it with composure, and then turned to McClure and said, "I'd like to give you a copy of this." [*Laughter*] And McClure treasured this copy; and over the years, he said, along with other later writings of John's, followed his career with delight.

Tate: I remember Curry in those days—well, of course, he was a bachelor and I think perhaps he was the last one of our teachers, you see, to get married— he was enormously hospitable to all the younger people. I remember Red and I used to practically live in his room there and—
Warren: Borrow his typewriter.

Tate: —we'd borrow his typewriter. And he had infinite patience with us.
Ransom: A very good talker.
Tate: Excellent talker.
Elliott: Wonderful man, always with his pipe, smoke-curing our learning.
Tate: Yes.
Warren: There's one factor, I think—I don't know how to assess it, really, but in a small and close provincial college, anybody who's there who has quality on the faculty stands out like a diamond on a piece of black velvet, you see. I mean if you had five able students of philosophy on the faculty, it would sort of cancel out, in a way. It ceases to be something; it just becomes then a convenience for you for passing a course of fulfilling the requirements. And the limitations made a kind of personal focus on individuals and on ideas; I remember this quite distinctly, since some of these people represented the great world of ideas and the great world of geography, of wider horizons, in a very special way which is no longer true in educational institutions, I suppose. So once given, by accident, certain persons on the faculty, their impact is much greater than it would be otherwise.

Now, the other night I was at dinner at Northrop's house in New Haven. An eminent professor of law was there, and he and Northrop were talking about big world universities and certain small colleges. And they both had made surveys and had been around a lot, and this professor of law had actually made trips around looking at small colleges. It started by Northrop saying that when you had very large departments of philosophy, or other large departments where there were a lot of high-powered people, the students didn't learn how to think, because they didn't follow one man closely enough to see how his mind worked, for better or for worse, on a problem. They only took his view and put it down as "that's what he thinks"; they didn't follow the process, because they were never with him enough. If you had five different courses in philosophy with five different people—and all of them splendid, let us say, or not splendid, or something, but they are different—you'd never learn how one of them thought at all. You never followed his thinking.

Tate: Red, you remember—
Warren: And they had no sense of the process of his mind—Excuse me [*to Tate*]. Northrop was saying, well, something is lost by the accumulation of a lot of really first-rate people under one academic roof. It becomes a cafeteria of intellects, then, rather than a good square meal where you follow through the way a few people think or feel, and have a model to accept or reject.

Tate: I think there were three men like that at Vanderbilt in our time: John, Tolman, and Sanborn. And we had them right through from the beginning. We weren't shopping around.
Elliott: We took all the courses that they offered—
Donald Davidson: And I'd like to add, too, that we had very easy personal access to them, at any time—
Warren: That's right, and all the personal relations. . . . One thing that strikes me in recollection, now: a few years after I left Vanderbilt, and people began to refer to those people as a unit, you see, as if there were a church or an orthodoxy; and I was so shocked by that—

Tate: I was, too; I had no idea—
Warren: —because I was so aware of the differences of temperament, and the differences of opinions, you see, in conversation—the Fugitive meetings were

outside—but the notion of a unity had just never occurred to me, really, except that the unity was just purely a unity of friendship and common background.

Warren: . . . Greatness is not a criterion—a profitable criterion—of poetry; that what you are concerned with is a sense of a contact with reality. And it's maybe a pinpoint touch or a whole palm of a hand laid, or something; but the important thing is the shock of this contact: a lot of current can come through a small wire. And there you are up against, well, big subjects and little subjects. It's just so it's a real subject, and, of course, you've got this word to deal with; you've got to have something that will actually create human heat in that contact. Well, language can in certain ways, because language drags the bottom of somebody into being, in one way or another, directly or indirectly. But if I had to say what I would try to hunt for in a poem—would hunt for in a poem, or would expect from a poem that I would call a poem— it would be some kind of a vital image, a vital and evaluating image, of vitality. That's a different thing from the vitality you observe or experience. It's an image of it, but it has the vital quality—it's a reflection of that vital quality, rather than a passing reflection, but it has its own kind of assurance, own kind of life, by the way it's built. And when you get around to talking about the scale, it's not the most important topic. It is an important topic, but it's something that comes in very late in the game.

Now, I think we started last night with that, and it's really not our province to discuss that, except in the realm of theory—late in the game. That is, I see no difference in the degree of reality between, say, "Janet Waking" and *The Dynasts*. One's a little poem, a short poem, and one's a big side-of-beef of a poem; but the significance of one can be as great as that of the other in the sense of your contact; the stab, the flash, the— I'm not arguing for short poems, now, mind you; I'm not doing a Poe thing about that, and the scale may be necessary in certain things to get the sense of reality. But there's no virtue or defect in the size one way or the other. The question is: Where do you get that image, that speaking image, the walking statue, and how would we interpret that? I would interpret it myself, but it would bring on, of course, a lot of wrangling and hassling about individual poems and a lot of other things. I'm not interested in getting anything said here except that— But when this problem of scale comes in early, I always begin to lose my bearings; I have to go back and start over again and try to see what

it's about for myself—I don't mean writing, but I mean reading. It's that stab
of some kind, early; that's the important thing for me in the sense of an
image that makes that thing available to you indefinitely, so you can go back
to it, can always find that peephole on the other world, you see—that
moment of contact with the . . . well, with reality, or realness, or something.

Tate: . . . The Fugitives' objective was the act of each individual poet trying to
write the best poetry possible. I'm afraid we're getting highfalutin again. I just
don't— May I speak a little to this point, John, just to something that Red
said? It seems to me this test of reality is the test by which we determine
whether a given work is poetry or not; and the scale is of importance only
after we decide that question, because if we dissolve the poetry into the subject matter, then I think that in the long run—
Warren: We have a document.

Tate: —we have a document; and what we call the literary tradition is dis-
solved into its historical flux again. Now take—If I may refer to one of your
poems, "Janet Waking" or "Bells for John Whiteside's Daughter"—in both
of those poems there is a very intense reality which exists in the language,
created in the language. That same thing happens in *The Divine Comedy*
throughout, not uniformly, but by and large throughout all the hundred
cantos. Now, we've got there not the difference of reality but a difference of
scale. The scale is important only after we decide that difference of reality,
or discern that reality. Otherwise we lose the whole conception of literature.
It's all gone.
Warren: May I break in here for a moment? Two things. I would string along
on what Allen has said about the prior question: it's a question of its existence out of the poem. That's really what I was fumbling at saying. And the
other things follow. Another thing: poetry is an exploration; the process of
writing is an exploration. You may dimly envisage what a poem will be when
you start it, but only as you wrangle through the process do you know your
own meanings. In one way, it's a way of knowing what kind of poem you can
write. And in finding that you find out yourself—I mean a lot about yourself.
I don't mean in the way Merrill's [Moore] talking about: I mean in the sense
of what you can make available, poetically, is clearly something that refers to
all of your living in very indirect and complicated ways. But you know more
about yourself, not in a psychoanalytic way, but in another way of having

dealt with yourself in a process. The poem is a way of knowing what kind of a person you can be, getting your reality shaped a little bit better. And it's a way of living, and not a parlor trick even in its most modest reaches; I mean, the most modest kind of effort that we make is a way of living. And I think Bill has something important when he insists that there is such a thing as a poetic condition, which is the willingness to approach a poem in that spirit, rather than in the spirit of a performer, when you get down to the business of writing a poem, or even thinking about poetry.

Tate: In that sense a man is a poet all the time.
Warren: All the time, insofar as he brings that spirit into his reading or thinking about poetry or about other things as well. It's a tentative spirit, and a kind of—well, I don't know exactly what's the word, except a lack of dogmatism in dealing with your own responses and your own ideas as they come along, a certain kind of freedom and lack of dogmatism under some notion of a shaping process. The other thing I had to say is more along what Merrill said. I believe that what Merrill, quite properly—now this is again not controversial, but just to make distinction—what Merrill has been talking about deals with the psychology of the process of writing and not with a literary question at all, it seems to me; that it's a psychological interest that has no bearing on the good poem or the bad poem as such.

Elliott: Yes, that was what I—
Warren: The bad poem or the good poem could be equally interesting in terms of the way the mind works in creating it, or in the stuff that may call the attention of any of us to the poet himself, or to Merrill Moore—what his psychic history has been. But I can see, I can imagine—this is guesswork, of course—no point-to-point equation between the psychological interest such a process would have from one case to another and the quality of the work that came out of it. That is, the clinicism of it, the clinical interest, would have no relation to the poetic value, necessarily; in fact, it might work the other way.

Cleanth Brooks: If I may break in for a moment with an illustration: Hulme makes a point that Rider Haggard's *She* is almost as interesting to the psychologist as—
Andrew Nelson Lytle: More so.
Brooks: —Melville's *Moby Dick*, or perhaps more so.

Lytle: More so. Yes. May I say something here, in extension to this, or support of it? Red, in this self-exploration, it's both intuitive and deliberate, isn't it? And you may start out with what you think is a subject—say, a subject matter larger than you really end up with, or you can reverse the thing.
Warren: Yes, you've got to be willing to always shut your eyes and then deal the cards. Just don't look yet.

Lytle: That's right. And you know Lubbock in *The Craft of Fiction* makes the point that the form, really, uses up all the subject, and the subject all of the form in the ideal situation—
Warren: In heaven, in heaven.

Lytle: —in heaven, you see—
Tate: You approach that—
Lytle: —but you have to approximate that kind of thing. . . . But in this self-exploration there is one danger: if the poet limits it to too close a self-exploration, then it becomes a kind of narcissistic thing, and you digress, you see.
Warren: Oh, yes—excuse me. You can't think you are interesting while you are doing it.

Lytle: No, that's right.
Warren: You've got to think of something else.

Lytle: Don't you really have to raise against the discrete objects the word, you see?
Warren: Yes, your self is not involved.

Lytle: No, that's right.
Warren: But when you get through you find out that you ate that, too.

Ransom: Couldn't we say that he [the poet] creates a new experience—that's empirical—a new happiness. He finds, he compounds experiences, or he takes, he's on the verge, he feels an experience; and he stays with it until he realizes the experience. He does it over and over. Other poets akin to him do the same thing. And presently the philosophers will come along, and they are not creative, and they have no existence until the creative people have refined and perfected types of experience. But evidently there is a universal, in the Aristotelian sense, within those—

Tate: Yes.

Ransom: —experiences, and the wise philosopher can find them out.

Tate: I would have to agree with that. I think that is right.

Ransom: But that is distinct from the work that the poet does.

Warren: But you might say their availability depends on their—let's use this word *depend* a little bit—that their availability depends upon that faculty of the universal; but he is not working in those terms. He's working in quite different terms, and probably even in terms of ideas, ultimately. When Wordsworth was getting along in years, there's a tale I think Crabb Robinson gives, of a clergyman—whose name I think was Miller—calling on him, very reverentially, and telling him while they were taking a walk one morning, "Mr. Wordsworth, I want to tell you how much I admire your poems for their fine morality." And that stumped Wordsworth for a moment; and then he said, "I don't value them for that. I value them for the new view they gave of the world."

Ransom: Not bad.

Warren: That's almost the phrasing, not quite. But that's the sense of it— unless I've very badly forgotten the episode—which I think is pretty good. Wordsworth knew what he was up to, I guess.

Warren: May I nag this communication business again, just a little bit? If a thing is made right, it's going to be available to a lot of people—if it's made right. But you can't make it right by thinking of those people.

Lytle: That's right, that's right.

Warren: You see what I'm getting at. I think you are trying to find the principles of creating that object somehow, out of what? I mean, you are bound to be in there somehow; but you cannot take it from the side of the communications. It's going to communicate: you create the thing, and there it sits on the mantelpiece, or wherever it is—

Lytle: Red, that's what I meant when I said—

Warren: —and then everybody can look at it. And if it's made right, it's going to signify, so that we can all look at it.

Alfred Starr: Well, Red, you are talking—
Warren: It'll make us all feel something significant, big or little. But what you have to keep your mind on is making that "thing." And making it significant to me would not make it significant to somebody else. Working at the object is finding the laws of that object that you are working with.

Lytle: Yes. If you think of anything outside of the thing that you are doing, you are lost. You can't do it; you'll never do it.
Warren: It's all right to think about whether it's going to be in it or not. [*Laughter*] But that doesn't matter. You see what you get.

Warren: I can only speak of what it signified for me—what Agrarianism signified for me. And of late years I have tried to give it some thought, and I must confess that my mind tended to shut up on the subject for about ten years. It seemed irrelevant at one stage to what I was thinking and feeling, except in a sentimental way—I mean at the level of what these things signify; I ceased to think about it during the war years. Before we got in the last war, just before it and several years after, there was the period of unmasking of blank power everywhere. And you felt that all your work was irrelevant to this unmasking of this brute force in the world—that the de-humanizing forces had won. And you had no more relevance in such discussions as we used to have, or are having this morning, except a sort of quarreling with people over the third highball.

Well, as I remember the thing as it came to me, there were several appeals in it. It hit me at an age when I was first away from this part of the country for any period of time, having lived in California two years, and a year in New Haven in the Yale Graduate School, and then in Oxford. And I had broken out of the kind of life I was accustomed to in that part of the world I knew. And there was a sentimental appeal for me in this. It happened to coincide with my first attempt, my first story about Southern life—a novelette which I was writing at that time at Oxford. And it had coincided, a little earlier that is, with a book on John Brown. But this book led to fiction—that's what the Brown was: a step toward fiction. It was a sentimental appeal and an attempt to relive something—to recapture, to reassess. This was not thought out; it was just what happened in a sort of an instinctive way. And that tied in with some perfectly explicit speculations, in conversation with friends, such as Cleanth at Oxford—and, I must say, this topic would never appeal very much to anybody in California.

But the question of—well, there are two questions: one, the sense of the disintegration of the notion of the individual in that society we're living in—it's a common notion, we all know—and the relation of that to democracy. It's the machine of power in this so-called democratic state; the machines disintegrate individuals, so you have no individual sense of responsibility and no awareness that the individual has a past and a place. He's simply the voting machine; he's everything you pull the lever on if there's any voting at all. And that notion got fused with your own personal sentiments and sentimentalities and your personal pieties and your images of place and people that belong to your own earlier life. And the Confederate element was a pious element, or a great story—a heroic story—a parade of personalities who are also images for these individual values. They were images for it for me, I'm sure, rather than images for a theory of society which had belonged to the South before the war. They became images for that only because they are lost. There was a pretty tough practical guide involved in that; they were out to make power, and money interested them. They can only become images for this other thing insofar as they could not participate later on in their version of a gilded age, probably. I'm not being simple; I mean this is an overstatement that I'm making. There were some correctives in Southern society as a matter of preventing that—the excesses of the seventies, eighties, and nineties, and so forth, and some that we enjoy now, perhaps. But as to how these elements related in their personal appeal to me? Now, I don't know how much that situation would be shared by others; but I was no economist and didn't fancy myself as one. But for me it was a protest—echoing Frank here—against certain things: against a kind of dehumanizing and disintegrative effect on your notion of what an individual person could be in the sense of a loss of your role in society. You would take it a loss that you had no place in that world.

Well, later on I began to read people like Bertrand Russell, during that time—about their idea of how the individual was affected by the state: in the power state he lost existence, disappeared, was a cipher. All of that was involved. And your simpler world is something I think is always necessary—not a golden age, but the past imaginatively conceived and historically conceived in the strictest readings of the researchers. The past is always a rebuke to the present; it's bound to be, one way or another: it's your great rebuke. It's a better rebuke than any dream of the future. It's a better rebuke because you can see what some of the costs were, what frail virtues were achieved in the past by frail men. And it's there, and you can see it, and see what it cost them, and how they had to go at it. And that is a much better rebuke than any dream of a golden age to come, because historians will correct, and imagination will correct, any notion of a simplistic and, well, childish notion of a golden age. The drama of the past that corrects us is the drama of our struggles to be human, or our struggles to define the values of our forebears in the face of their difficulties.

Dorothy Bethurum: It's also encouragement.
Warren: It's encouragement.

Bethurum: But the thing that impresses me is that I can't see that it isn't always possible in any period under any circumstances to live the life of aristocratic humanism. I feel very strongly all these things, but I think that the Agrarian movement was too pessimistic, was too unhappy about the future.
Warren: I thought we were trying to find—insofar as we were being political—a rational basis for a democracy. That, I thought, was what we were up to.

Frank Lawrence Owsley: I agree with that.
Tate: Yes, I do too.
Warren: And not to try to enter into competition of whether it was five slaves or five hundred slaves. In fact, that question was relevant only as an image—which Faulkner has now made available even to Frenchmen—for something else, for the crime against the human that we were expiating in our history. And I think that the word *aristocratic* used in a Jeffersonian sense is fine; but that was my notion—that aspect of it at that time. We were trying to find a notion of democracy which would make it possible for people to be people and not be bosses, or exploiters, or anything else of other people, but to have a community of people, rather than a community of something else. And Bill Elliott years ago, I mean at Oxford, was I think the first person who ever called my attention—when I first met him, our first meeting in a college there; which one it was I forget; Balliol, I guess it was—

Elliott: Balliol.
Warren: —it was your place; where you were staying that time you were on a visit. Well, anyway, he used to say that the great problem of democracy is a problem of responsible leadership. And he developed that and went on to the question of the role of the individual. I remember the conversation distinctly.

And that was in no relation to Agrarianism; but this thing, to me, started something that tied right into that when we began to talk about and write about the Agrarians.

Warren: Last night, Charlie Moss [Executive Editor of the *Nashville Banner*; Vanderbilt '24.] and I were talking, after you all had left his house. He said, talking about Agrarianism, "The question of civilizing and making progress amounts to a moral progress, or civilizing progress, and is a matter always of a fifth column in a society." And the effect is slow; if we had any function, we were a fifth column. We couldn't step out and take over the powers of the state. Poetry is a fifth column—
Elliott: That's right.
Warren: —in the same way. Universities should be fifth columns, but usually aren't.

Warren: Randall, may I lower the tone of the conversation? [*Laughter*]

[Randall] Stewart: Yes, you certainly may.
Warren: Not quite to the smoking-car level, but a story occurs to me. It's a little indecorous, but we're among friends and all of that. There was a socio-logical survey made several years ago I saw a news account of juvenile delinquency among young girls, girls in New York City. And they had many thousands interviewed, and asked them why they did it. And there were about seven or eight hundred said, "My mother doesn't like me," and about two thousand of them said, "My father doesn't like me"—Merrill probably can give you the proportion of these things—and another seventeen hundred said, "Well, they quarrel at night, and I have to go outdoors to keep from hearing their quarrels," and "I don't like my baby brother," and one thing and another. This got down to four thousand, nine hundred and ninety-nine of them. And then they had one more little girl to talk to—and they asked her why she did it, and she said, "I likes it." [*Laughter*] Well, I think that's what the Rockefeller Foundation's going to find out—[*Laughter*] We haven't got any alibis.

An Interview with Flannery O'Connor and Robert Penn Warren

Vanderbilt Literary Symposium / 1959

From *The Vagabond*, 1960. Reprinted by permission of Vanderbilt University.

During the annual Vanderbilt Literary Symposium, an English class and members of the faculty talked with Warren and Miss O'Connor. The interview was originally published in a Vanderbilt student magazine, *The Vagabond*.

Joe Sills: I would like to ask either or both of you: when you set out to write a story, how much of an outline do you have? . . .
Flannery O'Connor: I just don't outline.
Warren: I had an outline once, and it took me two years to pull out of it. You think you've got your work done.

Sills: What about the novel? How much outline do you work from? How do you write a novel?
O'Connor: Well, I just kind of feel it out like a hound dog. I follow the scent. Quite frequently it's the wrong scent, and you stop and go back to the last plausible point and start in some other direction.

Sills: Are you aware of how it is going to end?
O'Connor: Not always. You know the direction you're going in, but you don't know how you'll get there.

Edwin Godsey: Do any of you begin with the theme first, and hunt for the story, or do you do it the other way around?
O'Connor: I think it's better to begin with the story, and then you know you've got something. Because the theme is more or less something that's in you, but if you intellectualize it too much, you probably destroy your novel.

Warren: People have done it the other way, in cases: starting out with an idea, and hunting the fable, as they used to say. Coleridge is a good example of it. He says he had his theme for *The Ancient Mariner* for years. He kept casting around for the appropriate fable. He even made a false start or two, until he hit the right story. Those are not contradictory things, I think, because the theme was in him. He had at least reached some pretty clear intellectual definition of it before he started.

Godsey: Theoretically, which do you think is better for the young writer?
Warren: Let's don't say "the young writer." Just drop the phrase; not just for here, for always. Any writer who is not young had better shut up shop. He'd better be trying to wrangle through what he is up to, and pretend he's young anyway, or quit. Once he thinks he's an old writer, he's finished. About which is better: I don't think there's any choice in the matter. It's just a matter of temperament. I think people can freeze themselves by their hasty intellectualizing of what they are up to.

Walter Sullivan: Red, to get back to this novel business: your books are awfully well put together. The opening sequences contain so many images of the book as a whole, and prepare for so many things to happen. You've got to know a whole lot or you couldn't write that way.
Warren: There's no law that makes you put the first chapter first, though.

Sullivan: Well, I know, but . . .
Warren: Some of them have been written first, yes. I don't think it's knowing how the story comes out that's the point. As Flannery just said, you know what you want it to feel like. You envisage the feeling. You may or may not know how it is going to come out. You may have your big scenes in mind before you start. You may even be moving toward them all the time. You don't know whether they will jell out or not jell out. But it seems to me the important thing is to have enough feeling envisaged and prefelt, as it were, about the way the book's going to go. If that feeling isn't there: unless it dominates your thinking, somehow . . . you know, be the thing that is behind the muse, the thing that keeps it under control: if you ever lose that feeling, then you start floundering. But as long as that feeling as to how the book is going to end is there, something is guiding it. And then your mechanical problems have a sort of built-in correction for error. I mean you have fifty ideas, but

somehow you know they're wrong. If you keep this feeling firmly in you . . . I don't know how you will it . . . but as long as it is there, you have something to guide you in this automatic process of trial and error. You know what the book ought to feel like. Of course, you're going to modify that feeling.

Sullivan: I know exactly what you're saying, and I think you're exactly right. But it seems to me that there is a considerable danger in not knowing enough about where you're going, especially insofar as the structure of the book is concerned. In *All the King's Men*, did you write the first chapter first?
Warren: No, it was the second chapter originally. There was a shift in material there which the editor did. The present opening chapter was the second chapter, or part of the second chapter. The original opening got off to a very poor start, with the narrator talking about the first time he had seen Stark, the politician. He goes back into the scene which now appears later, in the second or third chapter, when he comes into town to get a political favor, make a political connection, in a restaurant or beer hall in New Orleans. There is this portrait of him coming in, the boy with the Christmas tie, you know, and his hat in his hand. Well, that was a very predictable kind of start. It had no urgency in it. So expository in the worst sense. I was trying to step that up by a kind of commentary on it, and the commentary was pretty crude, and that's the way the thing remained when it went to the publisher. And Lambert Davis said, "Look here, this is a very poor way to start a novel. You've got a natural start in the second chapter, and what's in the first chapter that's important, you can absorb very readily." And I think he was right. I know he was right about its being bad.

Sullivan: Well, now look, when you started the book, certainly you knew that Judge Irwin had been very culpable in his financial dealings.
Warren: No, I did not. No, I didn't know it at all. That came quite a while along the way.

Sullivan: Well, then, did you know that Adam Stanton was going to kill Willie?
Warren: Yes, I knew that.

Sullivan: You knew that Sugar Boy was going to kill Adam?
Warren: Yes. The point is, I am mixing up two things, the novel and the verse play which preceded it. There you had the germ: the politician, his wife, his

mistress, her brother were in the play. It was a very small cast, you see, and then it became a novel, but there was no Judge Irwin in the play at all. There's no mother, nothing of that personal stuff. In fact, there was no Jack Burden. He came in as a nameless newspaperman with two sentences to speak, a boyhood friend without a name as the assassin is waiting for Stark, who is then called Taylor. The newspaperman just meets this man and says "Hello, Hello," just a few words between them, a way of killing time, of having a little nostalgic reference to their boyhood. Kind of a hold, you know, until the action could happen. You've always got to do that, you know. If a man goes to kill a man, if a man goes to get an ice cream soda, you can't just let him go and get it, or go and kill him. You have to stop it, hold it a minute, distract it a little, delay it, get a focus from the side, and nudge it a bit. You try to make the reader forget what you put the man there for. If you say, "I am going to get the ice cream soda," and just go do it, there's no story there. Jack Burden came in there just the way I described. I just can't go shoot him. I've got to stop him. I've got to do something, and so this guy appeared there to stop him. Having him in there filled a dramatic need of fiction, a need of pace. When the novel idea started out some years later, I couldn't do it as a straight dramatic novel. I tried that. I thought on an idle Sunday afternoon: that newspaperman might be useful. The moment of nostalgia might be made into some kind of feeling by which to tell the story. That was how he got in there. I remember that distinctly.

O'Connor: When you write the thing through once, you find out what the end is. Then you can go back to the first chapter and put in a lot of those foreshadowings.
Warren: . . . If a person just does ordinary, hard, commonsense thinking about writing in general . . . I don't mean about writing only, but about books, novels, poems, stories that he's acquainted with—if he asks himself what he likes or doesn't like about them: that sharpens your wits; it goes deep down into your innards somewhere. It stays there, and is supposed to come out and affect your whole view of things, your whole practice, isn't it?

Harry Minetree: Can you really be that objective about something you're writing?
Warren: I think you have to be at some stage. People are different, you know. Some people pour it out and it is fine; some people pour it out and it's awful.

And some people grind it out very hard, and it is awful; and some people grind it out very hard, and it's good. I don't see any generalization. I do think one thing is always true: the degree of self-criticism is only good for a veto. You can throw out what you've got wrong, and you can even try to say why it's wrong, but you can't say, "Now I am going to do it right." At that point you're alone with the alone, and the alone had better come and do it, because you can't. Where the alone happens to be living, I don't know; he's backed up in your nervous system, or a must, or something. You need help at that point. It's got to happen to you, but the way you can make it happen to you, it strikes me, is just by keeping your eyes open about the way the world operates about you, and the way a piece of writing operates that you like or dislike: some know of an awareness as to how they operate. All the critical thinking you can do has to be forgotten as critical thinking whenever you sit down to write. It's bound to affect you, bound to be in you somewhere. Just as everything else is bound to be in you. I'm not disparaging hard critical, or other, thinking, but I think there's a right time and a wrong time for it.

James Whitehead: Sir, may I ask a question in two parts? You said that your nostalgic feeling about Burden may have been central. I wonder first, how much of that first chapter, after you had seen it as such, you felt was in a sense the enveloping tone of the novel. It struck me that this is the music that comes before the action in a sense you never forget, and that's in the first chapter. The other part of the question is: were you living in Louisiana when you got that out—from your inside, so to speak?
Warren: I had been living in Louisiana for several years when I started to write. I started the play there, and I finished it in Rome, and then I laid it aside for several years and wrote two other books in between.

Whitehead: It is the man who is the referent, the kicking-off place, not the sense, the sense of the land which you got across in the first chapter.
Warren: No, I can't choose between those two things. It started as the simplest kind of idea. A man who has the gift for power gets his means and his ends mixed up, and gets some power, and there's a backlash on him. He gets killed. It starts with that. Huey Long and Julius Caesar both got killed in the capitol, and there you are. It's as simple as that. It's a germ, an anecdote. And teaching Shakespeare in Louisiana in 1935, you couldn't avoid this speculation.

Cyrus Hoy: It's appropriate that you should have finished writing the play in Rome.

Warren: Yes. The troops were under the window every day. But the tone of the play had not been the tone of the book. For better or for worse. And the tone of the book turned on the question of getting a lingo for this narrator. I remember that fact quite distinctly. It was a question just of his lingo, and fumbling around with how he's going to talk—he's got to talk some way. A straight journalistic prose would not do. That is the trap of all traps. There has to be an angularity to any piece of writing that claims to have a person behind it. The problem was to find a way for him to talk. It was really a backward process. The character wasn't set up—aside from the lingo, and trying to find a way for him to talk.

Whitehead: Then the man saw that the country existed.

Warren: His ambivalence about what he saw—as a road, as people, as things—was a start. His division of feeling was the way it came out of the start of the lingo. That was the germ. It didn't start with a plot, or conception. This guy gets power, and he gets shot. All the details of Burden's life were improvised. They were improvised in terms of some envisagement of his feelings about everything at the end. But I didn't know what the last chapter was going to be until I got there. I didn't know how I wanted it to feel. Just as Flannery was saying: you go back a little bit, and keep looking back. After you are along the way, keep looking back, and your backward looks along the way will help you go forward. You have to find a logic there that you pursue. If you can't find it, you're in trouble.

Warren: I must say that I don't want to nag at a point here that has nothing to do with the one we're discussing, but thinking of oneself as a young writer: it's wrong. I mean, stop boasting. You see, you think you know everything, and you've got to put it down. Don't play yourself for a coward, play for keeps. I think you have to do it that way. Not that nice little exercise I am doing because I am young, and ought to be forgiven. Nothing will be forgiven. It will stink just as much if you did it as if Hemingway did it. It will be just as bad. "I am a young learning writer, and I mean well" is a terrible way to think of it. You're full of urgency and wisdom; you've got to spill it, and set the world aright.

A young man I knew some time ago was such a talented young man, really, and so bright. He knew everything. He knew about Kafka and Aristotle; he had read everything. He was the most educated young man I had encountered in years. He was twenty-one years old, a senior at Yale, scholar of the house, prize product of an expensive educational system, and he was leaving his studies, he was so bright. "You just go write a novel or novelette for your project, no more classes for a year," and things like that. He wrote well; he knew all about how he should feel as a young writer of twenty-one. Like that cartoon I saw in *The New Yorker* some years ago of two little boys reading a book of child care, and one little boy saying, "Jesus, I'm going to be a stinker two years from now." This boy was writing just like that, that kind of self-consciousness, you know. He had dated himself, you see, along the way.

He was writing a novel, a love story, and the boy got the girl after certain tribulations that were casebook tribulations, it seemed to me, because I am sure he couldn't have gotten them out of real life. Nobody acts like that. They were all so right, intellectually. He knew what people should feel at the age of eighteen, nineteen, twenty, and twenty-one, and fifty-three, and fifty-nine, and seventy-six. He had it all worked out—the life pattern for the fruit fly there at his fingertips. He had a wonderful last paragraph. They got in a clinch and everything was fine, and then they were going to get married. Then this last paragraph: I found it sort of chilling. He said he knew of course this was not really love; he knew that love would come after years of shared experiences: you know, walking the baby with the colic, and the mortgages. Now, just imagine a young man twenty-one years old who knows all about Kafka and Aristotle writing like that. The girl ought to run screaming into the brush. He's dated himself as a young writer, you see, a young human being, a post-puberty adult, some kind of thing like that. His life, everything, was all dated and sealed up. Romeo would never have thought of himself in that way: "This is not true love—that would be seventeen years from now, when we pay off the mortgage." I think it's a dangerous way to look at things. You've got to feel you know the truth, got to tell it—it's the gospel. Hate your elders.

Minetree: What term would you suggest in preference to "young writers"?
Warren: I don't know. That's not my problem.

Sullivan: What do you call yourself, Red?
Warren: I say I am trying to be a writer.

George Core: Mr. Warren, how did you finally hit upon the form of *Brother to Dragons*?

Warren: This is awfully like a dissecting room, where the corpse is scarcely able to fight back. To answer your question: by fumbling. It started out to be a novel. It clearly couldn't be a novel because the circumstantiality would bog you down, would kill off the main line. And then it started off to be a play. I was doing it in collaboration with a dramatist and producer, and we couldn't quite make it, couldn't agree. I couldn't get a frame for it—the machinery got too much in the way for me. And I was thinking of the wrong kind of problems at the wrong time. But what I was concerned with were the characters, and the emotional sense of it; I didn't want to be bothered by the pacing of it, that technical side. In other words, I didn't naturally think in dramatic terms. The next step was to throw away the notion of the stage play, and keep what was to me the dramatic image, which was the collision of these persons under the unresolved urgency of their earthly experience. All the characters come out of their private purgatory and collide; everybody comes to find out or tell something, rehearse something; it becomes a rehearsal of their unresolved lives in terms of a perspective put on it. That is what the hope was. Then there was the need to tie this to a personal note, putting the writer character in so he could participate in this process, the notion being that we are all unresolved in a way, the dead and the living. This interpenetration, this face [fact?] of a constant effort to resolve things, came back to the idea of a play again.

Randall Mize: Miss O'Connor, yesterday you spoke about the problem of introducing a definite theological motivation in writing in a society which is somewhat religious only on the surface. Do you think it is possible to write from a definite theological point of view?

O'Connor: Yes, if you're a writer in the first place. If you are a writer, you can write from any point of view. I don't think a theological point of view interferes in any way unless it becomes so dominant that you're so full of ideas that you kill the character.

Warren: Flannery, would this be true about theology or anything else: that by the sort of deductive way of going at it—illustrating the point—you're a dead duck before you start?

Betty Weber: Miss O'Connor, I was interested in what you said yesterday about the grotesque in fiction writing, particularly in Southern writers.

You say that the South can still recognize what a freak is, but perhaps thirty years from now we will be writing about the man in the gray flannel suit. I wondered if you would talk a bit more about that. Perhaps you'd explain why you think that's true.

O'Connor: I think as it gets to be more and more city and less country—as we, everything, is reduced to the same flat level—we'll be writing about men in gray flannel suits. That's about all there'll be to write about, I think, as we lose our individuality.

Warren: Did you like *Augie March*?
O'Connor: I didn't read it.

Warren: In Bellow's book I had the sense, particularly in the first half, that it was very rich in personalities. An urban Jewish South Side Chicago world, and the people had a lot of bursting-off the page. They were really personalities. They were anything but people in gray flannel suits. That he could in that particular work catch this vigor—this clash—of personality: that's what I liked best about the book.
O'Connor: I shouldn't say "city" in that sense. I mean—

Warren: Suburbs, yes.
O'Connor: I mean just the proliferation of supermarkets.

Warren: The city has sort of a new romance after the supermarket civilization of the suburbs; it's the new Wild West. I think Saul caught that in a way. Certainly there's a richness in his book.
O'connor: That's his region. Everybody has to have a region, and I think in the South we're losing that regional sense.

Warren: Well, you can't keep it for literary purposes.
O'Connor: No, because everybody wants the good things of life, like supermarkets—

Warren: —and plastics—
O'Connor: —and cellophane. Everybody wants the privilege of being as abstract as the next man.

Walter Russell: We've talked a good bit about this flattening out of personality. For reasons that are undefined to me, I have a good bit more faith in—what do you want to call it?—the resilience of individuality, and I think it must find its way of cropping out between the divisions of the country some way. Do you?

Warren: I think there is danger in our talking about it at all. In a way, as individuals, or people who live in one place or another place, we can't avoid talking about it, I guess. It's clearly a dehumanizing of man. All the philosophers know about it, and we've heard about it, too. And you see it going on: the draining away of all responsibilities and identities and those things. But it is a little like that scholar of the house, you know: the plan he got from the mental health center, or the university, or wherever he got it, and this is a kind of self-consciousness again. Anybody who sets out to be an individual, a real character, is intolerable. You can't bear the posiness of the crusty old character. "I have a role. I'm going to make my dent on society by having a role. I know my function, my kind of joke, my kind of this, my kind of that." It can run off in that direction. Then you have professional Californians, and all sorts of high-heeled-boot boys.

Russell: But they're working at it.

Warren: Everybody is working at it. Every place has its own kind of professional exponents—those who are going to be characters. Characters are the last thing in the world, it seems to me. They're the anti-individuals. They're substituting something for the notion of individuality, for fundamental integrity. We begin to talk about this, and we're singing the swan song. The mere fact that we're talking about it is a danger signal. We're made too self-conscious about it.

Whitehead: I've a feeling that it's an unfortunate thing if some boy in Manhattan hasn't seen a cow or smelled a cedar tree. I'm not quite sure why—

Warren: He feels pretty sorry for you, too.

Whitehead: Yes, I know. That's the thing that bothers me.

Warren: Maybe you're both right.

Thomas McNair: I think that what Miss O'Connor and Mr. Warren have been speaking about, this dehumanization, becomes a problem to the writer, because he perhaps is one of the surviving individuals. Perhaps, like Huxley in *Brave New World*, he may write about the whole man, he may write about other individuals, and his dehumanized readers can't even recognize his creation. They can't understand what he's writing about.

Warren: I think maybe we're giving ourselves airs to think we're writing about the whole man.

McNair: Well, comparatively speaking.

Warren: I think it's really what Flannery was talking about yesterday. You write about the whole man by writing about freaks. If you want to write about the whole man, write with this negative approach. By "freak" I mean anybody you know who is worth writing about.

McNair: You shifted the terms around, but I think you mean the same thing.

Warren: You occasionally get a very complete man, and he has no story. Who cares about Robert E. Lee? Now, there's a man who's smooth as an egg. Turn him around, this primordial perfection: you see, he has no story. You can't just say what a wonderful man he was, and that you know he had some chaotic something inside because he's human, but you can't get at it. You know he was probably spoiling with blood lust, otherwise he wouldn't have been in that trade, wouldn't have done so well at it. We can make little schemes like this, and try to jazz it up a bit, but really what you have is this enormous, this monumental self-control, and selflessness, and lots of things like that. You have to improvise a story for him. You don't know his story. It's only the guy who's angular, incomplete, and struggling who has a story. If a person comes out too well, there's not much story. Whoever wants to tell a story of a sainted grandmother, unless you can find some old love letters, and get a new grandfather? In heaven there's no marriage and giving in marriage, and there's no literature.

McNair: Don't you think perhaps it is easier for us in the South to recognize what is important in the freak to be written about?

Warren: We've gotten some good documents.

McNair: Easier for us than for a person in New York, in Manhattan.

O'Connor: I don't know. I had a friend from Brooklyn who went out to school in Indiana some place, and he said all he saw out there were healthy

blond youngsters. He went back to Brooklyn and he saw a little old man about this high with a cigar in his mouth, and he said, "Ah! I'm home."
Sullivan: There's Cheever. He knows some freaks.
Warren: And he knows he knows them. I think his point is, they don't know they're freaks. Until they read his stories about themselves. They think it's the man next door.

Whitehead: In a sense, we're trying to say we can't get too involved in geography. You never know—you make a value judgment on something like that—you speak of something you never have seen—
Warren: I think there's a real problem about your relation to your own world, but I don't think it's a matter of saying what's better and what's worse, because everybody is stuck with his own skin, and his own history, and his own situation. I think he's got every right to think about that, but I don't think it's a matter of choosing up sides for this purpose, this idea that you have to be chosen for this point or that point. I think self-congratulation is a mighty poor way to celebrate human nature. Joyce didn't hang around Dublin pleasing the Dubliners, yet Dublin is always there. Flattering yourself and your community is a mighty poor way, it seems to me, to write anything, or to be a good citizen, for that matter. Your own concern is in the defects, the jags.

Whitehead: Yet it's possible you can find a piece of geography, which makes you more aware of your own skin.
Warren: You're just stuck with it. You can't choose it.

McNair: That may all be true, and theoretically you can say that a writer in one place will write about the people in his place, bringing out the man in man, as well as the writer in another place.
Warren: He has to.

McNair: But is the best literature written in the South today or not? And why is it best?
Warren: It is not our business to speculate about that point. It's not my business, at least. I am second to no man in admiring a lot of writers that happen to be born in Mississippi and contiguous states, but this sort of speculation doesn't do a writer any good. It leads right away to "Where's my piece of cake?" Something like that. It seems to me it's a very poor way to think about

it, unless you want to be a social historian, or a critic, or a literary historian, or something like that. But it's no one's business to think about it very much. To think of how a person is related to his society is a very important point, but I think it should be thought about not as a writer but as a person. Thinking about it as a writer is the wrong level for going at it. Any important question should be thought about on its own merits, and not in relation to one as a writer.

Chris Boner: When a writer sits down to write, should he be more conscious of himself as a writer, or as a person?
Warren: He shouldn't be conscious of himself at all. It seems to me he ought to be trying to do his job. A guy learning to catch a baseball has to learn by trial and error. A guy doing a broken field run has to have some training in this. When he's in there he'd better not stop and say, "Am I pretty or not?" When the tackle is bearing down. His business is speed at that point, and nothing but speed—and a little deception.

Warren: There's no stupidity it seems to me, at one level, in saying "All right, there are "Southern writers' (in quotes)," and start saying what they do share. That is a reasonable thing to say, and a reasonable field of speculation, just so long as you don't equate them. Some clearly are synthetic, and write by imi-tating, trying to pose as another writer; some are purely imitators and have no personality except a synthetic one they're attached to. They use the group label as a way of trying to achieve some identity, of trying to be writers at all. But that is universally a problem; he's got to learn from somebody else. It is very hard for him to find any kind of voice of his own. That's his big trouble, it seems to me. But he can't find it except by saying he's going to find it, he's got to work around the problem, not head on into it. If he heads on into it, he's probably going to be the worst kind of imitator. Or he'll invent some-thing to get a difference. But I don't see anything reprehensible in grouping a whole lot of—no use naming names, you know all the names, just say the "Southern writers." They do share something; what they do with what they share is a very important thing; what they are from one to another is a very important difference. That is what makes the fact that you can group them together a rather piquant thing. If you look at the next step, an ordinary writer on the subject says what they share, and then makes the group. The interesting thing is, having made the groups, seeing then what the differences are within that, in terms of all sorts of things: kinds of talents, temperaments, philosophy, and God knows what. But that is the next stage, and it's rarely done.

Sullivan: There seems to be some sort of tacit agreement here that the South is a rich land of images. Could you say something about the dangers of this attitude of not transcending the image. It seems to me that the great danger here is that the Southern writer will be so busy being Southern that he won't be anything else.
Warren: It's certainly a trap.

Sullivan: Do you think it's as great a trap as I seem to think it is?
Warren: Well, it couldn't be worse.

Sullivan: How about that, Flannery?
O'Connor: I don't know. I think if you're a real writer, you can avoid that kind of thing. There are so many horrible examples of regional writers, and the South is loaded. There's one behind every bush. So many awful examples. It's the first thing you think of avoiding.

Warren: Yet you're stuck with your own experiences, your own world around you.
O'Connor: You have to keep going in deeper.

A Conversation with Robert Penn Warren

Frank Gado / 1966

From *First Person: Conversations on Writers and Writing*, by Frank Gado (Schenectady, NY: Union College Press, 1973). Reprinted by permission of Union College.

Interviewer: Thomas Hardy was happy when he could put aside his novels and write poetry. Do you prefer working in one genre more than the others?
Warren: Depends on what I'm working on at the time. I've thought about this some, and I think that writing poetry is more fun for me. It's so much more personal. I don't mean the material is necessarily more personal, but that it's a closer, more private activity. And technically it's a more exciting challenge: getting the words into the arc of the line and coordinating the meaning with the rhythm. I write poetry until it runs dry and the lines stop coming. Then I'll switch to a novel and ride along with that, sometimes for six or seven years or maybe more. I don't have any theories about this beyond riding with the impulse.

Interviewer: It seems historical events have a special hold on you. *At Heaven's Gate, All the King's Men, World Enough and Time,* and *The Cave*—there may be others—all contain recognizable historical figures or occurrences. Why is this?
Warren: Recognizable figures? I don't think they are recognizable from my treatment of them. I'm not being facetious. Writing a story about an actual person and using him as a kind of model are really not the same. I don't pretend that Willie Stark is Huey Long. I know Stark, but I have no idea what Long was really like. I heard him speak once at an enormous official luncheon celebrating the seventy-fifth anniversary of the founding of Louisiana State University—he had not been invited but walked in anyway and took over, and he was very funny. Then on another occasion I saw him—or I think it was he—in a passing car.

I knew stories about Long, but that's quite different. What happened with the real Long and what his motives were is between him, his God, and his conscience. There's no way in the world for me, or you, to know that. But I know water runs downhill; and if a bomb explodes, I know that someone lit the fuse. Events don't cause themselves. I saw the end products of Long and I know that men's motives and actions are triggered and operate in certain ways.

Interviewer: Ducking the question . . .
Warren: I'm not ducking it . . .

Interviewer: No, I mean, let me ask the question in another way. What was it about the Kentucky tragedy that caught your eye?
Warren: That came right out of a historical situation. Sure, there is a relationship in almost all of my novels with something that was a germ of fact. Individual personalities become mirrors of their times, or the times become a mirror of the personalities. Social tensions have a parallel in the personal world. The individual is an embodiment of external circumstances, so that a personal story is a social story. The mirror business has always struck me as being pretty interesting. I didn't frame this concept early in the process of writing novels, but I have discovered it works as a principle over a long time. . . .

My choosing the "Kentucky tragedy" tale was an accident. I was at the Library of Congress—I had the chair of Poetry—and Katherine Anne Porter, an old friend, who was a Library Fellow in American letters, had an office near mine. One day she said, "Look, here's something for you," and handed me the *Confession of Jeroboam Beauchamp*, and I read it. I had vaguely heard of this before, I guess through the two novels by William Gilmore Simms. It has been treated by others, too. Poe wrote a play about it, in Renaissance disguise. Then there was a book called *Grey-slaer: A Romance of the Mohawk* by a fellow named [Charles Fenno] Hoffman—from this neighborhood [i.e., New York State] as a matter of fact. He changed the scene from Kentucky to the Mohawk Valley. He had earlier reported the trial in a book called *A Winter in the West*, a travel book published in 1826. This story, you see, has had a lot of literary adaptations, but I didn't know that before I got interested in it and began to look around. Without realizing the story had played such a role in American letters, I was caught right off by the character and by the situation, the conflict between what was called the "New Court" party and the "Old Court" party in Kentucky, between new and old, and by the "mirror" thing I mentioned before. Then, too, I shouldn't underplay the importance of the fact that it had happened around my home section. Beauchamp got into trouble in my home country, and I had some sense of what that world had been like. I could bring to my surmises a certain body of feeling.

Interviewer: When you write novels based on history, do you think of your reader as knowing the stories in the way that Greek audiences knew the stories on which the tragedies were based?
Warren: Well, no. You can't, really. You have to carry a context. Oh, at a certain level, yes, you expect some familiarity with the period, but hardly anybody would know about the Old versus the New Court party in Kentucky in 1820.

Incidentally, the New Court party reminded me of the New Deal. The issues were somewhat the same: adjustments of debts, economic crises. You can sometimes see one political era in terms of another.

Interviewer: I hadn't realized that your use of history also involved a dialogue between the real and the ideal.
Warren: If I understand you, this would mean adjusting historical "fact" to fictional need. I can give you an instance in which such a change was deliberate. I found that my historical man, Jeroboam Beauchamp, who killed his ex-sponsor and benefactor, Colonel Sharp, had belonged to the Old Court party and that Sharp belonged to the New Court. Now, that didn't suit my scheme. The older man should be with the Old Court, the young man with the New— the "idealistic." In terms of my theme, that was the wrong layout, so I shifted them around. I had no compunction about doing this, because the historical Beauchamp was merely a prototype of my hero, and besides, was of no historical importance.

Interviewer: Your comments about a dialogue with history remind me of Faulkner. Faulkner said somewhere that there were only two nations in the United States—the South and New England. At least in part, he seemed to have meant that this sense of nationhood, of a people united by a common body of myth, was tied in with the region's closeness to its history.
Warren: Americans in general have a more highly developed sense of history than the Europeans because our history is so short. A man my age has known,

right in his own family, people whose memories go back farther than the midpoint of our history as an independent nation. Now, that's bound to have an effect on our thinking about the past.

The South is a special case. It lost the war and suffered hardship. That kind of defeat gives the past great importance. There is a need somehow to keep it alive, to justify it, and this works to transform the record of fact into legend. In the process, pain, dreariness, the particulars of the individual experience become absorbed in the romantic fable. The romance, you see, becomes stronger than the fact of any one story and changes it; even if you are only one or two generations removed from the event, it's hard to see through the romantic haze. Maybe that's one of the reasons Southern writers are so concerned with history. They've heard the stories since they were kids and later on they try to understand them in terms of their own range of experience as human beings. And in terms of scholarly history.

Interviewer: *All the King's Men* was first written as a play. What virtues did it gain in its recasting in novel form?
Warren: My approach to the question would not be abstract. The changes had to do with how the recasting happened. As you said, I wrote the play version first. I showed it to a friend who knew about drama, Francis Fergusson, who worked on it quite seriously and gave me a brief concentrated course in drama based on my play. But then I laid the story aside and wrote another book. It kept nagging at me, however, and I decided to revise it and make it a novel.

It was a tight little play. When I read it over, I missed part of my feelings involved in the original idea. The significant context for the action, the world in which these things could happen, was not there. Formulation of the context grew in the process of writing a novel. It was this instinct for a context that drove me on. Besides, I knew more about novels than I did about plays. The notion—or *a* notion—behind the play was that a man gains power because he is drawn into a vacuum of power. In one sense, is a creation of history. There was the germ of this in the first version, but in the novel this became more and more important—as "context." The narrator, Burden, has a "vacuum"—purposelessness—that Stark can fill. The bodyguard stutters, and Stark "talks so good." And so on with the mistress and others. For each individual, the "strong man" is a fulfillment. Here the individuals are the mirrors to society, in a sense.

But to return to the narrator, as an aside. He was the key in this respect. But he originally came into existence as a kind of accident. As a matter of fact, technical requirements often dictate character and meaning. It may be an aside here, but I'll tell how this particular character came about. In the play there is, of course, the assassination scene, in which the young doctor waits in the lobby of the capitol for the political boss to appear. You know he's outraged and that he has a gun in his pocket, and so you know he's going to shoot this guy. Now what happens? Let's take the play. A man comes out onstage, hand in pocket, hat dripping rain. He stands there. Stop. Let's pretend we're in the audience; we have all the information—couldn't have missed it—and as we sit there watching we say, "Go ahead and shoot him." Well, he hasn't come out yet. To which we say, "Come out and get shot, coward." Of course, you see the problem. The author has to satisfy the demand to get on with the play, yet he can't go too fast or it would kill the play. It can't happen rapidly—automatically, according to the expectations. A barrel, rolling down a hill, hits a tree, breaks up. That's action, but it's not drama. You've got to find some way to make the barrel bounce off here and bounce off there. Will it hit? Will it not? In short: distract attention. Throw something across the path of the driving object. A competing interest which serves as a "hold" to make the inevitable, when it happens, come as unforeseen.

This principle of a "hold" and distraction is rudimentary to dramatic art, to any form of telling which is not pure lyric poetry. It's as natural as breathing, but still it's very difficult to devise. You are not working out a syllogism or adding a bridge score; you are trying to fool people. You work toward something which is *expected* and at the same time *not expected*; you want a double take on it. You want shock or surprise, and yet a sense of its being logical. You want variety, and you want the obvious line of a simple plot.

So here we are in this scene: "Come on out!" If he comes out and it's bang-bang, then there's nothing to it, nothing but a blank spot. If you wind up this way, the play is dead. So I had to find something to fall across this movement when the assassin is waiting. Something both natural and distracting. So I brought in someone and tried to get a conversation under way. "How are things going?" "All right, I guess." "We had a lot of good times when we were kids, didn't we? Sure had good times." And the assassin says, "We certainly did."

That's the sort of thing you build on. Now, even at the moment before the act which means his own death too, he takes a backward look on life—boyhood, innocence, and all of that. "Yes, we had nice times"—and in that little moment of speech there's retrospect to a lost world. Then out comes the victim. Bang! Bang! But you've gotten something across there, some current of feeling running counter to the other drive.

So when I first began to think of starting over with a novel, I had to decide on the "voice." The idea of an all-knowing author felt all wrong; no principle for dramatizing development, no internal dramatization of the "vacuum." So out of the air I pulled the nameless newspaperman, an old friend. Give him a role—"vacuum." Why not make it complicated? Make it an employee of the victim: his hatchet man. I've known men from the newspaper world and their theatrical stances. So, okay, put him in and let him start talking. You're on your way.

So, you see, the play got switched over to a novel because of a defect of meaning, because it didn't have a context, and because of a technical consideration. But told this way, things sound a bit too deliberate. They are arrived at by trial and error usually. You rule out one possibility and then grope around for something else. You follow some hunch rather than a line of abstract reasoning.

Interviewer: Did you recognize the problem with the play before or after it was first produced at the University of Minnesota?
Warren: That production took place after the novel had been out six months or so. A friend of mine, Eric Bentley, who is now an eminent critic of drama, was one of my colleagues there. He asked me, "Didn't you write this as a play once?" I said, "Yes." "Let me see it," he said. So I did and he took it around to the drama school, where they decided to introduce it. It was a very splendid production.

Interviewer: When the movie was made, was there any use of the play version?
Warren: No, but when I sold them the book, I had to sign the play over to them, too, to prevent any chance of my coming out later and claiming that they had taken something from the dramatic version.

Interviewer: Perhaps you could settle an old argument. When I was in graduate school, a girl was writing a thesis on *All the King's Men* which maintained that Burden was the existentialist hero of an existentialist novel. To me, this was nonsense, and I was secretly delighted when our advisor, on

returning from a colloquium with you at Yale, told her the underlying philo-
sophical scheme was Hegelian. She almost assaulted him physically.
Practically called him a liar.
Warren: It's instructive for me. I wish I had known it.

Interviewer: Neither existential nor Hegelian?
Warren: I didn't know about it, either way.

Interviewer: Didn't using Burden as narrator change the novel's center of
gravity? In one way, he's more important than Stark.
Warren: There is, of course, a vast difference between the two. Stark is the
control point of the narrative, the first impulse, so to speak. But I had to set
him within the context of a world. I needed an efficient cause. Power moving
into a vacuum. So I got my vacuum fellow, or, as it were, my partial vacuum
fellow, into the story. But the real center of gravity in the novel is the dynam-
ics of power. The newspaperman helps illustrate it.

Interviewer: Burden is fundamentally a decent man. What leads him to be
an agent of evil?
Warren: He is a man with a grave defect of character and personality—and
he knows it. He's blind in certain ways and he's ready to be a tool, to enter
someone else's magnetic field. Sounds awful, doesn't it? But it's a constant
thing—power operates that way. Even nice people like Adlai Stevenson oper-
ated that way. All the people I knew wanted to do something for him in their
spare time, even if they had to push doorbells. They were in love with Adlai.
He filled their "vacuum." I voted for him, too. In 1952, that is.

There is a natural need to build something, to be part of a cause, to gain
meaning. This can get to be an evil thing when the great blankness of life is
filled by terrible forces. Look at what happens when this sense of cause is
stimulated by a Hitler or Mussolini. I was in Italy when I was writing the
play—I finished it in Italy in the first year of the war—so I couldn't help but
relate these things, being right in the middle of it. I was cut off from my own
world and I suppose this made my senses more acute. I was bound to wonder
what made these events, what blankness had made it all possible.

Interviewer: I'm still confused. Which theme struck you as most important:
Burden's quest for self-knowledge or Willie's political corruption?

Warren: Well, it wasn't so back and forth, you know, in the process of com-position. Things don't come as clear options—rather, as aspects of a single complex process.

Interviewer: Which one provided the forward movement?
Warren: Well, I wanted them to be related. I wanted to make a story, rather than have the story make the relationship. It never crossed my mind that Burden . . . No, that's not true—I guess it crossed my mind. Let me put it this way: Stark was the conscious focused image.

Maybe I didn't succeed very well. I remember going to see Bernard Berenson and being quite shocked when he said, "I want to tell you about your book. That fellow Stark is not very interesting." Well, I was taken aback because I thought I'd done my level best by Stark. He gave me a real lecture on this, a real lecture. The book, he said, was all Burden; for him, Stark was an excuse for Burden's existence. He liked the book fine, but not for my reasons.

Interviewer: You were also criticized for doing too well by Stark, weren't you?
Warren: Well, I've been called a fascist off and on all my life. That's what happens to a Jeffersonian Democrat in this crazy world we live in.

Interviewer: Why did you choose Huey Long as a model? Was it because the events of his life made for an exciting novel, or was there a particular moral issue about Long himself?
Warren: What I say might sound rude, but I don't mean it to be. It's not at all a matter of choosing in most cases, but of being chosen. The natural thing is for the story to be about you—it's always about you. You don't really start off: It's time to write a novel, what shall I write about? Now, there may be instances—Hollywood or some commercial writing—where the writer is that objective. But I don't think most writers, good or bad, work that way. They tend to have a lot of stories available to them just because they are human beings. Anybody here knows a lot of stories—whether he knows he knows them or not, he knows them. Now, when a writer decides on one of the many stories he has encountered, he doesn't just say: I'll take the third from the left. He sees his material in terms of a type of story that somehow catches hold of him, like a cockleburr in his hair. Why it's this story instead of that one that he picks to work on may be accidental, but waiving that consideration, it's

really because it has a germ of meaning for him personally. An observation or an event snags on to an issue in your own mind, feelings, life—some probably unformulated concern that makes the exploration of the connection between that thing and the issue rewarding. This can happen without your being conscious of why some particular scene makes it happen.

I don't for the life of me know why the Long cockleburr got hold of me, but the accidental reason is easy: I was living in Louisiana where there was a world that was very dramatic and about which I had very ambivalent feelings. One gang was saying, "Oh, this savior!" and another was saying, "Oh, this son-of-a-bitch!" You couldn't help but speculate on what accounted for this social situation. But you could be certain of one thing: it didn't happen out of the blue. There had to be a context beforehand. When you have incompetent or bad government long enough, you get Willie Stark. Somebody had to move in to fill the vacuum. It doesn't have to be a vacuum of power; it can be thought of as a vacuum of social goods. A felt need will be satisfied, one way or other, and it doesn't matter whether Stark is just making promises or is actually trying to deliver on them.

Now, this was going on in Louisiana in a very dramatic way. But it was happening everywhere in the world. The New Deal—same thing. You see, somebody has to provide the bread and circuses; if not, there's going to be real trouble. You won't just have bad government but maybe no government at all. And I don't mean to sneer at the democratic process. When the voters have a need they want immediately satisfied and somebody says, "I can do it for you," why, it's natural for them to elect him. Of course, you can have a leader who is fulfilling justified needs merely as a means of seizing power, or who uses corrupt means to fulfill the legitimate needs, and that raises the question of what price tag you're willing to put on the fulfillment.

The situation in Louisiana prompted my amateurish speculation about history and morality. It feels strange talking about it now—it was all so long ago; it's like talking in your sleep.

Interviewer: You suggested before that the method of narration in *All the King's Men* presented a problem. Did any of Conrad's works furnish a guide?
Warren: I've known Conrad since I was a boy of fifteen or sixteen and I like him very much. He's a wonderful novelist. But I don't think he influenced me, not so I was conscious of it. But that sort of thing enters the public

domain—after Conrad, novels could never be quite the same; he was in the air.

Interviewer: Getting away from fiction for a moment, would you comment on your view of political power as something shaped by an existing vacuum as it relates to the desegregation of the South?
Warren: Sure. In 1954, if there had been any leadership out of Washington— that is, if old Ike had been even half aware of his obligation to exert his authority and leadership—a great mess would have been avoided. But he retired from the issue, and instead of giving a rallying point for moderate and liberal opinions, he put his head under a blanket for almost a whole year. There was a vacuum in leadership from Washington and on the local level too, and this enabled a hard-nosed segregationist minority to charge right in.

I remember talking to the Secretary of Education in one of the Southern states at the time. He said, "Look. Shut that door and I'll tell you right now that sixty percent of all my county superintendents would like nothing better than to be desegregated tomorrow. They're all bankrupt, and integrating the schools would save them no end of money. What they need is for somebody to get up the right legal suit so they can turn around and say, 'I didn't do it— they made me.' If they could save face, they'd be glad. We can't afford segre-gated schools. But if you print that I said this, I'll call you a liar."

I remember, too, going up into a little county in Arkansas that had deseg-regated voluntarily. It was 1955, late '55, and there had been a lot of violence there. The people were poor; I remember seeing people lining up in the streets for government beans. I spent a very long time with one of the offi-cials—chairman of the school board, I think he was. I asked about the deci-sion to desegregate, and he said, "We didn't have any theories. We were broke. It cost sixteen thousand dollars a year to move them niggers to a Negro school and we didn't even have sixteen thousand dollars, so we figured if we integrated, we'd save sixteen thousand dollars a year. But then the speech-makers started stirring things up and soon my business was being boycotted. They were getting ready to bomb my house, my wife was threatened, and my kids were being chased by little ruffians. I reached the breaking point. One day I was coming out of the post office when some guy stopped me and called me a nigger-lover. Well, I let him have it. Now I don't care—I'll take the consequences." This is an interesting story, you see. This man had a problem in responsibility. He worked it out logically and defended his position, even to standing up to the bomb throwers. In the end, he came out on the side of a principle. If there had been some real leadership in the land, his story might have been multiplied many times over.

Interviewer: But if a man is a convinced segregationist from the start, how much of a possibility is there for his conversion on the basis of principle? Doesn't prejudice rule out logical deductions?

Warren: You can ask a man, "Are you for segregation?" and he may answer, "Yes, suh, segregation forever." Well, what he's really saying is that he's for segregation—everything else being equal. Would he be for segregation if it cost him a considerable amount of money? If it meant not educating his kids? If he had to go to jail? When things get sorted out, segregation is probably not at the top of his list of priorities—and leadership should sort things out.

There's danger in looking at the white Southerners and writing them off as Negro-hating segregationists. People, you must remember, are awfully complex creatures, and you may be in for some surprises if you divide the cast into heroes and villains. History plays some pretty cruel jokes. Remember when all the liberals in England were wringing their hands over the plight of the poor Boers in South Africa? You should: it's in the history books. Not too long ago the Boers were the persecuted people. Not much sympathy for the Boers nowadays. The same Boers are now the prime racist villains of the world. And remember that wonderful book *Let Us Now Praise Famous Men*, with pictures by Walker Evans and James Agee's text? Everybody's heart bled for those poor people—the white sharecroppers of Alabama. The book exposed the poetry and pathos of their lives for us to weep over. Now those who then were doing the weeping go down to Tuscaloosa or to the march on Montgomery and see those same people and they become the hounds of hell in the public eye. They're no worse and no better than they ever were, but you change the question and you get a different perspective.

Interviewer: Getting back to novel writing: have you ever used actual persons in your writing and then been embarrassed when you met them again later and they told you they recognized themselves?

Warren: No, they don't know it at all, and I don't tell them about it. Sure, you use things—you even use yourself and try not to tell yourself about it. You use whatever you can get your hands on; but you're not really using a person, you use something attached to a person—some suggestion, some episode, some quirk or trait of character. Take Jack Burden. I used a model, but he doesn't know it yet. I know him very well indeed. I even know that he doesn't know what I know about him. And that's knowing a man mighty well.

Interviewer: Why did you have Stark start out as an idealist? Was it because one of the stories you heard about Huey Long was that he began this way?
Warren: In a way, it seems there was a deep mixture of impulses in Huey, which is only a way of saying he was human and stuck with himself. But Huey aside, dramatic considerations would have dictated the "idealism." I remember a lawyer I was interviewing in Arkansas. He said something like "I started out to make a little money—to study law and make a little money. Then I wanted to square things up and I got caught up in it, you see." This man simply stumbled into idealism. You encounter such things all the time.

Interviewer: If you draw on real people you know, doesn't your novel, when you reread it, have a depth it doesn't have for us who aren't acquainted with the models?
Warren: Oh, I know where the materials come from and I could trace them down, but the people in the book aren't the people I drew on. Bits have been projected, whole aspects of character have been filled in, basic changes have been made.

Interviewer: I'd like to ask a question about criticism. People are always asking, "What does this mean?" And critics write all their articles trying to explain away the confusion. Now, I don't read a novel to get at any real meaning behind it. I read for enjoyment. Is that so wrong? Isn't there a danger that literary criticism will get to be like logical positivism in philosophy: a concern with meaning that winds up just being a study of words? Maybe a book should confuse you just to make you think.
Warren: Do you mean you're confused when you think?

Interviewer: No, I mean that confusion inspires new patterns of action.
Warren: I'm not trying to make a joke when I say I'm so confused that I would welcome some clarity, or some help towards clarity. What we want, I think, is not added confusion but a mental experience that gives a sense of moving from disorder to order, to a moment of poise. It isn't a matter of just

getting to some resolution tagged on at the back of the book. What we basically get out of a novel or play is an imaginative involvement in experience. The novel, say, starts with "confusion"—that is, with a problematic situation; otherwise, there would be no "story." But you must move through the "confusion" to the point when you can say, "Ah, now I see." This is an image of the possibility of meaning in life. It's a metaphor for meaning. To me this is a key notion. There is a satisfaction, a lift, a liberation in reading a good novel, seeing a good play, or reading a good poem. I feel, "Oh, things *do* work, after all!" Most of life is a hodgepodge in which it's very hard to feel meaningful. Seeing life in some way reflected in a guise that implies order gives a heightening of energy, of relief. It's a liberation. *Not*, I should emphasize, because of particular "solutions" offered, but because the process is an image of the possibility of meaning growing from experience—an image, that is, of our continuous effort to make sense of our lives.

Interviewer: But I can't construct a philosophy in books. What they do is to make me seek more, to give me new ideas.
Warren: Not by confusing you, though, do they?

Interviewer: Yes. If I'm complacent, I won't go anywhere.
Warren: Oh, but that's another matter. Every story, to be a story, must put you in trouble. The other day I read a remark attributed to—I think—Kathleen Norris. She said writing her novels was perfectly simple: put a good girl in bad trouble and then get her out. Well, she may not write the best novels, but she had the best idea. You want somebody in trouble and you want to wonder if he'll make it through or not. No trouble, no story.

Interviewer: Let me try to synthesize a bit. You maintain that significant fiction deals with trouble and that art represents an attempt to lead from confusion to understanding; would you be subscribing to the theory that great periods of art coincide with periods of stress in history? And might this help account for the Southern renaissance my colleague John Bradbury has been writing about?
Warren: I don't think there's much doubt about it. But let me try to say what I mean here. Certain kinds of stress do not permit immediate artistic manifestation. As the seventeenth-century poet Abraham Cowley put it, troublous times are the best times to write of but the worst to write in. When the house

is on fire, you don't sit down to write a sonnet. But a period of cultural and moral shock, short of the final cataclysm, does breed art. See New England of the great days, or Elizabethan England. Deep conflicts of values can release tremendous amounts of energy. When the pieties are shaken, you are forced to reexamine the whole basis of life. A new present has to be brought in line with the past, and the other way around.

The rapid rate of industrialization of the agricultural South had profound and sweeping effects. Smokestacks were rising—right in the bosom of the Jeffersonian ideal, and, it should be added, in the bosom of a good deal of poverty, pellagra, and illiteracy, not to mention the local variety of racism.

Interviewer: When you've written a book, do you feel you've surrendered it to its audience? Should a reader be at all concerned with what you meant when you wrote it? I guess I'm really asking: Do you believe the so-called intentional fallacy is a fallacy?
Warren: Stated that way, it's primarily a question of semantics. I would prefer to approach it from the other side. A writer doesn't know what his intentions are until he's done writing.

Interviewer: So, in a way, writer and reader are approaching the work on a similar footing?
Warren: If you look on a work as the writer's exploration of possibilities, then the question takes on a different complexion. A work represents a growth of meaning. You, the writer, are chiefly involved in finding, in growing toward meaning, but you haven't got a fully organized intended meaning when you start off. You have a certain body of feelings you are hoping to control, but not a specific intention. Intention is closer to result than to cause. A reader can infer an intention—that's well and good and part of the way we react to art—but that doesn't mean it was created according to the reader's impression of intention projected into form. I should add that this impression is exactly what the writer wants the reader to wind up with.

Interviewer: Guide us a little further. When you are writing, are you directing yourself to the work of art, or are you using it as a means to approach your audience and reveal something of yourself and your view of the world?
Warren: I don't think about my audience when I'm working. This doesn't mean that the audience isn't important. It is, but not right then when I'm

concerned with trying "to make it right." I've heard many writers say the same thing. Now, making it right, of course, means making your vision available to somebody. But if you see it's not being made available, if it's going off the rails, it's not because it isn't grasped by an audience but because the thing isn't right itself. You are your own audience, but because the thing you've written doesn't conform to what you think you wanted to express during the process, then it's wrong and you had better start over. No, I'm not saying what I mean. The question is not whether the thing being done fails to conform to a preconceived notion. It is whether—and let me emphasize this—the thing being done is violating a logic implicit in the process of composing it. Or worse, because you have not discovered the internal logic.

Conversation: Eleanor Clark and Robert Penn Warren

Roy Newquist / 1967

From *Conversations* (New York: Rand McNally, 1967) by Roy Newquist.

Warren: Born, April 24, 1905. Guthrie, Kentucky, in Todd County, fifty miles north of Nashville, Tennessee. Population, 1206 or 1305, I forget which. It's still the same—hasn't changed to this day. Half in Tennessee, half in Kentucky, half black, half white.

I went to public schools through my third year of high school in Guthrie, then went away to prep school for a year, and from there to the university. . . . As a writer I arrived fairly late. I wrote one or two things as a youngster. I remember an overwhelmingly passionate desire to write a poem when I was twelve years old and had a fever. This proves the pathology of art. I actually wanted to be a naval officer; I had an appointment to Annapolis, but had an accident and couldn't go, so I went to Vanderbilt University instead. For three weeks I intended to become a chemical engineer. Then I fell into bad company. I had a freshman English coach named John Ransom. He was the last man to recruit, to want to recruit, anyone to writing, but he couldn't help it because he made it so interesting.

Lots of young people took his courses and decided it would be nice to be a writer, and I was one of them.

I wrote a great deal during college, and went on to graduate school at Berkeley, California, for two years, then to Yale graduate school, then to Oxford for two years. . . . I came back to the South in the middle of the Depression. I had to go back. I wasn't programmatic about it; I just felt I had to go there. It wasn't really home, it was simply a part of the world I had a stake in. At Oxford, probably out of homesickness, I began to write fiction. . . . But something happened to me at Oxford that simply took me back to the South. Perhaps it was because of the fact that when I was in college in Tennessee I became so involved with the university world, and to misuse a big word, the philosophical world, that even when the Scopes trial was held a few miles away

52

I didn't go to it. Five years later I thought I was a damned fool not to have gone to it, so I came back from Oxford and became wedded to the South again. I could have gotten a bad job elsewhere.

Newquist: That was during the period when such a disproportionate number of our writers originated in the South.

Warren: It's true, I suppose, that for a while we did produce more than our share. And you're bound to wonder why, if you have lived in the South a great deal of time. I think it happened this way: The world of the South was frozen from 1865 to 1917, when the First World War came along. Things happened there, but the pattern of thought wasn't disturbed. There were no new ideas, no basic changes in society. The First World War shattered the frozen quality of the South. The key element in the South, the most obvious element, at any rate, is the race business. Once the First World War had been fought the South had to recognize the fact of Negro mobility, labor mobility. The Negroes would move from one place to another in the South where they were needed, and leave the South for opportunities up North.

A comparison (a more drastic thing, but nonetheless a comparison) is what happened in fourteenth-century Europe, when the Black Death struck and the labor ratio was changed. Society couldn't be constructed along the same lines afterward. But all sorts of shocks came to the South, beginning in 1917. I remember the people I knew, the college students and older people of the 1920's; they didn't look to New York or the Middle West, wonder what they were like, admire their writers. I madly admired Dreiser, and still do; he's a great writer, but I didn't look to him for guidance. In a strange way the relationship with the Irish and French writers was more important. Particularly the Irish, because ours is a provincial area, speaking provincial English. Our attention was focused on the European rather than the U.S. Northern. The writers, the Southern writers, of my generation, had a European orientation; Pound, Eliot, Crane, Stevens. Yeats and Joyce and the French novelists were our world. I never heard the word "Marx" used except in Hart, Schaffner and Marx until after I left college. This was a strange contradiction; every Southern freshman, literarily inclined, knew *The Waste Land* by heart in 1922. We sat up all night reading Baudelaire, but Marx and Freud were only ugly rumors.

Then our insular world ended. Strange tensions and ferments were bred, running from the question of a "new conscience"—"new discomfort" was the better description—regarding the Negro situation, and new notions of economics, and a sense of a world existing outside us. Just acquiring a sense of the world outside was challenging.

Hope came, too. The poverty of the South was immense, and the mere fact that the possibility existed of improving one's lot was an exciting thing. Even the black man felt this, as the possibility of change took hold.

Actually, I should think that all literary or artistic revivals, or new states of awareness, are based upon shocks of consciousness or moral shocks. You stir a man to a point where he wonders what he can do about an existing state. This happened in New England in the 1830's and 1840's, and in Elizabethan England of the eighteenth century. The Renaissance was a period of change through shock.

Results are always evidenced at different levels and scales. The society that is frozen, fixed in its values and procedures, begins to think about itself in a new way when it is kicked in the can. In literature the society can objectify the issues it finds most urgent. It's not a parlor trick, not a game; it's both a cause and effect of the society waking up to its own problems, its own inner nature. The South had this experience. It was shocked out of what it was. But you can't shock people too much, as Toynbee has noted. Too much challenge is like shooting a man in the heart. It doesn't make him do anything; he's dead. The Civil War, with its dire poverty and total shock, didn't bring change. It had to be just enough shock, the right shock treatment. The war genera-tion in the South during World War I was the real carrier of the shock. Younger people like me benefited from it. We were picked up in the backwash. But the generation of John Crowe Ransom, Allen Tate, William Faulkner— they made the real crossover.

World War II hasn't affected the South as much. Economically, yes—you can see the new prosperity. But there's been less social change. The big thing has been the civil rights movement of the 1950's, which could be regarded as a delayed backwash of World War II. The new mobility, the new investment of money in the South, has benefited Negroes in a backhand, corner-of-the-table way. Without World War II and the new education for whites and Negroes through the GI Bill, you wouldn't have had the civil rights move-ment as it is known in the South and elsewhere; so I suppose that the second war did have deep and significant effects, after all.

Newquist: In *Who Speaks for the Negro?* you examined the civil rights move-ment in an extremely frank and intimate manner. What motivated the book, and how was it done, and what did you hope to accomplish?

Warren: In one sense it was a purely personal book. You can't be a Southerner and not have the whole race question on your mind in one way or another. It's bound to be there. I simply had an overriding interest. I have my own feelings, and they were informing me of what was happening, but I guess I just wanted to know more, to really inspect my own feelings. I didn't go at it in a "Which side am I on?" approach; that wasn't the point. I knew where I stood at that time on that question. But I wanted to know the shades of feeling. You can't walk into Martin Luther King's office and say, "Let's go out to lunch and have a conversation." He'd say, "I'm busy; what do you want?" You have to have a reason for the project, a reason for yourself.

The key motive was to find out about that world as deeply as I could, to find out about myself as deeply as I could. The only way of "finding out" is to write a book or a poem; if you're a writer you will only do your thinking because you are writing. I must say that I have never had a more fruitful experience. The mere fact of seeing that number of people who feel such an extraordinary degree of commitment; the intelligence, the gaiety that sometimes entered. When you think of the great number of young Negroes of the highest intelligence, the strongest drive, devoting themselves to civil rights, you can only wish they didn't have to fight spooks. I'm not saying that what they've done and what they're doing isn't crucial and valuable, but what if all this energy was put to another purpose? To cancer research, for example? But they're committed to fighting the spooks of society instead of dealing with the real problems of nature, the real problems of man at another level.

America is a story of release of energy at different levels. One can see where each wave of immigrants has had a perfect release of energy, a sudden full entry into American life. The most recent and best-advertised release, artistically, is the Jewish literary impact. A Negro literary impact is just beginning; we are feeling the first stirrings of some extremely talented people. But think of this release of energy not in terms of just a few talented people, but a bang, a racial release. This is what has happened, stage by stage, to the various groups of immigrants. We don't even think about it any more. It is simply assumed. Now the last great reservoir of human energy, ethnically, is the Negro. Once that vast reservoir of energy is released we should run over with vast strengths and talents.

The Negro in a secret and suppressed way has made great contributions to American life, even when he was supposedly cut off from participation. The effect of the Negro has been enormous. We can't even guess what America would have been like without the Negro. No Civil War, a totally different structure of American life, different language, different music. Yet while the Negro has made an enormous impact racially, he's been cut off individually. This full recognition, the full release of energy, could come anytime in the next fifteen to thirty years. And it will be tremendous.

Newquist: To turn to *All the King's Men*. Could you explain its genesis?
Warren: I was writing novels and living in Louisiana, so there you are. It was just that simple. I was living in a melodrama. But all of my novels have come out of the same sort of thing, out of a world I knew something about.

If something doesn't interest me deeply I don't want to fool with it. It never crosses my mind to find a good story to write a novel about. I have to have enough interest in the subject matter to make me want to, have to, write the novel. Anyone knows a thousand good stories, but when you can get worked up about a thing that has a special rub, a special concern, then it simply has to be written.

Newquist: As a poet and novelist are you aware of a conscious obligation, to whatever quarter that obligation might be owed?
Warren: Yes, and I can say it very quickly. Two obligations. One is not to lie. The other is to write as well as I can. You're trying, imaginatively, to set up a world that feels like truth to you. This is the way it really is. It must be that way. And you have to do it as well as you can. You're not going to whip out something worthwhile without feeling it through.

I think your obligation begins at home, always, where you're trying to tell the truth as you see or feel it. And I'll make a remark on the side: I think that if more obligations began at home there would be fewer public troubles. If home truths were applied we'd have a great deal less trouble in the world.

Newquist: You've done a considerable amount of teaching at the university level, creative writing and literature courses. Has this been satisfying, on the whole?
Warren: Let me go behind your question, if I may, without trying to under-mine it. I don't see any difference between teaching classes in Shakespeare or classes in writing. It's all the same process: trying to teach people to apply their wits to the problem at hand. Fortunately, most of my teaching has been straight teaching; I can't imagine a worse fate than teaching just writing.

By and large, over the years, I've had an extraordinary range of talented, intelligent students. When you're teaching seniors or graduate students you

expect this, of course. As for really memorable experiences in teaching, I
don't recall a more extraordinary group of people anywhere than the students I had at Louisiana, seniors and graduate students. What this proves,
I don't know. Perhaps I was lucky.

Newquist: As far as your own body of work is concerned, which works have
given you the greatest satisfaction?
Warren: I have to take two views, a short view and a longer one. When you're
doing something, you're committed to it and the work is it. To think beyond
that would be death. As far as the long range is concerned, the novels that
seem to have brought the most satisfaction to me are *World Enough and Time,*
Flood, and *All the King's Men.* But when it comes to choosing fiction against
poetry, it's more complicated. I have to change my metabolism. Many years
ago I talked to Moravia about his first novel, and he told me that he thought
of it as a poem. I know what he meant. All the novels I have written have
seemed to me like big poems, with the chapters and events as metaphors rather
than documents. This is the way I think of fiction, from one perspective.

Newquist: How do you evaluate literary criticism and reviews?
Warren: I don't. I don't know how to survey it or analyze. It's possible to pick
up the paper on a day when something's right, another day when something's
wrong.

On the academic side I think that "high-brow academic criticism" as
opposed to straight reviewing has passed through a very strange phase where
exegesis of a certain sort has become the order of the day, and this is a necessary phase, but it's about run its course. They're moving to something else.

You see this when the works of a particular writer are dealt with. Take the
works of Faulkner, now. They've about done the exegesis of most of his novels, for better or worse.

Newquist: To turn to the younger writer: what advice could you give him, or
what would you hope for him?
Warren: I'm not an advice-giver. I'm not even an advice-seeker. But I would,
above all, make him an honest man. If he's a genius, I suppose he can be a
little crooked now and then. But anyone who wants to write is going to pay a
price, a damned big price. The gamble is big. Anybody with common sense
and a reasonably solid character and reasonably good health can make a

comfortable living these days, but the aspiring writer has to put a lot more on the line. The gamble is bigger, and I suppose the reward can be bigger, too. If he's honest and he works, advice is beside the point. He'll merely do what he must do, and that is everything.

Newquist: In considering American literature as a whole, which writers or books or specific events do you regard as landmarks or turning points?
Warren: This is a question I shy away from in my own mind, because I want to prowl around the question rather than plow right into it. The context swamps the question for me. I could pick off things for a textbook immediately, but I wouldn't feel the answer would be quite true. You can say *Huckleberry Finn,* and be true and untrue at the same time. It was *the* novel when it came out, and it was and is important, but to regard its enduring popularity is one thing, and to try to evaluate its influence is another.

When Hawthorne wrote his first few stories, nobody read them. Now we look back at them and say, "Ah, that was a great moment," but nobody read them when they came out. They were published in obscure magazines. His best stories were published that way. So at what point do they become a turning point? We now say that those stories were new and fresh, extraordinary and revolutionary, but when they were first published nobody read them.

Melville's poems, published in 1866, now look like world-shaking events, but nobody read them then.

It isn't as simple as saying, "This particular writer changed things when he wrote such-and-such."

The fact that Hawthorne existed is the important fact, but we can't talk about his particular stories because they weren't read or understood or even thought about for years. They had a slow effect. It wasn't until 1850 that *The Scarlet Letter* had any effect at all, and then it was misunderstood. Melville's *Moby-Dick* is great, but 115 years ago, when it came out, it was a failure. Now it's a great influence. Conversely, for many years Longfellow was appraised as some sort of god, but nobody could be of less influence than Longfellow for the past seventy-five years.

This is the tangle I get into when I try to answer this question. Just look at the 1930's. *In Dubious Battle* and *Citizen Tom Paine* were talked about in American literature classrooms in the tone of voice reserved for Shakespeare. Now we have to think hard to recall who wrote them. And at the time, the same time, you couldn't get anyone to speak well of *Light in August* or *The Sound and the Fury*.

Note: Later in the evening Eleanor Clark, Robert Penn Warren, and I returned to the subject of the young writer who seems so inclined to seek help from older ones.

Newquist: Perhaps it's from isolation that the young writer tries so hard to establish contact. There must be a feeling of working in a vacuum if you live apart from fellow writers.
Warren: It's true that Eleanor and I were very lucky in having a lot of friends our age, and many who were somewhat older, who were very bright and literary. We didn't have to go out and knock on doors. Rapport was built-in. I don't think we felt lonely or dependent. I could talk about things, the important things, with people my own age, and Eleanor and her sister and their friend could even start their own magazine [at Vassar]. I suppose, if you're isolated in a non-literary community, it can be a different matter entirely.

Clark: It's something else we're talking about, really. Who could have been more lonely than Sherwood Anderson as a young man? Or Dreiser? Actually, I don't know all the details of their early lives, but they certainly couldn't have lived in a very stimulating environment. And when you think of France, of the great writers of the nineteenth century, it seems they all studied in loneliness in some provincial town.
Warren: They didn't stay there long, though.

Clark: Even so, reaching out for communication is not the same as reaching for a handout. Let's make this distinction.
Warren: I was speaking of the necessity for communication as a thing that comes first—

Clark: But these people who write to us don't want you to talk; they're writing for a handout. They're writing for a synopsis of your own novels, or an introduction to someone here or there, or for help in getting a grant. This isn't asking for communication—
Newquist: Or as your friend Peter De Vries says, "While you're up, get me a grant."

Warren: Boy, that's true. You have to dodge getting grants, these days. They're like atomic bombs, all over the place. Few of us have survived the grants. The world is being blighted by them. It's a war against art.

Clark: This is another important difference between now and the time when we were making it, and starving in garrets. Nobody starves in garrets anymore; there's too much money around.
Warren: There's no romance in art anymore. So many ways of getting an easy berth.

Newquist: What do you think of the mechanics of so many best-sellers? The personality-oriented book that is sold to paperback and motion picture before it's ever written.
Warren: And then turns out to be a bad book.

Clark: The analogy of this very sort of thing is found in almost any poor section of Italy. People come to you wanting a job, and their idea of a job is this: Since you presumably move in a bigger world and have friends in Rome, your friends will know friends who know people in the ministry of something-or-other and, therefore, they will get a back-door job. This is the normal process of thought. Not to go out and do a job well. Of course, there are economic reasons for it, in these cases. And a certain involvement of historical procedures.
Warren: Not as a saw, but as a way of life.

Clark: It is, and it becomes a rather depressing commentary on a society. The business of today's young writer has become strangely analogous to this for very different reasons. There's no dire poverty behind their coming to the older writer to say, "Give me a hand." Something else is involved, but the psychology is the same. You go to somebody to get influence. Instead of sitting down and writing the best poem he can write, which is all that goddam well matters, all that matters. You write it or you don't. You're capable of it or you're not capable of it, and this should be all that matters. But in so many cases, it isn't what matters at all. They think first and foremost of climbing the ladder like some sort of awful worthless vine without roots.
Warren: This is true. Most of them haven't written anything at all. They're not the compulsive writers who have to write. They are people who don't write, but who do want a swimming pool in California.

Albert Erskine at Random House is a subtle and witty man, and he would say that most writers he knows want to have been writers or to have written. They want the contract, the swimming pool, but they don't want to work. They don't want to live the process.

Clark: We were talking to John Hersey the other night about students taking LSD and all that. He remarked that what saddened him as much as anything was the way LSD, in so many cases he's seen, is a surrogate poem. It gives the illusion of being a poet and producing a poem without having written a bit of poetry.
Warren: I wonder if it could ever lead to an A-plus on a term paper.

Newquist: As far as the young writers are concerned, wasn't there more emphasis on the literary quarterlies—the *Southern Review, Antioch Review,* etc.—in the days when you, Mr. Warren, were an editor?
Warren: You've got to remember that most of the wonderful things that appeared in the quarterlies and reviews weren't things that could be published in popular magazines. There were exceptions; the *Southern Review* published several stories by Katherine Anne Porter and two of her finest novelettes, *Old Mortality* and *Pale Horse, Pale Rider.* She could have published those elsewhere, but she preferred that they be in the *Southern Review.* We published five stories by Eudora Welty, five of her best. This was her choice, too.

Clark: But a lot of us couldn't have published our stories anywhere but in those reviews and quarterlies. Someone once sold me on the idea of having an agent. It was a disaster. This poor agent looked at my things and she didn't know what they were all about, much less could she sell them for real money. Those stories were at home only in the *Kenyon Review* and the *Partisan Review* and *Life and Letters Today* and the *Southern Review.*
Warren: Young writers may have had more patience then, more ambition; we had a natural set of contributors, and they seemed proud to have their stuff appear in our little magazines. In Louisiana we had the cream of fiction flowing into the office. Extraordinary first stories—they don't seem to be written any more. We never had a problem filling each issue with prose and poetry we were proud of. I don't really know if the young writer's approach to writing is that much different today. In the money sense everything seems more acute. The *Southern Review* has been revived, and they are paying. But

money—I saw this during the few years I was at the Yale drama school. The shadow of Broadway fell over it. The students weren't aiming at writing the play they really wanted to write, or could write; they were trying to write next year's big hit. But perhaps the situation in the off-Broadway theater will change that prestige symbol.

Newquist: I wonder if young writers get star-struck any more; fall under the influence of someone and worship—
Clark: That could be so exciting. I remember when I was about seventeen, and discovered T. S. Eliot. I'll never get over it; I would say it was the guiding influence of my whole career. Eliot was the introduction to Marx and everything else. He broke up the conventional world I had known and presented a literature from which one could assemble a whole new fluctuating world. When he died last year I read all the obituaries I could find and I was absolutely overcome.
Warren: Ralph Ellison says his life began with *The Waste Land* when he was at Tuskegee. That it changed his world.

Newquist: A final question for both of you: If either of you were to chart your careers over again are there things you'd do differently?
Clark: I'd have married him earlier.
Warren: Very much earlier.

Clark: As far as undoing career mistakes are concerned, wouldn't you make others?
Warren: I'm sure I'd make worse mistakes. I think a man had best settle for what is done the first time around.

Clark: I feel very lucky in my life. Woman, writer, and mother. I haven't formulated all this, not even to myself, but I'm sure it's a crucial sort of trinity.

Writing is removal; it's got to be. And being a mother is the opposite; it's an involvement. It's got to be, or you're a monster. A man is better able to remove himself from such involvement than a woman; perhaps it's the nature of the male.

But hardly anyone talks about one aspect of motherhood, and I haven't put it into terms for myself. When you have children you're surrounded by an endless and extraordinary creativity all of the time. It's a fantastic experience, and goes on at a pace adults cannot even remember. No experience as a single person can possibly prepare you for the barrage of creativity. It may be the total difference between being a single woman writer and a mother woman writer. Your time is chopped into: you're chauffeuring, you're worrying about colds and measles, you love them and practice piano with them and hundreds of things. And it's all time-consuming but it's lovely. But it isn't the big question as far as one's own writing life is concerned. You learn to accommodate your own impulses to this barrage, and it's a vital and difficult thing; yet if you are living with children who are pouring out inspiration by the mile every single day, it's as though you are looking in on God creating the universe. You somehow must accommodate the nature and proportion of your own creativity to this immense fact. How it is done, I don't know. One does manage—on some days.

Warren: I think this matter of isolation and involvement is a constant struggle between poles, so to speak, for the writer. This is why we have to get away by ourselves, just to have a relaxation from conscience. But hasn't this always been true? The Anglo-Saxon artists, poets, painters of the nineteenth century were forever flocking to Italy. Now we're flocking to a village in France just to get away from too much social consciousness, and to have our children in a French school for a year.

But we're not expatriates. We're rather the opposite of that. We just have to live and work for awhile away from here, away from tension.

The Uses of History in Fiction

C. Vann Woodward / 1968

From *The Southern Literary Journal* 1 (Spring 1969): 57–90. © 1969 by the Department of English of the University of North Carolina Press at Chapel Hill. Used by permission of the University of North Carolina Press.

Warren: I want to say that I am appalled and honored to be invited to a group of historians. It makes you feel that the writing of fiction is more important than you thought it was, and that your writing is, too. I am honored to be here and it is a great pleasure to be among my friends—three old and dear friends.

What I want to do now is simply to try to state a few principles that occur to me about the relation between history and fiction—in a way, between history and art, as I see the problem, as a background to what may happen later.

First I should like to say that the word "history" is a very ambiguous word. Clearly it means on one hand things that happened in the past, the events of the past, the actions of the past. And the word also means the record of the past that historians write. So whenever the word is used, we have to sort out its meaning. I myself use it differently, in each sense, as the occasion may demand, and I'm afraid my friends do the same thing.

As Vann has said, history is in the past tense. That sounds simple enough. It is about the past. But it is not simple, because it is not merely about what happened in the past, it is also the imaginative past.

History and fiction are both in this past tense. History is the literal past tense. The historian says, "It was in the past; I prove that it happened." The fiction writer says, "I'll take it as it has happened, if it happened at all—which it probably didn't." But the mode of the past tense is the past tense of a state of mind—the feel of the past, not the literal past itself. It is a mode of memories. It's the mind working in terms of memory. The history of the past that the historians write is the racial past, the national past, the sectional past, all kinds of pasts, including economic history—but the past, always. To the novelist, say Thackeray writing about Becky Sharp, the past may be merely a little personal past. But it is past. Even science fiction is about the past; the writers tell about the future as though it were past. In science fiction, you get yourself to a point beyond the story that you are telling. It is never in the future tense. It is in an assumed future which has become a past.

This fact points to a particular stance of mind: it has *happened*, and we are trying to find its meaning. It's a mode of memory we are dealing with, an actuality as remembered. History is concerned with actuality; its past must be provable. The fiction writer's past is not provable; it *may* be imagined. His characters *may* be imagined. But historical characters are imagined, too. They are brought into the picture of an imagined world. For how do we know the world of "history" unless the historian has "imagined" it?

Now, the big difference here between history and fiction is that the historian does not know his imagined world; he knows *about* it, and he must know all he can about it, because he wants to find the facts *behind* that world. But the fiction writer must claim to *know* the *inside* of his world for better or for worse. He mostly fails, but he claims to know the inside of his characters, the undocumentable inside. Historians are concerned with the truth *about*, with knowledge *about*; the fiction writer, with the knowledge *of*. And neither of these "knowledges" is to be achieved in any perfect form. But the kinds of "knowledge" *are*. This is a fundamental difference, it seems to me.

This leads to another distinction. Fiction is an art, one of the several arts. I want to read a little passage—the most radical passage I could find—about art as distinguished from other human activities. "Either art is a pure, irreducible activity, one that provides its own peculiar content, its own morality—it includes itself in its own meaning; or art is, on the other hand, a pleasanter form of presenting facts, meanings, and truths pertaining to other realms of reality like history, sociology, morality, where they exist in purer and fuller forms." This states the distinction quite coldly. For fiction is an art, like painting or music—with one difference. Its materials are more charged with all the human commitments and recalcitrances and roughnesses.

Now, here is where the rub comes, I think. The materials that go into a piece of fiction may be drawn from history or human experience, but their factuality gives them no special privilege, as contrasted with imagined materials. They have, as "materials" for it, the same status, and nothing more than that. But they come in with all the recalcitrances and the weights and the passions of the real world. The simplest example I can think of is this. Take *Hamlet*, or any tragedy we all admire and respond to. It is dealing with the recalcitrances of human pain, confusion, and error. We know these things all too well: the pain, confusion, and error of our own lives. But we come out of the play not weeping, but feeling pretty good, and we go down to the beer parlor and talk about it. Something's happened to the pain, confusion, error. It has happened only because we put the pain and error into perspective, and look at it—to see it and at the same time not quite feel it. We see it as if it had happened a long time ago—to us, but to somebody else, too.

There is, however, always a point where the exigencies and the pains of the materials of fiction or drama or poetry are too great to be absorbed. This recalcitrancy, which is the basis of contention between the form and the content of literature, can become too great. The really bigoted Catholic cannot read Milton; the really bigoted Protestant can't read Dante. In reading literature we have to make allowances for our theologies and our beliefs. But there is a point where it cracks. Let's recognize that. There is a form in which the recalcitrant material—that is, the practical commitment in relation to it— violates the vision of humanity, the long-range beauty of contemplation that is art. Let's leave it there for the moment.

Warren: Our little girl, who is about eleven years old, was studying for an exam in American history, and she said to me, "Hear my lesson." I heard her lesson and she said things I thought were pretty preposterous, but I didn't say anything about it, because I knew she was saying her lesson for an exam. I was too smart to say anything about it, but she was watching my face. "Oh, Poppy!" she said. "This is for an exam; this is not the truth. I know better than this."

Now, this is not the historians' fault. This is the people who write textbooks of history. It's very different. Official histories may be tests, or orators at the Fourth of July, or textbook makers, but not historians. They are very different, you see. And girls of ten years old get this point quickly; they understand it perfectly. By the time they are seventeen or eighteen, in college, they may lose it. But they know it at ten years old. They watch things much more shrewdly than their elders; they have no stake in it except truth—truth, and grades. They are quite different: they know this, you see.

The historian is after this truth, and it's a good truth. So is the novelist. They are both trying to say what life feels like to them. They have different ground rules for it. Let's assume that both are conditioned by their societies at every given moment—at every moment in history, in time. Now, the breaking-out process is always an act of imagination for both the historian and the novelist. The rules are different, though, in this sense: the historian

must prove points, document points, that the novelist doesn't have to document. Yet without that sense of documentation, the knowledge that It Is
Possible, the novelist can't operate either. He is conditioned always by the
sense of this documentation—that it is historically possible. He himself is
tied to the facts of life. He must respect them. Insofar as he departs from
them by imagination, he departs in terms of the possibilities laid down by
these ground rules of fact—psychological fact, historical fact, sociological
fact, all the various kinds of fact. Those are his ground rules. He can take a
new view of them, but he cannot violate any one of them to a point which
invalidates acceptance. That's the big proviso here. It varies a great deal. The
materials that go into his work come from the rough-textured life around
him, made up of beliefs and facts and attitudes of all kinds. A bigoted
Catholic can't read Milton, and a bigoted Protestant can't read Dante, but a
civilized Catholic can read Milton with joy. There's a point, though, where
one's commitment to basic ideas and basic materials, by reason of bigotry or
something else, makes one incapable of accepting the total vision of an
art—of a novel or a poem, or whatever. Let's face this fact. The autonomy of
the art is always subject to the recalcitrance of the materials and to your own
lack of self-understanding.

William Styron: I don't know what I'm going to say to add to this confusion.
We've been dealing in very intelligent abstractions, all of which make me feel
that maybe we should get a little bit more concrete. I like that phrase of Red
Warren's just now: "the autonomy of the art is subject to the recalcitrance of
the materials." This is something that I have had preying on my mind for
some time, in regard to a private argument, which became extraordinarily
public, having to do with a book I wrote not too long ago. It occurred to me
in thinking of this particular book, *The Confessions of Nat Turner,* that in all
of the extraordinary flak and anti-anti-missile barrage that has surrounded
it, no one, insofar as I know (and I don't mean only people who criticized
it from the black point of view, but a number of my white commentators
as well; and I bring this up not out of any immodesty, but simply because
I'm more comfortable in talking about particulars rather than aesthetic
abstractions)—no one has conceived of this book, which does deal with
history indeed, as a separate entity which has its own autonomy, to use Red
Warren's phrase, its own metaphysics, its own reason for being as an
aesthetic object. No one has ventured, except for several people in private

(bright people, whom I admire), to suggest that a work which deals with history can at the same time be a metaphorical plan, a metaphorical diagram for a writer's attitude toward human existence, which presumably is one of the writer's preoccupations anyway—that, despite all the obfuscation which surrounds the really incredible controversy about the rightness and wrongness of racial attitudes, wrong readings of Ulrich B. Phillips, Stanley Elkins, and so forth, a work of literature might have its own being, its own fountain, its own reality, its own power, its own appeal, which derive from factors that don't really relate to history. And this is why, again, I'm intrigued by Red Warren's phrase, "the autonomy of the art is subject to the recalcitrance of the materials."

I would like to suggest that in the endless rancor and bitterness which tends to collect and coalesce around controversial literary works, it might also be wise to pause and step back (I'm not speaking of my own work alone)—and regard a work as containing many metaphors, many reasons for being. This is true for all the literary works I admire. They are works (and I would include, among modern works, books by my distinguished contemporaries to my right) which do exist outside of history, which gain their power from history, to be sure, which are fed by a passionate comprehension of what history does to people and to things, but which have to have other levels of understanding, and have to be judged by other levels of understanding. It may be that in our perhaps overly modern and desperate preoccupation with history, which can be so valuable, we lose sight of the ineffable othernesses which go to make a work of art. At the risk of repeating myself once more, I would like to say that these factors have been forgotten.

Warren: May I say something, Vann? It strikes me that the question is one of the basic tensions of our whole lives. We can't have an easy formulation for this, an easy way out of the question. We are stuck with the fact that life involves passions and concerns and antipathies and anguish about the materials of life itself—whatever goes on in our hearts and outside of ourselves. This is what good literature involves. If you couldn't carry these things into literature, literature would be meaningless. It would be a mere parlor trick. All this—the concerns, the confusion—goes into literature; it goes into the arts. It exists in terms of the experience that the writer describes in literature, presented there in and of himself. They are not the same thing for everybody; a little different, you know, for each person, frequently quite different. But they all go in as passion, as commitments of various kinds. Yet at the same time the thing described must be made objectively itself. Now, take Glendower, to whom Ralph was referring. Now, nobody here is a Welsh nationalist, I trust. If there is one here—

Ralph Ellison: Ralph Ellison is.
Warren: No, you're not; *you* aren't Welsh.

Ellison: I'm a Welsh nationalist. But I also admire art.
Warren: I'm a Confederate. So here we are. We have personal loyalties and problems, you see. But in *Henry IV,* Part One, Glendower didn't bother us in terms of the great theme of the play. People are not living and dying over Glendower today. This is a purely pragmatic approach to it, you see; what can we surrender, what immediate needs can we give up, how can we withdraw our commitments in a given region of this play—in materials of the play—to gain a larger view? Now, I couldn't care less who won the battle at Shrewsbury, personally. It was a long time ago, and it isn't very important now. . . .

What I care about is the pattern of the human struggle there—as we know it in relation to Hotspur on one hand, and to the cold calculators on the other hand, and to Hal, as a kind of Golden Mean, and then, at last, to Falstaff, with all of his great tummy and great wit, and his ironic view of history and morality—outside of all schematic views. We are seeing a pattern of human possibility that bears on all of our lives, a pattern there that we see every day—the Hotspurs, or those cold calculators like Westmoreland, and then the people like Hal, who try to ride it through and in their perfect adaptability be all things to all men, and drink with Falstaff and kick him out at the end (in the next play, of course). We see this happening all the time. Shakespeare wrote a great vision of human life, but it's not about Welsh nationalism.

C. Vann Woodward: I'm interested in this question of fact myself. One of our distinguished novelists present, Red Warren, has written a novel about an historian. I think that Jack Burden was an historian, really. At least he was the narrator of *All the King's Men,* and he had two historical investigations in his career. One of them, you'll remember, was the investigation of the truth about an ancestor, I believe a great-uncle named Cass Mastern and he said that the investigation was a failure. It was a failure because he was simply looking for the truth. The second investigation was about a man who turned out (though he didn't know it at the time) to be his father, Judge Irwin, and this investigation proved to be a great success. And he said that the reason for that success was that he was only looking for facts. The facts resulted in the suicide of his father, and a tragedy. So an interesting distinction was made there between facts and truth. Jack Burden, incidentally, was an historian, a seeker for a Ph.D., as some of us have been.

Warren: He didn't get it.

Woodward: He didn't get it, and the reason, as you say, was he did not have to know Cass Mastern to get the degree. He only had to know the facts about Cass Mastern's world. I would be interested in hearing you discuss this distinction between fact and truth. I think it's to the nub of our discussion, perhaps.

Warren: I'll tell you how it happened. I'll do it in two ways. One is how it happened to me, and the other is what could be said about it afterwards; they are quite different things. Jack Burden himself was a pure technical accident, a way to tell the story. And you stumble into that, because you are stuck with your problem of telling a story; you have to make him up as you go along. But that's another problem. The question about his peculiar researches, as I look back on them, is simply this. Being a very badly disorganized young fellow, he really didn't want the Ph.D. anyway. He stumbled on his family history, involving a character in his family, a couple of generations back, who had devoted his life to trying to find a moral position for himself. And this young man, without any moral orientation at all that I could figure out (he's an old-fashioned lost boy, not the new kind—there have always been these lost boys), didn't want his Ph.D., and he didn't know what to do with himself. He didn't know his mother, he didn't like his father, and so forth. At first he couldn't face the fact that in his own blood there was a man who *had* faced up to a moral problem in a deep way. He couldn't follow it through, could not bear to face the comparison to the other young man. Then, he couldn't face the truth otherwise, without this piece of research. Later, when he had the job of getting the dirt on a character in the novel, he did get all the facts. He gets all the facts, and the guy turns out to be his father, who commits suicide. It's a parable, I didn't mean it to be one; I wasn't trying to make a parable of truth and fact. It just worked out that way. You sort of stumble into these things. It's a parable, as you pointed out to me tonight; I hadn't thought about this before. Well, the facts Jack Burden gets are deadly things. Facts may kill. For one thing, they can kill myths.

Speaking Freely
Edwin Newman / 1971

From *Speaking Freely*, January 3, 1971. © National Broadcasting Company, Inc. 2004. All Rights Reserved. Reprinted by permission.

Edwin Newman: In one of your books, you quote Hawthorne on the Civil War: "It was delightful to share in the heroic sentiment of the time," Hawthorne said, "and to feel that I had a country—a consciousness which seemed to make me young again." Is that missing now, do you think? Missing from many of our people? Obviously, we don't want to have another war to achieve that, but—
Warren: We haven't got that kind of war right now [in the Vietnam conflict]. The war is different.

Newman: Do we have a sense of country at all? Is that still with us?
Warren: I'm quite sure we have a sense of country, at a level not evoked by this war. This war doesn't evoke it. Pearl Harbor evoked it. Overnight, automatically. This war doesn't evoke it. This is a policy war, and a policy war can never evoke a sense of country.

Newman: There must be a more fruitful way to evoke a sense of country than by war.
Warren: Indeed. I should say. But it's a very painful fact that usually a war evokes it more than anything else. William James said, "The only tax men pay willingly is a war tax." This applies to the emotions, too. And quite rightly, I think, in one sense. In peacetime you should be critical of everything your country does. You should try to keep it straight. And in a moment of great crisis you forgive your country its errors, in order to let it survive. But William James is right. The war tax is the only tax men pay willingly. This applies to your emotional relationship too.

Newman: You're willing to have your emotions taxed, as well as your—
Warren: That's right. That's right. And normally, I think, any intelligent person is inclined to criticize his country more strongly than he will criticize

anything else. And he should. He should. It's a way of criticizing himself, too. Trying to live more intelligently, and more fully.

Newman: During the Second World War, when you were the consultant on poetry for the Library of Congress, were you not telephoned one day to advise on what was represented as poetry by a general?
Warren: I sure was. I was feeling pretty well out of it, because the Navy didn't want me, and the Army would have to come and get me if the Navy didn't want me, and so I was waiting. They never came. But a general called me up one morning and said—rather, a captain called me up and said General So-and-So wants to talk to the consultant on poetry. The general is writing a poem for a song to inspirit our boys—

Newman: To inspirit . . . ?
Warren: To inspirit our boys, he said. This is what the captain said. He was a very educated captain. And a very fancy captain, clearly. And the general came on, and he said, I want to find out about the meter. What do you think of the meter of my poem? And he read the meter on the telephone, from some place—and he tapped it out, and I tapped it out, and we tapped it out. Did four or five times. I thought it was fine meter for his purposes. So we didn't go into anything beyond that. I remembered part of this. I remembered a lot of it at the time, but it tends to leave my mind now. Well, all I can remember now is a couplet, which was a refrain. It kept coming back in. "We are the boys who don't like to brag, / But we sure are proud of the grand old flag." That's good wartime poetry.

Newman: Is that poetry, by the way?
Warren: No, it's wartime poetry. It's a general's wartime poetry, you might say. It's about as good as General Patton's poetry, though. Did you ever hear his poetry?

Newman: No, I haven't.
Warren: I read a fragment of it once. And Sitting Bull was a pretty good military man; he wrote some poetry too.

Newman: Patton's poetry was all addressed to the God of War, was it not?
Warren: Um-hm.

Newman: God of Battles, I think.
Warren: Something like that, yeah. Very much like very bad Kipling.

Newman: Mr. Warren . . . the American South gives the impression of being a particularly rich, fertile field for literature. If it is, if indeed it is, what is it that makes it so? Why have so many celebrated American writers come from the South? Is it the climate? Is it the War? Is it the fact that it had slavery? Or is it possible to say?
Warren: Yes. I'll make a guess. If you have a very—a firmly organized society, aesthetically organized, fixed, rigidly fixed, with little sense of change in it, and little opportunity—limitation of opportunities of various kinds, with unremarked, unobserved, undefined pressures there, building up, usually moral pressures of one kind or another, or partly moral pressures—you suddenly introduce other forces that are very shattering to this, morally shattering, morally disturbing, plus a sense of shifting ranges of opportunity for feeling, for all sorts of things—you are apt to get some reaction. It may be literary in part. Some kind of cultural shock, cultural collision of a rather static world, against a world more fluid and provocative, which involves a moral issue of some kind, it's apt, very apt—probably, you can judge from history—to get some kind of literary expression.

Newman: So the more flexible society is less likely to produce—
Warren: Well, I wouldn't say that, exactly. I'd say a society waking up is more apt to write than it is to do anything else. . . . In the earlier part of the nineteenth century you have something almost parallel to that—a very rigid society suddenly brought in contact with European and Eastern thought, and suddenly money was also a different part of it. And a whole shift took place in the structure of New England society, from the old, the preacher-teacher-farmer, you suddenly had State Street and finance, and people going to Germany to study, like—like Longfellow being sent to study and coming back to teach—this world, shock of ideas, plus people taking those ships out to the Orient. Suddenly a great shock and a change of the social center of gravity. There is a whole theory about this, how firmly based I don't know, but it's a theory backed by a very eminent historian, that you have this shock of a change of the nature of power in New England. It's the key to the whole ferment of ideas from 1830 on.

Newman: It's the flowering of New England.

Warren: That's right. From that point on. In the South, with its deep, very deep moral ambiguities around slavery—it being a very democratic country, with terrible slavery in the middle of it—and the home of our republic—because Jefferson was Southern, and so was Washington—carrying on a tradition outside of the American tradition. Slavery again. This whole question of an internal struggle, usually glossed over, but central to the whole life of the section; and then a very frozen world, cut off from modernity up until the First World War. And the First World War, you had this great, great shock of meeting the outside world, really meeting it. Also the shock of meeting the black man for the first time, in a new role. In one of Faulkner's novels, a returning black soldier (one of the early novels)—a returning black soldier was a shock. He was wearing a uniform. It was a different world. From that time on, it was a different world. This whole encounter with the outside world from Ireland—this is very important to the South, some part of the South, anyway—the image of Ireland as a rebellious minority, and the South as a rebellious minority, or French educations and experience in the war, and England—the explosion suddenly in all different directions. And I think you can make a case for this. You have the same thing in different ways happening with the sudden great burst of Jewish literary genius in this country; and black, the same way. The same kind of shock—the breaking up of a fixed situation, where some people have been more or less enclosed, brought into a fruitful relation and a shocking relation to the world outside.

Newman: And that's what we're having now, this—well, the Jewish outburst has been going on for some time.

Warren: For some time, and the black outburst is now in full swing. The release of all sorts of submerged and hidden capacities. Brought about by some strange, shocking relation to an outside world. It's a certain kind of shock, of course. But we see it, stage after stage. We see it in the first breakthrough of the immigrants, with Dreiser. He was the first immigrant writer in America. In the long time since America was established. And a whole new vein of feeling came from American literature with Theodore Dreiser.

Newman: I suppose you see it in another way with Willa Cather—in the West?

Warren: Yes. But that society was firmly fixed. It was rigid, you see, and it wasn't in the sense of minority society, as Southern society was, or Jewish society, or black society, you see. These are fairly firmly fixed, enclosed groups, with their own order of life, and their own special kind of limitations and deprivations, and their own inner problems and tensions.

Newman: In your own case, Professor Warren, both your grandfathers fought for the South in the Civil War—
Warren: And a grand-uncle, too, may I add. He got shot in the leg.

Newman: And I think you heard first-hand accounts of the fighting. Is that correct?
Warren: That's correct. Yeah, sure.

Newman: What effect did it have on you? Did it make the Civil War seem a very romantic thing? What notion did it give you of the South in which you were living?
Warren: It was very double. At the first, of course, a small boy of six or seven hearing about battles, it's all very romantic because he doesn't understand blood, but I do remember very distinctly the shock of discovering that the old man, my grandfather, who had fought battles, wasn't romantic about it. I remember that shock very distinctly. It was a story, an important story to tell, but it wasn't romantic. This was a great shock, because I wanted to make it all very romantic in my childish way. This shock was quite real. I even wrote a poem about it, called "Court Martial"—about that moment when the old man was not romantic at all, and I had been romantic, and suddenly he was realistic about it. So it carries a double thing with it. Though any defeated society is going to romanticize its war, that was done by the U.D.C., not the old men.

Newman: That's the United Daughters of the Confederacy?
Warren: Yes.

Newman: —who romanticize it?
Warren: Well, they are the carriers of piety, and they are the carriers of romance.

Newman: You yourself have written, in dealing with Herman Melville, an American writer to whom you've paid a great deal of attention—
Warren: Yes. Twenty years of attention.

Newman: You quote a line—I should say, you quote a line from Melville, in one of his poems that refers to the Wars of the Roses: "In legend all shall end." Melville thought that would happen with the Civil War. He said, "North and South shall join the train of Yorkist and Lancastrian." Do you think the Civil War is going into legend? Has it gone into legend?
Warren: It's there, I think, now. It's a legend, and a forgotten legend, in one sense.

Newman: May that legend be changed by the black revolt?
Warren: It'll be forgotten by it. It's being changed by it, yes. But it suddenly seems so remote, you know. It'll come back again as something not remote, but it's a great Homeric moment of our history, I think. You can't forget that story, but we lay it aside for the moment.

Newman: We can lay it aside politically, can't we?
Warren: Yes. It's now overlaid with so many ambiguous and confusing and, I think, destructive issues that have nothing to do with the War itself. The War is incomprehensible now to most young people who haven't made themselves historically instructed in it. They see only a kind of gross symbol, not a human experience of infinite complication. But I say this without grief or pain or surprise. It's an observation.

Newman: I suppose it was inevitable. It's usually thought to have become inevitable because of the industrialization of the South, but it probably happens for much less predictable reasons, doesn't it, when you get an historic development of that kind? It happens in ways that nobody can foresee.
Warren: You mean the role of the Civil War in the American consciousness?

Newman: Yes. There certainly have been times in American history in this century when it seemed that the Civil War would never cease to be a political factor.
Warren: Nineteen sixty-one, for instance. And suddenly it's only a thing in New Orleans to wave a Confederate flag for reasons that would have embarrassed Robert E. Lee. He would have been the last man to have been cheering on Governor Faubus in Arkansas. But his flag is being used by—was used for

the school in Arkansas, in Little Rock, or in New Orleans several years ago when desegregation proceeded in those two schools, those two places. But it takes time to reorder symbols, and that's the symbolism it now has. Only history courses will remedy that. Back to Melville. May I cut back there a moment?

Newman: Please do.

Warren: That particular poem—a wonderful poem, with some awful bad lines in it. It's such a poem of fundamental insight to me. It's called "The Battle of Stones River, Tennessee, as Viewed from an Oxford Cloister," and this bloody battle, fought outside of Nashville in the Confederate drive to retake Nashville late in the War, seen by the Oxford Don, a historian or a man aware of his own history, with thousands of miles of distance, it looks like time—he looks back to the Wars of the Roses in England, their Civil War of centuries before, and the poem really says (paraphrased and boiled down) that what we remember from history is human stances, the sense of human values, rather than issues. What remains is the nobility or ignobility of the human stance, the human gesture, the human passion. Not politics or even the moral issues. And this is what happens ultimately: All becomes legend. We see an image of human values, I think. I mean, all the past—I don't mean the Civil War—we have to analyze to bring back the issues. We are really concerned with the image of the passion, the devotion, the courage of human beings in any cause, rather than the weighing . . . distributing right and wrong in the cause. This is the romance of the enemy we always find. The brave enemy is always our best friend, not the rather ordinary fellow who is our ally.

Newman: Again, coming back to Melville, in *The Selected Poems of Herman Melville*, which you edited, you refer quite early in the Introduction really to poetic value. Is that something that can be defined?

Warren: Well, if I could define it today, I wouldn't accept the same definition tomorrow. Put it that way. I made a remark in the Introduction of this sort: In the course of years of reading Melville—sporadically, but off and on for many years—I took a different view of what conscious poetic values that I had when I started twenty-five years earlier, in '46, with my first piece on Melville; and I began to feel more dimensions in the question, just by living very closely with the work of that poet (and other poets). This is, I suppose, inevitable. I change in things all the time. But I was more—For one thing, Melville is a very imperfect poet. He was very unsure technically. And I was forced to think more and more about what survives imperfect techniques. An intuition somehow survives groping formulation, the imperfect formulation of it. And sometimes the imperfection of the formulation actually gives a peculiar poignance to the intuition. But I wouldn't have any clear-cut formula for this. I can report a certain shift in my basic feeling about poetic values, but my whole life, and, I suppose, all lives of people who read poetry, must record a shift of taste. A poet who is great when you're twenty-five is not great when you're fifty. You still admire him, but the infatuation is gone. . . .

Newman: Does this have anything to do with the growing sophistication on the part of the reader?
Warren: I don't think so. It's deeper than that, I would say, individually considered. It wouldn't be sophistication; it might be a new innocence, even, instead of sophistication. But the difference I would insist on, and what I would say about this, out of my own experience, is two symbols that make much sense. It's what nourishes me. There are certain poets at certain times that are necessary to me. And I soak in them. I feed on them. They are saying something to me, or giving me a way of life, a feel of life which another poet will not do at that time, that period of years. The poet I have known before may be remembered with affection and great admiration, but I don't want to read him then, any more. He's not for me any more. I may come back to him. Of course, there are a few poets where the reference is more or less steady—with different degrees, but more or less steady. But very few, I think, for me.

Newman: I remember at a news conference once, General de Gaulle was asked who his favorite poet was, and he replied, "The poet I am reading."
Warren: That should be the way it is, in a way. What you are wrapped up in. I mean, really reading, not just scanning.

Newman: May I go a bit further in this? You have written, with Cleanth Brooks, what I suppose is the most celebrated textbook on poetry in the English language, *Understanding Poetry*, so I don't hesitate to ask you. You take an example of Melville's poetry, and you quote the line "Like the fish of the bright and twittering fin," and you say that the word "twittering" converts

that line into poetry. Is it possible to say how it does that, or is it just something we know from reading it aloud, or rereading it—really reading it, not scanning it, as you said?
Warren: Well, I think I could say why for me. It's not going to be why for you, you see. How does the line go now?

Newman: "Like the fish of the bright and twittering fin."
Warren: If the fish has a bright and twitching fin, it's not poetry, you see. It's not poetry then. That's dead. Couldn't be worse. But "twittering" gives a new dimension to the whole thing, gives a new sense. It's not the only thing that makes poetry, but it discovers a new dimension of feeling. It's like—that little trill of a bird on the bough, as it were. The busy little twitch of the fin in the bright water, and the little warble or twitter of a bird on a bough are now tied together. We see a relation, feel a relation of the density and of resonance in nature. We have expanded our sense of life a little bit, just a little bit, by the twittering, [not] by the twitching.

Newman: It's an image, in the old sense of image.
Warren: That's right. It amounts to a concealed metaphor, a concealed simile of some kind. It opens up our sense of a vital density of the world, the resonance of life. Just a little bitty bit, you know; just a little bit. But enough to make it feel as poetry. A new dimension of feeling has been opened up to experience. And that is just a trivial little line; it's a nothing of a line. This is where he started, though, before *Moby Dick*. He could write *Moby Dick* and write the great poems of the Civil War, and the other big poems he was supposed to write.

Newman: Professor Warren, you have said that the hope was once tenable that a volume of poetry could sell like a popular novel, but that any poet who entertained such a hope today would have to be—would be marked out as a certifiable lunatic.
Warren: Barring Mr. McKuen, of course.

Newman: Yes, Rod McKuen, but what is bad about this change in taste, then?
Warren: This is a long and fumbling answer. If you— It's not a change of taste. It's a change in the world which is behind this. When Tennyson's *In Memoriam* was published, in the middle of the last century, the publishers

gave to Tennyson (for a poem he published anonymously, I think) enough money to marry Emily. He was engaged fifteen years; it was time to marry her. But he set up housekeeping on this poem. Imagine that. The advance on this little poem set up housekeeping for Alfred and Emily. But now I suppose that doesn't happen. Tennyson's poems were published over here during the Civil War. They couldn't keep count of the sales. They couldn't keep count. The book-keeping broke down in the thing so fast. Unbelievable. Unbelievable. Right in the middle of the War. And also, a very small percentage of the public was literate compared to now. But those who could read, read. That's one difference. Everybody reads now, and nobody reads. Or few read. But in any case, why? For one thing, poetry—it wasn't a matter of taste. It was a matter of what kind of needs poetry fulfilled in the broadest sense. It fulfilled the needs of our columnists, the daily columnists. It fulfilled the need that now gives us our weird news. It took the place of novels. It did everything. It was a jack-of-all-trades then, really. If Tennyson wrote a poem called *Maud* about women's rights—but Kate Millett does not write in verse, you see. All right, there we are. *Maud* is a poem. I must say it's not much of a poem. It's a lot of verse, with a few nice lyrical touches, like the bugle, I think, is in there nicely, but by and large this so-called poem, *Maud*, was, officially speaking, a poem, while Miss Millett does not write in verse. She writes in a, shall I say, sober prose. But that's one example right there. Or if you talk about science in the modern world, you don't write a poem like *In Memoriam*. Tennyson writes about science in the modern world, and he calls the poem *In Memoriam*. There are other things there, too, in the poem. Now, if you get Mr. Mumford, and Mr. Reich, and all the other pundits of science and technology—they don't write in verse. Some don't even write in prose. Some do. It's another world, you see. We have specialized out the needs which once put us in a lump. However imperfectly we acted, we acted in a lump, all together. Now we have specialized it out, so poetry is poetry, only poetry and very little else. Now, back in the 1930's you had a little social-consciousness poetry; in Vietnam you have a little Vietnam poetry. But by and large, poetry goes on being poetry, bringing to all of us some special satisfactions which are poetic.

Newman: There's even an enormous difference between World War I and World War II, wasn't there?
Warren: There certainly was. There certainly was. Now, I am not applauding this specialization entirely. I think we have lost certain things by it. And I

would guess we may regain a broader base, a richer poetry, by coming back
to poetry as a fuller reference to life than we have had it for a long time.
Without the awe. Let's look at it this way too. The poetry of Pound and Eliot
and Yeats, the three great masters of our century in English—they were writing about fundamental issues of our society, of our whole world. They were
the people who suddenly made the image of a glimmer of a technological
world emotionally available. Scientists . . . like Bertrand Russell had written
about it; several others had written about it. But it hadn't affected anybody.
But once the image of the Waste Land is there—You see, it's the Waste Land.
That's where it is. Why is it the Waste Land? So, however recondite and specialized we figure the poetry of Eliot was, it also gave us the big, dominant
image of an age. It is now a catchword among eighth-graders, and lies behind
street riots and hippie communes and group-gropes. Now, that irrelevant
poem is a very difficult poem. It took people a long time to understand it.
But what they finally understood was the very world they were living in. It's
very hard to say, in a way, that *The Waste Land* is more specialized or irrelevant than *In Memoriam*. It didn't sell as much. It has sold an awful lot over
the years now to this time.

Newman: Against the background of what you've just said, then, Professor
Warren, let me ask you to explain something else you have said or written.
You say there has never been so much poetry in existence as there is now. You
find poetry on the air, on the hustings, in folk ballads, in advertising copy
and public relations. What do you mean by that?
Warren: I don't mean good poetry. Sometimes it happens to be good. But I
mean the use of the language emotively to compel assent and arouse feelings.
This aspect of language is always there, except among scientists doing a specific job. And it's organized, highly organized, the advertising business. We
know this, you see. They are very, very clever fellows. They know a lot about
the techniques of poetry, and they make very good livings out of it. Some of
them do, anyway.

Newman: That's poetry in the sense of emotive language?
Warren: The manipulation of language to arouse emotion, in that sense.
Emotive language, or controlled for effect—poetry in that sense—or expres-
sive of emotion. In its broad general sense, the world is always full of it.
That doesn't make it good or bad. It may be used descriptively only.

Newman: Professor Warren, you have been teaching for many years. Everybody talks about how different young people are nowadays. Are they different from what they used to be? Have the students you've taught notice-ably changed over the years in a fundamental way?
Warren: Well, "fundamental" is a trick word there, you see. It's a trick word.

Newman: That's emotive language, perhaps.
Warren: I don't think it's emotive language; it's a word we have to deal with, I think. I think we have to deal with that word. There are differences. There are real differences, but I would have to preface any remark about that by saying that I don't want to put them in a lump. "The young" is a word. The actual young are people. They are all different, in their ways. Now, to break them into certain groups, you can generalize about—more than about the individ-uals—I mean, about the group as a whole. And I think, if you are going to have a kind of precocity, a kind of intellectual awareness before emotional maturity, you're going to have a certain number of liabilities with this. At the same time I say that, my observation is in a small range of students I see. I have very few students, really. But I know them pretty well, those I have, because I see a lot of them in a face-to-face way. In five years the level of what I've seen is remarkably higher. The best is no better, but the level is so much higher. And the kind of basic seriousness. I will say this, too—this is surpris-ing to me, and painful to me, that more and more I see a lack of vocation among even very, very brilliant young people. No direction, no passion for life. And this is, I think, a very shattering thing to watch.

Newman: Is that the so-called dropout . . . ?
Warren: I am talking, now, not so much about dropouts, though it applies to dropouts. I mean the bright dropouts—the young man who has taken his degree, has his B.A. with honors, and says, "Where do I go now? There's no place I really want to go." Or the senior saying, "What do I do next? I don't really care." Now a man with an expensive education, a first-rate brain, feels there's no place for him in the world—this is not an uncommon situation. Not uncommon at all. And expanded and multiplied, it can be tragic. At the same time, I know so many people of the same generation who have found the most rewarding lives, so far, in direct action of poetry, writing poetry, or giving two days a week out of his law practice to slum practice, and so forth. These are going on together. They are side by side. And we don't know what's

going to happen out of this. But I do resent the notion that the young are put in one package. There are many kinds of young. And the articulate young, or the noisy young (they're not the same thing, necessarily—noisy and articulate is not the same thing), aren't always fair samples. Think of all the boys in laboratories or libraries who are truly changing the world. The guys in the chemistry laboratories, the guys in the medical schools, the guys—Karl Marx, sitting around reading a book—

Newman: In the British Museum.
Warren: In the British Museum. We don't know where the world is being changed.

Robert Penn Warren: Willie Stark, Politics, and the Novel

William Kennedy / 1973

From *Riding the Yellow Trolley Car*, by William Kennedy (New York: Viking, 1993), 165–73. © 1993 by WJK, Inc. Used by permission of Viking Penguin, a division of Penguin Group (USA) Inc.

In 1946 Robert Penn Warren published *All the King's Men*, the novel that would make him an international literary figure. It was the story of Willie Stark, a Southern governor not unlike Louisiana's Huey Long, whom Warren had observed from a distance in the early 1930s at Louisiana State University. The book became a critical success, a best-seller, won the Pulitzer Prize, and was translated into at least seventeen languages.

Warren conceived Stark's story first as a verse play, *Proud Flesh*, then wrote the novel, then wrote a new play with the same title as the novel. The U.S. film version of the book won an Academy Award, and a Russian version also won a best-picture award. The book has been the subject of a vast amount of scholarship, and has been called the best political novel of the century.

Robert Penn Warren was sixty-eight, not all gray yet, tall, trim, and tweedy when we talked at his home in Fairfield, Connecticut, on February 14, 1973. I was writing the first of what was to be a series of interviews for a national magazine with writers on their masterworks; but the series never materialized and this interview was never published until now.

Warren had moved to Fairfield in the early 1950s, converting two old seventeenth-century barns into a spacious rustic-modern home with eighteen-foot ceilings. He had published nine novels up to this time, plus nine volumes of poetry, and had won a second and third Pulitzer (both for poetry; he is the only writer ever to win the prize for both fiction and poetry), a National Book Award, the Bollingen Prize, the National Medal for Literature, the National Humanities Foundation's Thomas Jefferson Award, and much more, all these for his poetry. In 1986 he would be named the first official Poet Laureate of the United States.

Warren's wife, the writer Eleanor Clark (*The Oysters of Locmariaquer*, a National Book Award winner), prepared lunch for us all in the midst of our Fairfield conversation. The Warrens both work at home, each with an office in one of the two converted barns. To reach Robert Penn Warren's office you walked past garden implements and fertilizer and then you arrived at what he called his boar's nest.

But we talked in tidier surroundings, a living room of the main house with a picture window that looked out onto a meadow with tall pine trees that Warren had planted in the 1950s. His Kentucky twang was difficult to understand at first, but then you quickly tuned in, and you noticed how often he laughed when he talked.

Kennedy: When you look back, does the book have a special place among your works?
Warren: It's a hard question. I don't think any of the novels had the intimacy of the poems, but putting the poetry aside, if I'm just rating the novels, I think it's one of the three I have to rest my case on, feel closest to.

Kennedy: And the other two?
Warren: *World Enough and Time*, the novel that came after it, and then *Flood*, which came out in '64. The first two were extremely well received, and *Flood* had, you might say, a controversial press. Lot of savage attack, and praise too. Those three, I think, are the novels with the most weight in them. Of course I always say the next one's going to be it.

Kennedy: In some ways it's not political at all, but it's been called the best political novel of the century. Why are there so few memorable political novels?
Warren: I don't think of novels in categories like that, novels about horse racing, about crapshooting, and lovemaking. I think of them in terms of the emotional tone or the thematic issues they propose, categories which are more inside.

Kennedy: But when you think of novels of substance with political content, what comes to mind?
Warren: I guess you could call *The Gilded Age* by Mark Twain a political novel and that's a memorable thing; it involved politics. *Democracy* by Henry Adams is an unreadable novel but a fascinating book. He sure

couldn't write novels but as a commentary on politics it's fascinating. *Under Western Eyes* by Conrad is political in one sense; revolutionary psychology is what it's about rather than the practical applications of it. Of course there's Shakespeare's plays, some intensely political, and they're quite memorable; but it isn't the first thing you remember about them.

Kennedy: Or your book either. Maybe in retrospect it's Willie Stark's story but when you're reading it it's Jack Burden's dominance, and the structure of a society.

Warren: When I was in Italy in '48 Berenson wrote me. I went to see him and he said, "Your book's not about Stark," and that surprised me a little because I didn't think it was about him either. And he says "Stark's not very interesting. The book's about Burden and that's what I like. That's your book." I hadn't thought of it so baldly, total dismissal of the Stark story.

Kennedy: But Stark did dominate your first work on the subject, the verse play.

Warren: Yes. I began that play in the shade of an olive tree in a wheat field outside Perugia in the fall of '37, finished a first draft just before Christmas in 1939. I rewrote it but then put it aside and started another novel, and when I looked at it again in early 1943, my whole feel for it changed. And I decided there were more things involved than I was able to get into a play. I began to see that one thing that caught my interest originally had not been the notion of a man of power, obsession of power, riding against the obstacles in his way to success and then disaster—but the context—his relations to other people. More and more I had felt more than a personal story here. The man of power is only half of the matter—the other half being the context in which power is achieved. The man of power achieves power only because he fulfills the needs of others, in both obvious and secret ways. In its most obvious form in my novel this appears in Sugar Boy, the little stuttering gunman, whose devotion to Stark comes from the fact that Stark "can talk so good," is an orator. And so on up to Jack Burden, who having lost a grip on his personal life, only comes alive when he identifies himself with the man who can act. The pattern that finally emerged—emerged because it was not according to a scheme but by a development, a slowly growing envisagement—was that Stark fulfilled some need in every person around him. And this, of course, has implications for politics, or history.

But who could tell the story? It had to be somebody who was intimately involved in the process, who had a deep personal stake and who was intelligent and detached enough to understand his own predicament. Then Burden came in almost as an accident. He had been in the original play as merely a technical device in the assassination scene. He didn't have a name even. He came in to distract the audience and in a sense distract the assassin, before the victim comes on and is shot. A newspaperman, an old friend of the assassin, Adam Stanton, they talk and Adam is caught at the moment of murder and suicide with one backward look to boyhood, to the other world, the unspoiled world.

Then two years after I finished the play I saw Burden as the key to the context I was after. The first morning I sat down with pencil and paper and started to write the novel, Burden started talking.

Kennedy: Would you explain why you decided to write the Cass Mastern section [a long flashback to a pre—Civil War episode].
Warren: I was jammed. I'd gotten to the point where I was going to have a flat, straightforward story. I couldn't see how I could give a new dimension to it. You know you don't think about things in these abstract terms at the time. You feel it rather than think it. At that point the story was going in a straight line to a preconceived climax. I had to have a new dimension to put the whole story against. The Cass Mastern story gave that. It came in a kind of flash.

Kennedy: How far were you in at the time?
Warren: At the exact point where the story is interpolated (about one-third in). I was reading a lot of stuff about Kentucky history at that time.

Kennedy: I wondered about your research on that.
Warren: It wasn't research, it was reading. I don't research a novel. I did no research at all for the Stark side of the thing, not a damn minute of it, didn't even read a newspaper. What I didn't have in my head I didn't have. I was not following Huey Long; I never did one minute of research on Long. I didn't care what Long was, in that sense. I was trying to make a character. But I was reading a lot of Kentucky history, just reading, at the time I was writing the novel and this character [Mastern] began to take shape.

Kennedy: You've credited your editor on that book, Lambert Davis, with changing it. What did he change?
Warren: He was an extraordinarily able editor at Harcourt Brace, my editor and friend. He was not much older than I but was farther along in the world than I was. The big thing was he said the novel is starting wrong. Cut that out and start right here, where I start now.

Kennedy: What was wrong about it,
Warren: Too wordy, too abstract.

Kennedy: Was it nonrealistic?
Warren: No, it was realistic, but rhetorical rather than specific. Abstract in that sense. I remember in that opening description, when Burden meets Stark the first time in a saloon . . . it was like Caesar described by Plutarch. The young man standing on a street corner of Rome, delicately scratching the top of his scalp with one finger; who would've thought he had any harm in him? That kind of crap. Now Lambert said, "This is where the thing begins, on this road, going to Mason City. And this [other] is all preparatory and obviously preparatory, and a lot of bad writing here too, inflated writing." And so I tried what he suggested. In the car going to Mason City the scene comes alive, something happens and you get into Stark's world immediately. Lambert was right. You had to take the author's promise that [the original opening] was going to mean something later. That's a very poor way to start a book.

Kennedy: How did the Elizabethans influence the book? You've written about that but without being specific.
Warren: Let me take an indirect approach to that question. Back then—and now—I was much more soaked in poetry and Elizabethan drama than I was in fiction, and that fact, no doubt, made me think of a novel in much the way I think of a poem. I think of a story, sure, but I also think of it as a metaphorical structure going at the same time as the narrative and other structure. And frequently this feeling I'm driving for seems to come as an image, even a scene, that is floating there, not tied to narrative yet. It's there ahead of me. It couldn't be dramatized directly yet it is somehow in the background. That's related to the Elizabethan stuff. The literal plays behind the novel were two Shakespearean political plays, *Julius Caesar* and

Coriolanus; they were there consciously. And then, less consciously, Webster's *White Devil.* Flaminio, a character in *White Devil,* was in the back of my mind in some sense, I'm sure. I did not realize it at the time but I now see it was. He was somehow behind Jack Burden. Flaminio is a man of blankness gone evil, who's taken refuge in evil to find meaning.

Kennedy: Did you consider Willie evil?
Warren: I wanted to make him a good man, a decent man. . . . He's gone so far into making the means defile his ends that there's a horror he can't dig out of in the end.

Kennedy: Have you ever written about a totally evil figure?
Warren: No, I have no desire to. This thing came to a head when they were making a movie from the book. There were two movies made in this country, one by [Joseph] Mankiewicz, a two-shot TV thing I never saw, I was out of the country; and Robert Rossen did the other, made a damn good movie of it. But about two-thirds through he left my character entirely and made a total villain out of Stark: the fascist brute. My man, you see, gets some redemption out of the novel . . . dies repentant. Now Bob had four or five endings and ran them all off and said "Now, Red, which do you like?" I picked one but said none of them represent what I said in the book. "Son," he said to me, "when you come to Hollywood you've got to learn one thing— there's not going to be anything called irony in the end of an American picture. It's gonna be cops and robbers, cowboys and Indians." And so Willie died muttering the last line from the Horst Wessel . . . tied right into the Nazi-Mussolini picture. Bob and I got along fine because we understand each other. It's his movie, not mine.

Kennedy: Did the book and movie make a big financial difference to you?
Warren: After the book I felt I could eke out a living without teaching. I'd tried it before but it didn't work out.

Kennedy: Part of the success of the book, its wide appeal, seems at least in part the Huey Long element, the politics, the feeling people have that they've got a window on something authentic. You've written about this but I wonder if you'd take it now into the question of fiction versus nonfiction, the appeal.

Warren: A lot of fiction from the start has been based on the fact that it must claim authenticity. . . . *A Journal of the Plague Year* . . . the manuscript found in the chest, the bottle, the thing being authenticated. This is the appeal to journalistic interest, in the best sense of that word. We want the facts of the case. . . . With the rise of modern journalism, in terms of the Civil War, the rise of big newspapers, the country put tremendous new weight on the fact, and this, associated with the rise of pragmatic philosophy, not only William James but the whole sense of the state of mind you associate with James's philosophy: the open-endedness of moving in to see what action means—this is all mixed up with it. By the time you get to the 1880s and the nineties, with the rise of protest journalism, organized muckraking, you have a new urgency about the handling of fact, fact as meaningful politically, in another spirit: we are exposing the hideous underside of life. You get a person like Stephen Crane as a young boy going down in the mines, standing in soup lines and sleeping in flophouses to see what it was like. He was saying the fact is better than the story. Now this became so acute that one of the reigning novelists at that time, H. B. Fuller, who is recognized by Dreiser as the father of American realism, said that the novel is dead, that novelists should become biographers, writers of fact; there's no reality in fiction anymore. Now in another aspect of the romance of fact you get Richard Harding Davis, this handsome, well-mannered, adventurous youth whose life is more interesting than fiction—war correspondent par excellence. He became an arbiter of taste and the model for young men to follow in their lives, the pre-Hemingway model. Davis was so famous it's hard to believe it. The old Oliver Wendell Holmes, the great autocrat of the breakfast table, the dictator of taste, would make a personal call on Davis. Now these two impulses [that Crane and Davis represent] are very strong and we've had them with a vengeance. But Crane is very mixed, on one hand in the flophouses to capture the sensation, to say the imagination can act, and on the other hand his most famous book [*The Red Badge of Courage*] is about a war he never saw, pure imagination. Interviewing a few old men down around Frederick and then reading the official record of the Civil War and thinking about it, imagining it, he gets a masterpiece. He made a very fruitful blending of these things, the technique of fact in the world of the imagination. The point I'm getting at is you find a world now hailing this as a new discovery.

Kennedy: What work are you referring to?
Warren: Capote, say. *In Cold Blood.* Touting this as new. It's an extremely effective book but there's no novelty to it. It's what Fuller was pulling for and others have practiced for a long, long time. . . . People read for a number of reasons. They want to find out how beet sugar is made or how to give a dinner party, or what's the best practice in bed. These are all marvelous know-how books, and they also tell about people, gossip books. But the immediate appeal is the newsworthy element. Fitzgerald's fame was based on his bringing news from the underworld of youth. That's big, and why shouldn't it be? . . . But one thing the fact novel or journalistic essay cannot do is give the inside, because only the imagination can do that. You believe the inside of Hamlet, or Marcel in Proust, or Ishmael more than you believe the inside of Henry Adams in the autobiography, or the inside of the *Cold Blood* killers. The killers you know a lot about, but you don't know them. You know Clyde Griffiths, though. You know him only because he's not factual, only because the fact of creation has made him credible. This is not saying better or worse, it's saying different. The fact novel is fine for decor, the milieu. When the real crisis comes it's always the thing seen from the inside that sticks.

Kennedy: But people don't seem to value that truth these days. Talk to publishers and they say, "What are you going to do about fiction, it doesn't sell."
Warren: One reason we can say is that there are not enough good novels.

Kennedy: But why is that?
Warren: I'm just making a guess, and I don't mean well-crafted novels but ones that take bold risks of imagination. Maybe too much depends on documentation. The novel approaches too close to journalism and forfeits its powers of imaginative creation to be more convincing at the level of reportage. And you can't compete with reporting.

Kennedy: You wouldn't think it was because of the absence of interest in the interior of the human being?
Warren: It may very well be that. At the same time the notion of the interior is news too. But [you find] people interested in inner life as treated by generalizations, by experts, by Kinsey researchers, by God-knows-who dealing with inner life. But they're not talking about individuals. They're

talking about patterns. And it may be that the notion of individualism is in decay, that your mass culture isn't interested in individuals at all.

Kennedy: What does this mean for fiction?
Warren: I don't know, but you find people as far back as Valéry saying that journalism and movies give you immediacy of fact and impact you don't get in a novel, and so literature can only become more abstract, move toward the patterns more or less like abstract painting. So you get the pattern in the art itself rather than art as related to life. And this is a very elite, very difficult kind of art which is not related to the meat and potatoes of living. Now this [move to abstract literature] is hailed today by some as new, but it's not new at all, it's an echo of Valéry. It's important to remember there's a history to these things. It gives a different feeling about the future of the novel. Maybe a more pessimistic one, or optimistic, I'm not saying which it'll be. We're in a process that's been going on a long time, and to gamble it has to be a long-range gamble. Meanwhile, I'm writing another novel, and I have to try to individualize it.

A Conversation with Robert Penn Warren

Bill Moyers / 1976

Warren: I'm in love with America; the funny part of it is, I really am. I've been
in every state in the Union except one, and I'm going there within a month.
Bill Moyers: Which state is that?
Warren: That's Oregon. And I've traveled in the Depression in a fifty-dollar
car, broken-down, old green Studebaker. I wandered all over the West. I spent
time on ranches here and ranches there and have been in all sorts of places.
And I've had change given back to me for gas in the Depression. Some guys
say, "Oh, keep the change, buddy; you look worse than I do." I really fell in
love with this country.

Moyers: *He is a rarity in American letters. The only writer to win Pulitzer
Prizes for both fiction and poetry. And he loves the country he often rebukes.
We'll see why tonight in a conversation with Robert Penn Warren.*

Moyers: The novel [*All the King's Men*] became a classic when Robert Penn
Warren wrote it at the age of forty-one. Almost three million copies have been
sold around the world . . . in twenty languages. The movie became a classic,
too. It won three Oscars. Its subject was politics; its theme, corruption.

Warren: It sort of grew out of circumstances. Grew out of a folklore of the
moment where I was and I guess also because I was teaching Shakespeare and
reading Machiavelli and William James. Everything flowed together. That was
a world of melodrama, the world of pure melodrama. Nothing like it since,
well, until Watergate, as far as melodrama's concerned.

Moyers: Oh, you think Watergate was melodrama.
Warren: Obviously, it was melodrama, tragedy. It was tragedy, too. You couldn't believe it. Well . . . only it happened to be true.

Moyers: Did you think that *All the King's Men* would become a classic?
Warren: I never gave it a thought; I just try to make an honest living.

Moyers: *It has been a prolific life since Robert Penn Warren arrived in Guthrie, Kentucky, seventy-one years ago this month. Since then he's been almost every-where, and written just about everything. Nine novels, ten volumes of poetry, short stories, essays, two studies of race relations. There's hardly an award he hasn't collected. The National Book Award, the Chair of Poetry at the Library of Congress, the Bollingen Prize, the National Medal for Literature, and of course, those two Pulitzers. He's still writing. Increasingly intrigued by the fate of democracy in a world of technology. We talked at Yale University, his base for writing and teaching this past quarter-century.*

As a poet and a novelist, as opposed to being the author of *All the King's Men,* how do you explain the vast disenchantment of our modern times?
Warren: I don't know. It's touched every country in the world; we're not alone, it's part of the modern world.

Moyers: Is there something in . . . ?
Warren: There's something in the modern world going on, and I don't profess to understand it. We can make guesses about it.

Moyers: Make some guesses.
Warren: Well, we are, for one thing—the whole Western world is undergoing some deep change in its very nature in what it can believe in. And one of those things is clearly how democracy can function in a world of technology. That's one thing. Another thing, it just seems the massive number of people involved. Government's designed, the modern liberal democracy is designed, to function within a certain limited world.

Moyers: How successful do you think we are in keeping some notion of democracy, and some concept of the self alive in a highly technological, scientific age of huge organizations?
Warren: Not successful enough. I think you can see many indications of that.

Moyers: What are some of the manifestations you see that deeply trouble you?
Warren: Now, this is a small academic matter in one sense: the death of history.

Moyers: The death of history?
Warren: Yes. History departments are on the decline, I'm told. I don't know the statistics. But certainly they . . . the sense of the past is passing out of the consciousness of the generation.

Moyers: What do you think will be the consequence of that?
Warren: I don't know how you can have a future without a sense of the past. A real future. And we have a book like Plumb's book, *The Death of the Past,* which is a very impressive and disturbing book. As Plumb puts it, in the past people have tried and learned what wisdom they could from history. They have tried to learn from what has happened before. Now, he says, social science will take the place of history. And the past will die . . . and the machine will take over . . . done by social scientists. That's his prediction. He says only history keeps alive the human sense, history in the broadest sense of the word. It might be literary history or political history or any other kind of history. It's man's long effort to be human. And if a student understands this or tries to penetrate this problem, he becomes human. If he once gives that up as a concern, he turns to mechanism.

Moyers: The machine.
Warren: The machine.

Moyers: Process?
Warren: Some process to take charge. Now he may have . . . there are many kinds of machines, there're many kinds of processes he can turn to. But the . . . the sense of a human being's effort to be human and to somehow develop his humanity, that is what history's about.

Moyers: Do you sense among the students you teach, and among the young people you know, this loss of the past, this disconnection from history?
Warren: Yes, I have. I have indeed.

Moyers: What is the effect of it?

Warren: It's a certain kind of blankness. A certain kind of blankness. But the past is dead for a great number of young people; it just doesn't exist.

Moyers: I know you once wrote that Americans felt liberated from time, and that it gave them a sense of being, gave us a sense of being on a great gravy train with a first-class ticket.

Warren: Well, we had the country of the future, the party of the future . . . we had the future ahead of us, and we had this vast space behind us on this continent. We had time and space. We could change the limitations of the European world. Such a simple thing as a man's hands becoming valuable. A man on the American continent in the eighteenth century was valuable, neighbors were valuable, hands were valuable, there were things for hands to do. And so the whole sense of the human value changed . . . right . . . beginning with the value of hands, what they could do. Or the value of a neighbor down the road a mile away instead of twenty miles away. These things made a whole difference in the sense of life. And it's a fundamental stimulus to our sense of our own destiny.

Moyers: They also were a power incentive, were they not, to human dignity?

Warren: To human dignity because the hands mean something. They're not just things owned by somebody else. They belong to that man. And then, all of the rest of the factors that enter into the creation of American . . . the American spirit. All of those things are involved.

Moyers: You said once . . .

Warren: We could always move, and the sense of time—being time-bound and space-bound—disappeared, but mitigated, anyway. A whole psychology was born; it'd never been in the world before.

Moyers: A very optimistic philosophy of progress.

Warren: That's right. As Jefferson said, in writing to his daughter Martha, he said, Americans—I think it was his daughter Martha, anyway—Americans fear nothing, you see, cannot be overcome by earnest application, you see, and what's the other word? Ingenuity.

Moyers: Ingenuity.

Warren: Americans assume that there are no insoluble problems.

Moyers: We've really been—we've really been trapped, in a sense, by Thomas Jefferson's definitions of America in those terms, haven't we?
Warren: That's right, we assume that we can solve anything rather easily. And we're always right. We think we're usually right about it. Since we can solve things, we're the ones who are right.

Moyers: I remember you wrote once that America was defined by one man in an upstairs room. Thomas Jefferson writing "all men are created equal," giving this great metaphysical boost to the American self-image.
Warren: Yes, he gave more than any one person, gave us our self-image. I think he was wrong about human nature in his emphasis on it. He wasn't a fool, of course; he knew that there were bad people. He knew there were stupid people because of six, I think, siblings in his outfit. Four had something wrong with them in the head. And the other one died young. Jefferson's genius was the only one of this brood of children who was even—I think this is right now—who was not in some way deficient. And so he was probably aware of the fact that all men are not born equal, right there at his own fireside.

Moyers: How do people who still live with that mystique of democracy, that mystique of the self, how do they come to terms with the world you have described as being large, impersonal, driven by science and technology?
Warren: They say that's the way to solve it, by and large. They say somebody will fix it up, the expert will fix it up some way. The magic cancer cure, there'll be this, there'll be that. The expert will come along and fix it up. And our faith has gone from God to experts. And sometimes experts don't work out.

Moyers: Well, you've written a lot about how to hold on to the sense of self when the world is changing this way. What do you say when the world enforces a beating upon us from many directions, forces we can't understand, forces we can't change, forces we can't even define? How do you . . . ?
Warren: Some forces we don't . . . even want to change; we want our technology and we should have it, should want it. It's how we use it, that's important. It's the attitude toward it, it seems to me is important, not its presence. From scientific speculation to the applications in technology represents a great human achievement. It's how we approach this and how we wish to use it.

Moyers: Well, I wouldn't want to abandon, would you, this material progress we've made, the things that make life so much more amenable.
Warren: God, no, I don't want to abandon it. My grandfather said he took a very dim view of the modern world—he was born in '38.

Moyers: Eighteen thirty-eight . . .
Warren: Eighteen thirty-eight, and fought the Civil War and wound up life as . . . he died in 1919, 1920, something like that—'21. He looked around the modern world and found it not all to his taste. But he said they have got two things that make it worthwhile. Fly screens and painless dentistry. Well, I'm for fly screens and painless dentistry too. I want that and I want some other things to boot.

Moyers: What is the proper posture or attitude from all the years you've lived?
Warren: The problem is finally a human problem, and not a technical problem. And we're back to the history again. The sense of the human as being the key sense. As we talk about education, this means the so-called humanities is the only place for students to find the point of reference for the application of their science and their technology. That is the sense of the struggle to define values.

Moyers: What are the values that are most important to you now?
Warren: Well, I can tell you what my pleasures are.

Moyers: What are your pleasures?
Warren: Put it this way. Because I'm selfish and want to fill my days in a way that pleases me. Well, it so happens that my chief interest in life, aside from my friendly affections and family affections, which is another thing—though they're related—is the fact I like novels and poems, as I want to read them and I want to write them . . . as I have an occupation which to me . . . I can go beyond that—now, why that occupation? It's the only way that I can try to make sense to myself of my own experience . . . is this way. Otherwise I feel rather lost . . . in the ruck of my experience and the experience I observe around me. If you write a poem or read the poem—somebody else has written one that suits you, that pleases you, this is a way of making your own life make sense to you. It's your way of trying to give shape to experience. And the satisfaction of living is feeling that you're living significantly.

Moyers: Does it . . . ?
Warren: That doesn't mean grandly; that means it has a meaning, it has a shape, that your life is not being wasted, it isn't just being from this to that.

Moyers: It also means imposing . . .
Warren: And understanding.

Moyers: . . . and imposing order, doesn't it?
Warren: Order.

Moyers: Some sense of order.
Warren: Some sense of order on it, yes.

Moyers: What does poetry and literature offer people in an age of technology and science?
Warren: I say it offers an inward landscape. Now, I've been talking about outer landscape, but it offers an inner landscape . . . it offers a sense of what man is like inside. What experience is like, he can see perspectives of experience. This may be in poetry or it may be in history or it may be in political science; it may be taken in historical perspective. Man's view of how he should govern himself over a period of time has changed.

Moyers: But how does it help us to see ways to deal with technology, with organization, with size?
Warren: It makes us ask the question how that light or this object or this automobile or this plane will serve our deepest human needs. Or whether it's a gadget, whether it's a toy. Now, when Coleridge has the Ancient Mariner shoot the albatross for no reason except he has a crossbow to shoot the albatross, he's dealing with that problem. The problem was already there, you see. A machine defines the act. The man shoots the bird only because he has a cross-bow. Why should he shoot the bird? He has no reason to shoot the bird. It's a gratuitous act. The machine defines the act. Because the machine will do so-and-so, therefore it must be done. See what I'm getting at there? Coleridge's poem is a criticism . . . man as victim of technology.

Moyers: How do we get control?
Warren: It's a constant struggle. It means trying to inspect the things that shape us, that make us. Once we understand it, we can sometimes do

something about it. Now, I'm not talking of psychoanalysis; I'm talking much broader than psychoanalysis, which is one—is a special kind of application of a principle that's always been functioning in the world. People look at what made their world tick or made them tick, and they achieve, may achieve, some sense of freedom from mechanical forces. I mean forces of machines, of mechanisms, but forces that have made them into machines and give them habits of doing this thing this way and that way. Religious conversion is one of the most obvious examples of this.

Moyers: Reconversion?
Warren: Religious conversion.

Moyers: Religious conversion.
Warren: . . . is an old-fashioned way of looking at it. A man's been one kind of man; he suddenly understands life differently . . .

Moyers: Do you believe that's still possible?
Warren: I think so. I think it can exist; it exists for certain people.

Moyers: Well, give us some help. How do we do it?
Warren: Try to see how you came to be the way you are. The poem of Randall Jarrell's "Change" ends "change me, change me."

Moyers: And you think it's still . . . is part of the creative process.
Warren: I still believe in such things as religious conversion . . . though I'm a non-believer, I'm a non-churchgoer, put it this way: I'm rather a common type, I think now, of a yearner.

Moyers: The yearner?
Warren: The yearner. I would say that I have a religious temperament, you see, with a scientific background.

Moyers: Pilgrims sought God and looked for a promised land in the hereafter. What do you yearn for?
Warren: I yearn for significance, for life as significance. Now, if I'm feeling with a poem or a novel I'm, in a small way, trying to do the same thing. I'm trying to make it make sense to me. That's all. That's one reason why I like teaching . . . I have a real passion for teaching.

Moyers: How's that?

Warren: I think there's nothing more exciting than seeing a young person moving toward the moment of recognizing significance in something. The inner significance of something.

Moyers: And it happens under what occasions?

Warren: It can happen under— In a classroom, it can happen in any class-room any time and very often. And very often, indeed. And I'm a parent and I've seen it happen to my children.

Moyers: How does it happen in an urban, complicated, interdependent city where life is crowded and services are poor, and a feeling that one is being acted upon by men and events over which he has no control? How does this yearning to signify find the creative satisfaction?

Warren: It means a whole regeneration of the feeling of our society. And it's not going to be done by just making a few appropriations. I knew one man whom I rarely see now—he used to live in this neighborhood—whose job was to explain the background of the National Merit Scholarship winners. What could he find in common among these boys and girls who were spec-tacular intellectually, you see, and had great drive. And he said he had worked on it for years. He had found one thing only was in common: there was always a person behind that child. It might be a friend or a teacher or an old grandmother who's illiterate. It has nothing to do with education. With some sense of recognition by an older person of this child's worth, this child felt valuable, felt valued. And some one person or maybe, maybe more than one had made him feel this was worth sitting at night reading, studying his book.

Moyers: And you're saying somehow we have to get that personal touch back into . . .

Warren: Some sense, something that will correspond to that. To humanize education, or to . . . maybe you can't create the home life again, maybe it's gone. I don't know. Now, I don't . . . I hesitate to be optimistic. But he said at least if they do anything, they know there was always one person or more than one behind that child . . . who suddenly seems like a miracle. He might be coming out of some lowly, illiterate, starving ranch in Wyoming and sud-denly this child appears and it looks like a miracle. But no, the old grandpa was there, talking to the child or some . . . or some teacher spotted him. Now,

Dreiser was the most unpromising boy you can imagine. He was just the most totally unpromising. He was a ferocious masturbator, he tried to get a wealthy girl, got money and . . . and sex tied up . . . tangled all his life. He was a poor student, he scarcely read a book, but some schoolteacher, a Miss Field, spotted him and said that boy has something. And she let him go on and graduate from high school. He got a job in Chicago as a clerk in the basement of a . . . of a hardware store as a stockboy. And she hunted him up a year or so later . . . said I'm going to send you to college. This old-maid school-teacher said I've saved my money and I'm going to send you to college, you've got something. She sent him to college for a year. He wouldn't go back, said I'm not getting anything here, said I'm just not learning anything here at all. So he . . . he wouldn't take her money any more, said I'm wasting your money. But that's the one person that put the finger on him, though, and says you've got something. Anything that will cultivate the sense of the value of a human being is the hope that'll make that man feel valuable, and that'll make . . . make it easier for someone else to feel valuable.

Moyers: Well, we've been for two hundred years a country that grooved on more and better progress, and that hasn't been all bad. It's had a big price. But the question, it seems to me now is, how do you hold onto the material abundance, spread it around so that more people share in it, but at the same time keep what you've written about so often, that sense of self and dignity and individual responsibility?
Warren: Also, we've got to quit lying to ourselves all the time. Now, the Civil War was the biggest lie any nation ever told itself. It freed the slaves. Then what did it do with them? And the big lie was told, and also, we're full of virtue, we did it, we freed the slaves and it came home to roost a hundred years later. But we lie to ourselves all the time.

The lying about Vietnam was appalling. There was an awful lot of lying about Vietnam. There've been all kinds of lying. Now, there's the lying about our dealing with Mexico from the very start. I'm not saying give California back to Mexico; if you have to give 'em somethin', give 'em California, is my motto . . . which I used to know very well. But the point is you cannot keep lying to yourself indefinitely. And my daughter studying her history lesson in American history several years ago when she was a little girl in school—not now; she's a senior at Yale—but I was hearing her lesson for the examination. And she said something that was so appallingly wrong, I must have flushed . . . she said don't say anything, Daddy (Poppy, she called me), don't say anything, Poppy, don't say anything, I know it's a lie but it's what you have to tell the teacher.

Moyers: Well, that was . . .
Warren: And this is the way half of our life is led in America. We have the right lies to tell ourselves.

Moyers: But haven't we stripped ourselves now of that pretense? I mean we were never innocent, but now the pretense is gone.
Warren: The pretense is . . . is going, anyway.

Moyers: You don't think it's all . . .
Warren: I don't think it's all gone, no. You're going to hear more lies the next six months than you ever heard in your life before.

Moyers: The stuff of another novel.
Warren: Well, the lies are going to be told. But see . . . I'm in love with America . . . the funny part is, I really am.

Moyers: What do you like about it? What . . . what does America say to you? Affirmatively.
Warren: Well, the story is just so goddamn wonderful. I mean the whole thing from the . . . the little handful of men, you know, who pledged their lives and sacred honor and set off the world. It's a great story. And it's the plain sweat and pain that went into this country . . . and integrity, the incredible integrity.

Moyers: Integrity.
Warren: There's just lots of it. The people . . . history's full of it.

Moyers: This is the man I'm talking to who wrote that piracy and go-getterism are part of this country.
Warren: They are. But at the same time, you find the other thing is there too. But even the evil is part of the story.

Moyers: It's the story you love.
Warren: I love the story, but also, you can't have a story like for the . . . you know, from babes and sucklings, all life is evil against good. And American history is interesting because that's the way it is.

Moyers: And often the evil and the good reside in the same personality.
Warren: In the same personality. On the one hand you have a man like
Houston who is a . . . is a pirate and a brigand but . . . but a boy who will read
Homer by the fireside of the Cherokee chief when he's . . . when he's thirteen,
fourteen years old and say that's pretty good. And he ran away from home
and was living with the Cherokees in east Tennessee when he was a boy in his
teens and reading Homer. And he turned out to be great.

Moyers: Well, he was very lucky because when he headed west he stopped in
Texas.
Warren: He stopped in Texas, he stopped at the right . . . in the right place at
the right time. But he started out . . . he and the same old Indian chief he met
later on after he had been governor of Kentucky . . . I mean of Tennessee . . .
and had this trouble with a woman there . . . with his wife . . . his wife had
left. But he lived with the Indians again. Now, he and the Indian chief plotted
to conquer the whole West, including Mexican west. And Jackson stopped
him. Well, this is almost verifiable, there's some doubt about it, but it's almost
certainly true. And when he crossed the river, when he plunged across the
river into Texas, his friend rode with him to the river and gave him a new
razor as a parting present. Razors were hard to come by in those days. And he
turned around and said this razor'll shave the President. Well now, this is . . .
this is America. I mean . . . I like these romantic stories of America. And the
incredible energy and the incredible humor of America.

Moyers: Humor?
Warren: Humor. The whole tale of the . . . the folk tales, incredible number
of folk tales, just an incredible number of folk tales. The whole sense of the
. . . the whole South-west . . . it's incredible. But it's the complexity that is . . .
is engaging. But what I hate is they destroy the complexity, to wipe out all
that past and see us outside the past like that. I know we've had heroic ages,
that it's Homeric.

Moyers: Is it over?
Warren: Well, that's up to us. Now, I . . . I felt a thrill with the moon shots.
I know that's not very sophisticated. But I think that's not the whole story,
though. Moon shots and poems are not very different. They're both totally
irrelevant to the ordinary business of life. The guy that devotes his life to

fiddling in a laboratory or fiddling with a poem, they're both outside the ordinary common-sense world. And they're both a little crazy.

Moyers: And yet you value them.
Warren: I value them, indeed. I . . . I think if you once get rid of the craziness in the world, you haven't got anything left.

Moyers: I remember in one poem you once asked yourself, "Have I learned how to live?" Have you answered that question?
Warren: I haven't answered the question, no . . . no, of course I haven't answered the question. How would I? I know certain things about myself that I didn't know one time. Some things I don't like, too, I've learned. But don't ask me which ones.

Moyers: I was just about to.
Warren: But I do know that I have to have a certain amount of time a day for myself . . . they're kept for special occasions, I mean I . . . I want to be alone with my scribbling, my writing . . . my swimming or something. And I don't know why. I . . . but I guess it's a lonely boyhood, I attribute it to that, anyway.

Moyers: But filled with the presence of ideas and people from the books you read.
Warren: That's right. I had a very happy . . . very happy boyhood actually. My summers were very happy, anyway. On an old run-down farm where old Grandfather was very bookish and quoted poems all the time when he wasn't reading *Napoleon and His Marshals* . . . or drawing the maps of Civil War battles with his stick in the dust. And reading military history.

Moyers: Most people don't know that about that part of the South. They still think of the violence and the terror of the South, and the racism. They don't realize that in the world, even when I grew up, it was filled with writing and reading and . . . and presences beyond the known and seen.
Warren: There was a lot of reading; it has declined a great deal too. It was declining already in the . . . my boyhood. But you can tell by the books in the house, the kind of books in the house, you know. Or the . . . or the correspondence of a family. I'd get hold of the correspondence of a family for a hundred years. And an old house being torn down, several times I got the

papers . . . the contractor tearing it down said got some papers for you. And I said I'd read them. But one thing that's impressive, at least in middle Tennessee and Kentucky, was the will toward, well, education or bookishness in the strangest communities. Well, even *Kidnapped* . . . a schoolteacher went to another at gunpoint to get one, you know. And a certain man named Allener, I think, had a big revolutionary grant near Bowling Green, Kentucky. He was a wealthy man with a vast estate; he . . . he had built himself a fine house, but he couldn't get a schoolteacher. So he . . . a man who had commanded a regiment, you see, of regulars in the Revolution, and a man of great wealth . . . said well, I can do something useful, I can teach school. So he taught school for no pay for the rest of his life. Any child that would come, could come. He was a schoolteacher. Now, that is a kind of heroism.

Moyers: Time to be alone, you say, is essential to answering that question: how to live. Do you have a television set?
Warren: No, I don't. I apologize. There's just not enough time in the day, you see . . . there's not enough time in the day . . . so much to do. And if it's television or books . . . what it would come down to be.

Moyers: And you've made your choice.
Warren: I made my choice. Also, I didn't want my children having passive enjoyments.

Moyers: Passive enjoy . . .
Warren: Passive enjoyments.

Moyers: Explain that.
Warren: I'll be honest with you; I didn't want TV around small children. Have the problem of discipline, you know . . . in monitoring it. And they took it; they'd never ask for one. They'd rush to one in any other house, but they would say to the teacher, if he said to you use this program for your course: But our family's not like that, my father won't let me. And there it was. But I . . . this is eccentric, I know.

Moyers: I remember now that you wrote somewhere about the danger of our becoming consumers not only of products but of time not wisely used. Is that what you mean?
Warren: That's part of it, yes. And children are very vulnerable.

Moyers: Well, that provokes me to think that most people aren't poets and writers, most people can't flee, and most people live in systems and institutions that give them very little time to themselves. And yet, as I travel the country and listen to people, they're saying, How can I create myself, how can I signify? Do you have any thoughts?

Warren: I think part of it is will . . . to look into something that opens the inside, that books or, oh, I could say perfectly well . . . I could see it perfectly well being done by TV, you see. I'll be arbitrary about that. But . . . I don't know, I'm not trying to remake the human race, I'm reporting myself as best I can to you . . . and what I find necessary to me.

Moyers: And pleasurable, you said.
Warren: And pleasurable, uh-uh. And pleasurable, yes.

Moyers: What about the process of writing, of creating poems and novels? Was it painful?
Warren: It's a kind of pain I can't do without. I can't say I like it, but I can't do without it. It's the old thing of scratching where you itch. We're trying to find out what the meaning of your experience is. I phrase it that way to myself now. I've already done it to you early today. I've been trying to find out some meaning of your own experience. Now, I often write about other people; of course, this is part of you too. I find . . . I find I can't do without it so far.

Moyers: Can you teach it? Can you teach a young person to write?
Warren: I don't think so. In one sense you can. I think you can teach shortcuts and what to look for. I think you can teach certain things which are peripheral to the actual process. You can't create the kind of person that will be a writer, but you can help a little bit. You can open eyes to certain things and you can show how certain pieces of . . . of literature work a little bit . . . can be helpful. What to look for . . . you can modify a taste to a degree.

Moyers: In more than thirty years of teaching, have you noticed any significant change in the ability of young people whom you teach to write and express themselves?
Warren: I find increasing illiteracy.

Moyers: Illiteracy?
Warren: Illiteracy. Yes, I do . . . right in Yale University.

Moyers: Kingman Brewster's not going to be very happy with that.
Warren: Well, I'm sorry. That's just true.

Moyers: Well, all of this: increasing illiteracy, discontinuity with the past, size, complexion, technology, even television—how does it all make you feel about the fate of democracy?
Warren: I'm an optimist. And I think God loves Americans and drunkards . . . keeps them out of the way of passing cars . . .

Moyers: But not of themselves.
Warren: Not of themselves, yeah. We're part of a whole great process, we're part of the whole Western world, we're part of the whole drive of technology, and we have a very tenuous . . . a very tenuous hold on our . . . our goods and our chattels right now in this world. It's a very dangerous world we're living in. And I wish to God I had some wisdom about it. But I think there is a streak of contempt in the American life . . . of things that are very valuable and . . . not only are valuable, are essential to our survival. We're driving fairly straight for a purely technological society, and with technological controls. And our government is in the hands, in the control of technologists who are not concerned about any value except mere workability . . . immediate workability.

Moyers: Utility.
Warren: Utility. And I'm not . . . not by any sense sneering at the . . . at the useful things of the world. Even the pleasant things of the world, I like 'em a lot. I met a young man a few years ago . . . a few years out of Princeton, such a nice young man, the nicest kind of a young American. He said [when] we were introduced . . . he said, "I'm Xerox." Now he has given up his identity already; he says, "I'm Xerox." He's not Mr. Jim Jones any more even in his own mind; he has no self.

Moyers: He's the organization of which he's a part.
Warren: He's the organization of which he's a part. I'm Xerox. And this is a symbol to me of the whole state of mind of the self ceasing to exist . . . it's part of a machine.

Moyers: Is there an antidote?
Warren: I think there is. I don't know whether anybody's gonna use it or not.

Moyers: What?
Warren: Well, I think the proper kind of education. I mean education that has something of the humanistic about it.

Moyers: That says you matter.
Warren: That says you matter. And the human being is this kind of a creature.

Moyers: You're talking about a rebel. What is it that makes a rebel? Aren't you?
Warren: I guess I am . . . I guess I am. Well, let me read you a little poem about the perfect citizen. I love this one by Auden, the man who is the perfect citizen. He was not a poet and not a scientist and not anything else, he's just simply a good citizen. [Warren reads "The Unknown Citizen."]

Moyers: Chilling.
Warren: It's chilling.

Moyers: Shades of George Orwell. What about the role of writers in our history? The writers who have shaped or questioned, contributed to these two hundred years. What can you say about . . . about writers in American history?
Warren: Well, I'll say this, anyway. If we start pretty early . . . let's start with Cooper. You find a man who creates the first great myth of America.

Moyers: James Fenimore Cooper.
Warren: James Fenimore Cooper. Now, he's . . . on one hand, he says, you see, you have the rape of a natural land . . . the destruction of a natural land. On the other hand, you have the destruction of man and brutality that he's aware of and talks about. And also the paradox, which he has no solution for . . . between the values of nature and those of civilization. He has no easy solution for them. Let's take a case or two and look at [it] right quickly. In *Deerslayer* you have two characters, named Hurry Harry, that's the go-getter, that's his name for the go-getter, the guy who's out to exploit anything, and Hunter, an ex-pirate who's been driven off the seas . . . hidden away on Lake Glimmerglass.

Now, these two guys are partners in the American story. The ex-pirate and the go-getter. Now, this is too pat, it sounds almost too pat. And then this deerslayer, the young deerslayer, he has never killed a man. . . . There's a camp of Indians, women and children at some point on the lake. There's a bounty on Indian scalps. So Go-getter Hurry Harry and Hunter set out to go into the camp—it's abandoned by all the braves—and kill all the women and children and sell their scalps. Now, this is Cooper's view of . . . of a myth of America. And . . . or another case, in running back to his first novel, that series of pioneers with people bringing cannon out to kill . . . to kill passenger pigeons— no reason except the killing of pigeons—with a cannon. They're not going to eat them; they let them rot. At the same time, they lock up in jail the now very old Leatherstocking because he's killed a deer out of season to live on. That episode appears in the first one of the books. But over and over again you have this. He's attacking; he's going at the things in the American society that he sees as incipient and with the same problems we're dealing with now.

Moyers: Well, other writers forged those myths.
Warren: It started with Cooper. You can go right ahead with William Faulkner and Cooper agreeing right down the line. And Frost not far off that line. And then you have another approach which is represented by . . . well, I mean most recently, most famously, Pound, who was concerned with American philistinism of another sort. And lack of a spirituality, if you want to call it that. You have a whole series of the major writers who are violently critical of America. Melville, for instance, violently critical, and they simply are not ordinarily read straight in school. They're just not read straight in school. What they say is not being . . . is not being told to the student. Over and over again you find it's true. And what the implications are of our American literature. It's an extremely critical literature, critical of America and constantly rebuking America and trying to remake it.

Moyers: And yet that's so American—to be critical, to take to task, to challenge.
Warren: That's right, that's American too, you see . . . the fact that they've produced the writers who could take this violent attitude toward their own people or to their own society. Let me tell you something . . . just an anecdote. A man I used to know in Italy—still know—he was a lieutenant in the Italian army when Italy got in the war in the summer of '40. He took to the hills with two friends. A rifle each and a few grenades and some pistols. And

finally joined the partisans, finally found some other discontented people to join with. And as a major with an armored train and an air fleet of his own. But he said that what got him off—his father had fled Italy earlier as anti-fascist (his father being a musician . . . concert conductor). This young man said I left because such a stupid fascist government allowed them to translate American novels. And all the novels were translated because they attack America, these American novels attacking America, you see. The Faulkners and God knows who. And he said to himself, A country that strong that could afford to attack itself and criticize itself must be very strong, so I think I'll leave the Italian army. He did.

Moyers: We're right back to that fundamental division again.
Warren: Right . . . right back.

Moyers: Now . . . we've always seen ourselves, if we read the novels, as we are. And we know now that the masks have been stripped off in the last few years, and yet I still find, Mr. Warren, hosts of people out there who want to believe . . . and want to affirm.
Warren: Well, I'm in love with America. I . . . I want to believe and want to affirm, too. And I just literally—I don't know any other way to describe it—I just fell in love with the American continent.

An Interview with Robert Penn Warren

Peter Stitt / 1977

From *The Sewanee Review,* 85.3 (Summer 1977). © 1977 by the University of the South. Reprinted with the permission of the editor.

Peter Stitt: You entered Vanderbilt at an early age, which leads me to think that you grew up in a home where the life of the mind was fully lived. Is that so?

Warren: Well, both my father and my maternal grandfather had books everywhere. I've got a lot of my father's books right over there. I recently reread Cooper for the first time since I was a boy, using my father's copies. And each book had the date he finished reading it—1890, '91, and so on. I spent my boyhood summers with my grandfather on a tobacco farm. He was an old man then. . . . He read poetry and quoted it by the yard. He was wonderful, an idol. His place was very remote, and he allowed nobody on it except our family: he was totally cut off from the rest of the world. For one thing, it just didn't interest him. I mean, he read books all the time—Egyptian history or Confederate history or American history, and poetry. But there was nobody to talk to: there were very few people in the community who had any interests like his. So I got the benefit of his conversation. I spent hours a day with him and I found him fascinating. He was against slavery but a good Confederate. He said, "I stand with my people." . . . He loved to relive the war with me: we'd lay it all out on the ground, using stones and rifle shells.

Stitt: Was it the literary activity at Vanderbilt that drew you there?

Warren: What I actually wanted to be was a naval officer. I finished high school at the age of fifteen—no great intellectual accomplishment where I went—and got the appointment to Annapolis. But then I had an accident. I was struck in the eye by a stone, and couldn't pass the physical. So I chose Vanderbilt. Then I had to wait a year; they wouldn't take you at fifteen unless you were living at home. I started out to be a chemical engineer, but they taught chemistry primarily by rote: there was no theorizing, no sense of what it was about. At the same time, I had John Crowe Ransom as a professional English teacher. He made no effort to court the students, but I found him fascinating. He taught ordinary freshman expository writing, but he had other things to say along the way, and he would shine. At the end of the first term he said, "I think you don't belong in here. I think I will have you go to my advanced class." There was only one writing course beyond freshman English at Vanderbilt. A few people in their sophomore year would study forms of versification, poetry writing, essay writing—things like that—with Ransom; and this is what I did the second half of my freshman year. He was also the first poet I had ever seen, a real live poet in pants and vest. I read his first book of poems and discovered that he was making poetry out of a world I knew: it came home to me.

Ransom was a Greek scholar by training. He had never taken an English course in his life except freshman English, which was required at Vanderbilt, where he had gone. And he always said, in a tony way, "I don't see any reason to take a course in literature when the language is native to you." He laughed at himself for being an English teacher. "I find myself completely superfluous."

Stitt: Was there much literary activity among the students at that time?
Warren: It was a strange situation, and I really can't understand it even today. There was just a tremendous interest in poetry among the students. There were two undergraduate writing clubs, junior and senior, where people would read poems and essays to each other. And there was an informal poetry club which met about once a week. We'd read each other's poems and booze a little, crack corn, and talk poetry. All kinds of people wrote poems then—I remember two all-American football players, a future U.S. senator, a man who later became chairman of the Department of Romance Languages at Wisconsin, and another who later became the only Phi Beta Kappa private in the Marine Corps. It is hard to believe now, but this is literally true: if an issue of *Dial* would come out, people would line up to get the first one. Freshmen were buying the *New Republic* or *The Nation*, to get the new poem by Yeats or the new poem by Hart Crane. This didn't last for very long, but it did last up to the thirties, when I was teaching there and people like Randall Jarrell were in as freshmen. And all this was going on outside of the curriculum. That's why I think graduate programs in creative writing are stupid. Sometimes I've been peripherally involved in them, but if people want to write, they will write. It is nice if they can show their stuff to their elders;

that's natural. But what we see is just an attempt to formalize what since the beginning of time has been natural.

Stitt: How did you become a member of the Fugitive group?

Warren: The Fugitive group was started before the First World War when some young professors, including Ransom, and some bookish, intelligent young businessmen got together to discuss literature and philosophy. But it really got going after the war, when the moving force became a strange Jew named Mttron Hirsch, an adventurer of no education whatever, except that he had read *everything*. He had been the heavyweight boxing champion of the Pacific fleet, and was a great friend of Gertrude Stein in her early days. He had also been a model for many of the painters of Paris: he was an enormously handsome man, very big, perfectly formed in his way—and he became the center, almost the idol, of the group. He was in his early forties then, and had, or claimed to have, a back injury. So he would lie flat on his back on a couch and be waited on by his kin. I think he made a good thing of it. He was the wise man of the tribe, and he liked to be able to talk with some learned friends, so he accumulated people around him. I guess that was the source of it originally.

I believe Allen Tate and Ridley Wills were the first undergraduates to be admitted to the group. They were five or six years older than I. Tate had been ill and had come back to college, which is why he and I overlapped. He couldn't pass, or wouldn't pass, freshman math and freshman chemistry, both of which were required. He had all A's in everything else, things like Greek and Latin; but he wouldn't do the others—it bored him too much. So he was around.

Then in my junior year, I guess it was, Ransom invited me to the Fugitive meetings. Greatest thrill I'd had in my life. By then it was mostly a poetry club—we read each other's poems and argued poetry. Everybody was an equal in that room; no one pulled his long gray beard. And it was a good time to be there: Ransom was writing his best poems then, and Tate was just finding himself. I myself was seventeen, and I said, "This is what I'm going to do." I had no interest in fiction, though, not until later.

Stitt: John Crowe Ransom must have been a remarkable man and a strong presence in the group.

Warren: He was an influence on everybody. He was a center of this without ever trying to be; we just automatically looked to him, you see. He was very learned and a student all his life. And not only that—he was also a great player of games, a crack golfer; and he played tennis, poker, and bridge. Sometimes he played bridge or poker for the whole weekend. People who didn't know him well sometimes think he was an unfeeling man, but that just isn't so at all. I recently had a letter from my goddaughter, who is Ransom's granddaughter. She said, "He is so often portrayed as being cold and self-absorbed that I wanted to write and tell you at least one thing that happened in my presence. When you were ill"—this was in 1972; I had hepatitis and they thought it was cancer—"Pappy either went or sent someone to the post office three times a day to see if there was any news, and he telephoned all over the country." He was a man of great warmth. I wrote an essay in celebration of his eightieth birthday, and the letter he wrote me in return is incredible. He said, "I find myself at last brushing away a furtive tear." He raised vegetables and flowers, and every morning he would decorate the whole house with fresh flowers. And he loved to cook breakfast—better breakfasts than I've had all the rest of my life. He always served them to his wife while she was still in bed.

Stitt: Why do you suppose Ransom stopped writing poetry when he did?
Warren: Well, I can tell you exactly what he said to me before he stopped writing. We were sitting by the fireside one night, and he said, "You know, I think I will quit writing poetry." Now, he was at his very peak, and I said, "You're crazy." He said, "No, I know what I'm doing." John was, in everything he did, intellectual and introspective—he knew his own mind. But this is one time when he did *not* know what he was doing. He went on to say, "I know I can write better poems than I've ever written; I know how to write my poems. But I want to be an amateur"—and that's what he was—"I want to love what I'm doing, to do it for pleasure"—that's his game business again. He said, "I hate a professional poet. I know people who have ruined themselves by being professional poets, because they end up imitating themselves. If I get a new insight, a new way in, if I grow into something different, I will start again, but I don't want to be same old John Crowe Ransom." That's the way he explained it to me. So I said, "Well, you're crazy," and I still think he was crazy.

Randall Jarrell had a different idea, and I think he was right. He said that being a poet is like standing out in the rain, waiting for lightning to hit you. If it hits you once—that is, if you write one really fine poem—you are good; if it hits you six times, you're great. Ransom wouldn't stay out in the rain.

Stitt: Do you think he was wise to go back late in life and revise his poems as he did?

Warren: I think frequently he did harm to the poems. He wanted to be back in touch with it, but he had lost the touch. The last time I went to see him was at the time of his eighty-fifth birthday. I went out there to give a reading and to see him. He was totally himself, not showing any sign of age. After we came back from the reading, we sat down and had a drink, and he said, "I've given myself a birthday present. I've written a new poem." It was a new kind of poem, you see—published in the *Sewanee Review*. He went back into the rain at the age of eighty-five. And that was that.

Stitt: I want to talk a bit about how you compose your poems. What gets you started on a poem—is it an idea, an image, a rhythm, or something else?

Warren: It can be a lot of things. More and more for me the germ of a poem is an event in the natural world. And there is a mood, a feeling, that helps. For about ten years, from 1944 to '54, I was unable to finish a poem—I'd start one, and get just so far and then it would die on me. I have stacks of unfinished poems. I *was* writing then—other things, *Brother to Dragons* and a lot of short stories. Many times the germ of a short story could also be the germ of a poem, and I was wasting mine on short stories. I've only written three that I even like. And so I quit writing short stories.

Then I got married, and my wife had a child, then a second; and we went to a place in Italy, an island with a ruined fortress. It is a very striking place—there is a rocky peninsula with the sea on three sides, and a sixteenth-century fortress on the top. There was a matching fortress across the bay. We had a wonderful time there, for two summers and more, and I began writing poetry again, in that spot. I had a whole different attitude toward life, my outlook was changed. The poems in *Promises* were all written there. Somehow, all of this—the place, the objects there, the children, the other people, my new outlook—made possible a new grasp on the roots of poetry for me. There were memories and natural events: the poems wander back and forth from my boyhood to my children. Seeing a little gold-headed girl on that bloody spot of history is an *event*. With the bay beyond, the sea beyond that, the white butterflies, that's all a natural event. It could be made into a short story, but you would have to cook up a lot of stuff around it. All you have to cook up in the poem is to be honest with your feelings and your observation, somehow.

This was a new way of starting poetry for me. I had been writing two kinds of poems earlier—one kind tended to start from a verbal and abstract place, and the other kind was a sort of balladry, based on an element of narrative. "Billie Potts" was the last poem I wrote before the drought set in. It was a bridge piece, my jumping-off place when I started again, ten years later. Now my method is more mixed. Some poems can start with a mood. Say there is a stream under your window, and you are aware of the sound all night as you sleep; or you notice the moonlight on the water, or hear an owl call. Things like this can start a mood that will carry over into the daylight. These objects may not appear in the poem, but the mood gets you going.

Then my most recent poem—I think it is one of my best—is a poem that was set off by a review of my work. Harold Bloom of Yale is kind enough to like my poetry, and he wrote a review for *The New Leader* in which he talks about the place that hawks occupy in my poetry. When I read it, I realized that it is all true. You don't know your own poetry, you know—working on it so closely, you see it differently. And so I thought about the fact that I had killed a hawk, a red-tail, in my woodland boyhood. I brought him down with what was a record shot for me. I was then a practicing taxidermist, among other things, and I stuffed the hawk and carried him with me for many years—I used to keep him over my bookshelf. This is the key to the poem, a factual event, a memory. It can be like that.

That's my most recent poem. Now I've had a break of several weeks—poetry comes to me in fits of a few weeks or a few months, perhaps a half-year, and then there is a break. I know when I am through with a certain mood, a certain thing—every book is based on a curve and I know when the curve is closing in and the book is over. It is purely intuitive. But I don't know whether this new book is over or not. I've got enough poems, but it is not quite the way I want it. But it will be a strange book and will look as if I've started all over again, in the way Ransom said. But I never know how the next poem will start; I don't want to fall into a formula.

Stitt: You have said, "For me the common denominator is always an ethical issue." This is clearer, I think, in fiction than in poetry.
Warren: It is much more obvious in fiction. But the relation between the abstract and the concrete is different in more recent poems. I have moved more toward a moralized anecdote—I don't mean to preach sermons, but I also don't want to be coy about it. I would like to show the problem of the abstract and the concrete in the construction of the poem itself.

Stitt: Do you write your poems out in longhand or at the typewriter?
Warren: Practically in my head. I do a lot of them when I am exercising. I find that regular exercise, any kind of simple repeated motion, is like hypnosis—it frees your mind. So when I am walking or swimming, I try to let my mind go blank, so I can catch the poems on the wing, before they can get away. Then when I have a start and am organized, I will sit down with pencil and paper, but never at the typewriter. I once had a bad shoulder injury, and must swim or exercise very heavily every morning in order to keep it functioning freely. And this I find is very conducive to writing my poetry.

Stitt: Do you revise your poems heavily?
Warren: Very heavily. I read them and read them, and do draft after draft. And I retain the drafts. Often if I am stuck I will go back to an earlier version to refresh myself—I may have been on the right track and taken a wrong turn.

Stitt: Have you ever had this experience some poets speak of, where a poem just comes to you in a burst, as though by inspiration, and all you had to do was write down the words?
Warren: The best parts of a poem always come in bursts or in a flash. This has been said by many people—Frost said in a letter, "My best poems are always my easiest." My notion is this: that the poet is a hunter on the track of an unknown beast, and has only one shot in his gun. You don't know what the beast is, but when you see him, you've got to shoot him, and it has got to be instantaneous. You can labor on the pruning, and you can work at your technique, but you cannot labor the poem into being.

Stitt: As you've reprinted your collections, you have often left poems out, sometimes many of them. Why is this?
Warren: Sometimes I think they are bad, and sometimes other people think they are bad. For instance, when I was preparing my *Selected Poems* of 1966, I consulted with Allen Tate, William Meredith, and Cleanth Brooks. If two of them were strongly negative about a poem, I would take it out, unless I had my own strong reasons for leaving it in. And my editor, Albert Erskine, is very helpful.

Stitt: Do you feel that your two creative activities, fiction and poetry, are complementary to one another?
Warren: I feel this: they have the same germ; they are very different in the way they manifest themselves, but they spring from the same source. I always

put the poem first: if a poem falls across a novel, I will take the poem first. I will stop the novel and go whoring after the poem, as I have done several times. I mentioned earlier how writing short stories kept me away from poetry. *All the King's Men* is a novel, but it started out as poetry, a verse play. The original idea was implicit in a single word, the name *Talus*, my first name for Willie Stark and also the name of the groom in book five of *The Faerie Queene.* I was thinking that people like Hitler or Huey Long are machines, executing the will of Justice. Reducing it to one word is purely private. As for the verse play, I later saw that it left out the action and complication necessary to show that power—the man of power—flows into a vacuum: a vacuum in society, government, or individuals. So my man Talus became Stark, whose power fulfills the weaknesses of others.

Stitt: Some critics feel that poetry has displaced fiction as your most important concern in recent years? Do you think that is true?
Warren: I don't know—I still try to roll with the punch and write what needs to be written on a given day. But I started as a poet and I will probably end as a poet. If I had to choose between my novels and my *Selected Poems*, I would keep the *Selected Poems* as representing me more fully, my vision and my self. I think poems are more *you*.

Stitt: You mentioned Harold Bloom earlier. Do you pay much attention to the critics and reviewers of your own work, especially poetry?
Warren: I have learned things from some of them, but most reviewers are just filling space. Sometimes a foolish critic will tell you a very important thing, almost by accident. But you've got to learn to live without counting the good reviews and the bad reviews, because sometimes they are right and sometimes they are wrong. I understand there is a weak review of my novel coming out in the *Times Book Review*, when just a few weeks ago they devoted practically the whole issue to praising the *Selected Poems*. So you just do the best you can.

Stitt: In rereading things written about your work, I found one critic who called your poetry cerebral and academic. How do you react to that?
Warren: It depends who says you are cerebral. Compared to Sara Teasdale, I would say I am cerebral, but John Donne would probably think I was not. Speaking more generally, I think you've got to forget all the things you know abstractly when you start writing. Of course, you never forget what you know

about novel structure or about the construction of a poem, but you put those aside and just do it. You may use material that is intellectual, but you are using it in another spirit entirely.

Stitt: Another critic I came across said that Richard Wilbur hates the "things of this world." Now, I would say that Wilbur, like Robert Penn Warren, loves the things of this world, and indicates that love by investing physical objects with an implicit spiritual essence.

Warren: I am a creature of this world, but I am also a yearner, I suppose. I would call this temperament rather than theology—I haven't got any gospel. That is, I feel an immanence of meaning in things, but I have no meaning to put there that is interesting or beautiful. I think I put it as close as I could in a poem called "Masts at Dawn"—"We must try/To love so well the world that we may believe, in the end, in God." I am a man of temperament in the modern world who hasn't got any religion. Dante almost got me at one stage, but then I suddenly realized, My God, Dante's a good Protestant—he was! Where have I gone? My poem reverses the whole thing, you see: I would rather start with the world.

Stitt: How did you come to write your beautiful poem on Audubon?

Warren: There is a little story about that. I never research a book, except if I get in a pinch on some detail, then I will look that up. But when I was thinking about writing *World Enough and Time*, I began to soak myself in Americana of the early nineteenth century, histories of Kentucky and Tennessee—that sort of thing. Well, Audubon appears in that history, so I went ahead and looked at his journals, and so forth. I got interested in the man and his life, and began, way back in the forties, to write a poem about Audubon. But it was a trap; I couldn't find the frame for it, the narrative line. I did write quite a bit, but it wouldn't come together, so I set it aside and forgot about it. Then in the sixties I was writing a history of American literature with Dick [R.W.B.] Lewis and Cleanth Brooks, and I did the section on Audubon. We all read everything, then one person would write up a given section and the others would rewrite the first draft to their hearts' desire—a continuing process. So I got back into Audubon. Then one day when my wife wasn't here, I was making the bed, when suddenly there popped into my mind a line that had been in the version of *Audubon* that I had abandoned. I never went and hunted the rest of it up, so I only had that one line to go on. But I suddenly saw how to do it. I did it in fragments, sort of snapshots of Audubon. I began to see him as a certain kind of man, a man who has finally learned to accept his fate. The poem is about man and his fate—all along, Audubon resisted his fate and thought it was evil—a man is supposed to support his family, and so forth. But now he accepts his fate. Late in his life he said, "I dream of nothing but birds." Audubon was the greatest slayer of birds that ever lived: he destroyed beauty in order to create beauty and whet his understanding. Love is knowledge. And then in the end the poem is about Audubon and me.

Stitt: Since the fifties your poetry has been mostly optimistic and affirmative, emphasizing the glory of the world and its promises. And yet you also have poems on ugliness, death, racial violence, and so on. How do these poems fit into your vision?

Warren: That's all part of the picture, just the other side of it. You have people like Dreiser, who are monsters humanly but who make great things. There is Flaubert, whose main goal in going to Egypt was to get the clap, and yet he had this inspiration for *Madame Bovary,* and he thanks God to be alive, approaching the curve of the wave. It is the complication of life—nothing more complicated than that.

Stitt: Do you think of a book of poems as a cohesive unit or as a collection of individual pieces?

Warren: I don't see them as pieces but as a kind of unit. Some time back I began to write poetry in suites of three or four units, and that has become more and more a mark of mine.

Stitt: The subtitle of *Or Else—Poem/Poems 1968–1974* would seem to indicate that idea.

Warren: Yes—it can be considered a long poem, or it can be considered a group of short poems. Some of the poems were written with my being unaware of their place in the sequence. It wasn't undertaken as a planned sequence; the true sequence grew. This kind of structure is related to how you feel your experience—I couldn't tell you exactly how, but is related.

Stitt: You have done a good deal of editing. I think especially of the editions of the poems of Melville and Whittier. What impelled you to undertake those tasks?

Warren: I don't know. Melville I have always been crazy about; one of the first critical essays I ever wrote was on his poems. Then someone asked me to do a little Melville edition for a series of poets in New York, and I said yes and started work on it. But when I showed it to them, they said it was too much, too big, so I thought to hell with you, and took it to Random House. I was just fascinated by Melville. Then Whittier: I had been rereading Whittier and felt that I had done him a wrong—I found his complexity more interesting in a cumulative text than what I had seen before. Now, Dreiser is an old passion. I've read all of Dreiser and have had many different opinions of him along the way. Humanly he was a monster. I have a psychologist friend at Yale whose chief study is the act of creativity. I got him to read first the auto-biographies of Dreiser, then some of the novels, and he was very helpful. He would say, "Okay, this is a lie, and that is a screening device for something else." But those are ways of being in contact with things that interest me—I'm not making a career of it, although I enjoy the work. I could spend my life very happily studying Coleridge, studying Dreiser, and so forth. I just like something else better. I have more need for something else.

Stitt: Do you find the writing of criticism a pleasant task?
Warren: Well, it's a little bit like teaching. I like to talk about books I have read, and I always liked the association with the students. I think that only in the university can you find a certain kind of humanistic temperament to deal with—I don't mean that everybody who teaches has it, but some people are quite wonderful. They know something disinterestedly, and know how to apply it, and it is a privilege to associate with them. But I couldn't have stood teaching beyond a certain point—I got sick of myself for one thing. And I have ceased to have any interest in writing criticism, even though there is a new edition of my *Selected Essays* in preparation. I have sworn that I will never write another line of criticism of any kind. I will write some fictional prose; I want to write a couple of more novels that are in my head, but I really enjoy writing poetry more now.

Stitt: Do you still consider yourself a Southern writer, even though you have been away so long?
Warren: I can't be anything else. You are what you are. I was born and grew up in Kentucky, and I think your early images survive. Images mean a lot of things besides pictures.

The South: Distance and Change

Louis D. Rubin, Jr. / 1977

From *The American South: Portrait of a Culture*, edited by Louis D. Rubin, Jr. (Baton Rouge: Louisiana State University Press, 1980). © 1980 by Louisiana State University Press. Reprinted by permission.

Louis Rubin: The two Southern authors who are with me here to talk about the South might be said to be of different literary generations. Robert Penn Warren was born in 1905. As a youthful member of the Nashville Fugitive poets he was publishing verse in 1924, a year before William Styron was born. Red Warren's first novel, *Night Rider,* came out before the Second World War, in 1939. Bill Styron published *Lie Down in Darkness,* his first novel, in 1951. Yet in addition to a close personal friendship, they share many things together, among them a fascination with Southern history. What is interesting to me here is that neither of them has lived in the Southern states for a number of years. Bill, you left Newport News, Virginia, well before your first novel came out, didn't you?

William Styron: Well, I'll put it this way: there's a split. I spent my childhood, boyhood, youth, and education entirely in the South, and in my early twenties I left. I've visited a lot, but I've never really been back.

Rubin: And, Red Warren, you grew up in Guthrie, Kentucky, and then you went to Vanderbilt University in Nashville, Tennessee . . .
Warren: Fifty miles away. It was in the same part of the world.

Rubin: But then when you graduated from Vanderbilt you went to California, and Yale, and then Oxford, and then you came back to the South to teach.
Warren: In 1930. And I lived in the South until 1942, with some trips abroad and other trips around the country—a lot of trips to the Far West during that period, and abroad a couple of times.

Rubin: You left Louisiana State University, where you and Cleanth Brooks edited the *Southern Review,* in 1942, and you went to Minnesota. So you've been away from the South for over thirty years.

Warren: Yes, I left Minnesota for Yale, and I've lived in New England now for twenty-five years, for twenty-seven years.

Rubin: And, Bill, you've been away almost that long yourself.
Styron: Yes.

Rubin: Yet what strikes me now is this: Red, you recently published a new novel, *A Place to Come To*. And, Bill, I've seen excerpts from the novel that you've been working on. Red's novel involves a Southerner who's been away from the South for a long time, going back and leaving. And while Bill's novel takes place in New York and Europe and involves a concentration camp experience of the Second World War, nevertheless the meaning of the experience is "happening," insofar as the narrator is involved, to a Southerner from Virginia. So obviously the experience outside of the South still seems to mean a great deal to both of you in terms of what it signifies to you *as* Southerners. Your imagination seems to be still very thoroughly grounded in an identity that geographically at least you abandoned a long time ago. Could you say that, as a fiction writer, Red, this is still the experience that is most real to you?
Warren: Well, "reality," I guess, is one word to describe it. Actually, it seems to me that though your basic images and attitudes may change in many ways, they are always fundamentally conditioned by what you knew in small and large ways very early in life. This remains important, at least to me. Now take a small, trivial thing. If I were writing a story about a Connecticut farmer, I wouldn't know where to begin. But writing a story about such a family, rich or poor, grand or miserable, in the South, I wouldn't have any hesitation. It would be as natural as breathing to me. I'd know what they did, I'd know what they ate, I'd know what they'd say. And also the matter of landscape is extremely important. I suppose I'm bringing in something now that may be irrelevant, but the nature of the land itself, in relation to the landscape of other parts of the world, other places, is very important to me, particularly in poems.

Rubin: . . . Red Warren, I notice that several of your recent novels have involved a man going back a long time later to the place where he grew up and noticing the difference, having had the experience of being out in the world. In one instance the old place has been covered by flood waters. In your

most recent novel he comes back at the very end to the town he had been
fleeing from all his life, where his mother had lived.
Warren: She had driven him out, because she hated where she was.

Rubin: In one of your poems there is an image that I find very striking—it
has come to my mind again and again. It is the image of the man who has
returned home and walks out by the railroad tracks at night and watches
the Pullman cars on the train go by—that memory. In both cases it seems
to me that so much of your experience of the South, and Bill Styron's
experience of the South, involves this sense of "Who am I?" in terms of
"How far have I gone from the South and where did I start from and how
did I come back?"
Warren: There's one difference between us; I don't know how important it is.
I wanted to live in the South, you see; I'm a refugee from the South, driven
out, as it were. The place I wanted to live, the place I thought was heaven to
me, after my years of wandering, was middle Tennessee, which is a beautiful
country, or *was* a beautiful country—it's rapidly being ruined. But I couldn't
make it work. When I went back to teach for three years there, I enjoyed
living in the country and driving in to do my teaching, and this was fine. But
I was let out of Vanderbilt University, and had to go elsewhere for a job. I went
to Louisiana State University, which was quite fortunately a very exciting
place. And I left Louisiana only because I felt I wasn't wanted. I felt pressure
to leave. It wasn't a choice. I had settled myself down and bought a house
in the country—settled down for life, I assumed. I left, shall we say, under
pressure of some kind or another. I wasn't fired. I left out of pride. I went to
Minnesota, which I enjoyed.

I've quit teaching several times—"never again." But I fell in love with
teaching along the way, so I always drifted back in again. I was out as long as
six years one time, two years another time, and again a year or so at a time.
But that's not the point. The point is that I, unlike Bill, didn't make a choice
of living outside the South. I always felt myself somehow squeezed out of the
South, which is a very different thing from Bill's conscious choice. That is a
generational matter, perhaps; I don't know.

Rubin: But I wonder whether Bill's choice was entirely a free one? In other
words, didn't the choice really mean: "Can I be myself and do what I want to
do while living here?" And the answer was no.

Styron: I think that was my decision. The decision I made had nothing to do with any antipathy toward the South; quite the contrary. It so happened that I didn't have many friends left in the South. I had very few connections in the South that I felt deeply. I was not in teaching. After I left Duke University I hung around Durham for a while and enjoyed it, oddly enough, because it's not the most attractive of Southern cities. But I left simply because most of the profounder contacts I had made with other human beings were in the North, and that was my decision.

Warren: The South never crossed my mind except as an imaginative construct before I left it. I was raised on the battles and leaders of the Civil War by a grandfather veteran who had a very active part in the Civil War, but he was also mad for Napoleon's campaigns, so I got a great dose of Napoleon's campaigns and General Forrest's operations all mixed up together. . . . I had it all tangled up together in my earliest years.

Rubin: That is also what the Confederates themselves did, you know. They thought of their Civil War experience, when they wrote about it, in Napoleonic terms. You know that story about the Battle of Shiloh, the surprise march, when the sun's coming up and the officers are saying "This is the sun of Austerlitz," and the soldiers didn't know what they were talking about— they thought they were saying "the Son of Oyster Itch."

Warren: This leads to another question. The South has one peculiarity: it was a nation once, and that makes a vast difference, though it can be forgotten that it makes a difference. Another thing that's forgotten that makes a difference is that Southerners felt that they had created the Union—Washington and Jefferson had created the Union—and the North was going to take it away from them. There were many Unionists in the Civil War who were still fighting in the Confederate army because they were fighting for their country, which was the United States of America.

Styron: Wasn't Robert E. Lee's conflict in 1861 based on that?

Warren: I guess it was based on that; many were. It was a double nationality that was involved there, and there's a vast complication—I don't pretend to settle it now—an emotional tangle in the role of the South in fighting the United States, and the role of the South as an independent nation. This is a complicated issue, and it has strong emotional ramifications, even for ignorant people.

Styron: The very idea that such an intense nationalism existed almost defines the individuality that the South still thinks itself to have, whether rightly or wrongly.

Rubin: I think it's still very much there. I don't think it's eroding. The fact that the South is becoming urbanized and industrialized, so that, let's say, the suburbs of Atlanta seem to resemble the suburbs of Detroit, or something like that—I don't think that they *are* the suburbs of Detroit. I don't think the South is losing its identity at all.

Styron: I don't think it's losing its identity, but I think it tends to be less well defined in certain areas. I've spent recently a lot of time in North Carolina, and I notice that in the larger urban areas there is a blur. I mean, except for the accents and so on, you find a kind of Northern overlay. On the other hand, the small towns, where I've also been, in eastern North Carolina, are maybe even more Southern than I once remembered, for some reason. A little town like Goldsboro, where I've spent a lot of time, which is in the heart of the Tobacco Belt, has barely changed an iota since the time I remember it as a little boy in the 1930's. So I think it's a matter of where you are in the South.

Warren: That may be true. I think there are vast changes in the parts of the South I knew best—middle Tennessee and the Cumberland River Valley— vast changes and changes of attitude. Now some are for the good, and I would be the first to grant that. I faced the question, actually, when I started to buy a farm in Tennessee, where I would spend half the year. I felt I'd be isolated. A lot of friends are dead and gone. But I also felt a real change in the whole nature of the world. And I felt it would be an idle dream for me to go back there. It would be ridiculous.

Styron: I feel the same way.

Warren: The one friend I know who did so shot himself.

Styron: *That's* the end of a dream.

Rubin: Aren't you really talking about the nature of time, though? I mean, about your experience of your childhood and the people you knew when you grew up as a child. If you had stayed there, they wouldn't have continued the same way, either. When you go back to Guthrie, Red, or you go back to Newport News, Bill, in a sense you are going back to your memories of a time. There are

a number of physical objects around that can trigger those memories, but you're really going back to a time even more than to a place. You say that everything has changed. What you're saying is that so many years have elapsed, aren't you? As for the people who have been there all along and who haven't left, they've changed too. They're not the same. You're now fifty-one, I believe. Let's say you had been fifty-one in the year 1935 instead of 1977. Don't you think that if you had come back to Newport News in 1935 at the age of fifty-one, you might also have said, "This has all changed. It's all gone. It's not like what it was"? In other words, isn't part of what we're dealing with here the nature of time, and when you look back it always seems that everything has changed?
Warren: Part of it is. That's partly true. But there are also other elements involved in it. One element for me was that I had no attachments to a town. My attachment was always to the country, and that made a difference. I was attached to the countryside, to rural life, not town life. I couldn't abide small town life from the start. I was always against it.

Rubin: In some ways it seems to me that a good deal of the strength of twentieth-century Southern writing in general, and your own work in particular, may lie in the fact that the literature itself has had to, and still has to, confront the tremendous phenomenon of change in time. It becomes almost an exemplar of the American experience as a whole. The change has been so swift, so bewildering, and in so short a period of time—in your own lifetimes—that a good deal of the strength of Southern literature comes out of the intensity and the power of that change.
Styron: I think you must include in that the quite obvious and single most significant social change in the South, which we haven't touched on yet—the rapidity with which the whole racial dilemma has been turned around, within the lifetimes of most all of us. Certainly that has been one of the most bewildering and, I might add, amazing and benignly revolutionary things that I think have ever happened in a civilized country.

Warren: And now Jimmy Carter can be elected president by black support, as he was.
Styron: Yes, of course.

Warren: Back in the 1960's I was traveling a great deal in the South, more than in the North for a while, interviewing Negroes for a book I was writing—all kinds of Negroes. More than once I heard Negroes say, "There's a personal relationship here, bad or good, which gives reality and holds some hope for the future. If a sheriff shoots you in Alabama, he probably knows your name. If a cop brains you in Detroit, he doesn't know your name. That makes a big difference." This was actually said to me by an Alabama black. "I see some hope in that," he said. "He knows what he's doing; he's stuck with it."

Styron: He might be a black sheriff now.

Warren: Yes, now he might be a sheriff himself. . . . Don't forget that segregation was a very late development in America, and it was not true of the Old South. There was slavery, but not segregation. Segregation did not come in until quite late. In the 1880's and 1890's, according to Vann Woodward's book *The Strange Career of Jim Crow*, the Charleston, South Carolina, papers, for example, were against segregation. They said, "After you segregate the trains, the next thing is there will be two Bibles to kiss in court." And it happened.

Rubin: That's true. On the other hand, I think that can be interpreted a little differently. Isn't it true that laws demanding segregation, and all these little artifacts—the front and the back of the streetcar—came about because with the end of slavery there was no longer any enormous institutionalized social fact which would create the distance, maintain the barrier, and therefore the white South felt it had to enact these things into little laws, and things like that? It wasn't even questioned, before, so that there wasn't any need for it in that sense.

Warren: Well, there was no need up North, because there was enforced segregation already.

Styron: But there was also the fact of Reconstruction, which was a trauma in many ways to the South, with on the surface often a very shocking insult to white Southern sensibilities. The idea of black men being in power, and being artificially put in power, was a traumatic experience after the hegemony of the whites. Certainly one of the reasons for Jim Crow, at least one of the elements in Jim Crow, was a redressing of that grievance.

Warren: It was also a change in the class system in the South, part of it.

Rubin: Very much so.

Styron: But all this aside, the fact still remains that for many of us, if we could have lived to be two hundred years old today, we would have known a phase in our lives when strict segregation would have been an unheard-of strangeness because in antebellum times it would have made no sense, emotionally or otherwise. But for those of us who are caught up in history, the experience of being brought up in the South, born and raised any time from 1900 right on through to World War II, was the equivalent—I don't think it's stretching it too far to say—of living in South Africa, certainly in the Black Belt part of the South where I was brought up. You had a total *apartheid*, and it had a severe, lacerating, and wounding effect on both races, black and white.

Warren: I agree with you about that.

Styron: And it wasn't our fault. I'm not trying to get off the hook. I'm simply saying that history treated a whole generation of us—maybe two generations—to this.

Warren: One other very important element in it, too, is the flinch from black flesh, dark flesh. Now the flinch was not part of slavery. The flinch from black flesh was very strong in the North. The word "miscegenation," for example, was a word cooked up by Copperheads and New York journalists, according to the *Journal of Negro History*, which is my only authority for this. They tried to get Lincoln and various other people to sign a document saying it would be nice to have miscegenation. They couldn't get a signer.

Rubin: What you're saying is that nineteenth-century America, North and South, was racist.

Warren: What I'm saying is that in the South there was little flinch from black flesh compared to that in the North, where there was a great flinch from black flesh and concubinage occurred quite frequently.

Styron: Aren't you saying also that this repulsion did not exist much in antebellum times, but did exist afterwards, even in the South?

Warren: That's exactly what I'm saying. It grew up afterwards in the South.

Styron: I remember noting this to my own surprise once, when I wrote an essay on this for *Harper's* a long time ago. When I reflected on my boyhood in a Southern town, not a Southern rural environment, in retrospect I was astounded by my total unfamiliarity with black flesh. I mean, even as a presence, even as a part of the ambiance of my life. It was nonexistent, except for

the ones who worked in the kitchen. After the day was done they evaporated, they went somewhere else. The myth was quite the opposite. This miscegenation myth you're talking about *was* a myth, because after the modern South began and after Jim Crow began, everything legislated against any contact.
Warren: In the earlier agricultural South, a lot of children played together. They had their black nurse. This was very common, in many segments of society.

Rubin: It seems to me that in your imaginative writings and in your journalism, too, both of you have chronicled this change. I don't say that you sat down consciously with the intention of doing so, but this is what your work shows. In Bill Styron's case, his first novel involves someone growing up in the South and leaving the South. His next novel involves someone who again grew up in the South but is a long way away from it and is trying to learn how to go back, but not really back to the same place—how to find a place, or a place to come to, to use the title of Red Warren's latest book. And in your next novel, Bill, you took a black man, a slave; here is the Southern racial experience, but looked at from a completely different point of view. In the novel you're working on now there is a man brought up with Southern sensibilities, coming to grips with a different kind of horror, a completely different kind of horrible situation—the concentration camps of the Second World War. And he says, "The particular kind of injustices which I'm indignant about may not be nearly so important as what race hatred can do to people like this." That's the insight to be drawn out of that experience of separation. And, Red, it seems to me in your instance, there are few if any other authors who have written as much as you have, consciously, about the problems of the South and the Southerner, the Southerner going away and returning, the Southerner living in the change from the Old South to the New South, and the various problems this involves. If I were a social historian, let's say fifty years from now, and I wanted to chronicle how all this happened, in both instances your works would be one of the best places to look, even though I would doubt very much that either one of you, especially when you are writing fiction or poetry, ever sat down with that conscious intention in mind.
Warren: Certainly it never crosses my mind. It's the story that counts. If it has a story it has a cocklebur in it that you can't understand and that you want to understand. It has a nag in it; that becomes the reason you write it, the nag in it.

Rubin: You wrote your first fiction about the South when you were in England, didn't you?

Warren: I did, and I did it because I was asked to write it. The farther I got away from the South, the more I thought about it. . . .

Rubin: And you, Bill, wrote your first fiction at Duke, in Durham, though that was apprentice fiction.

Styron: Yes, very much so.

Rubin: And you wrote most of *Lie Down in Darkness* living in New York, didn't you?

Styron: I wrote practically all of it somewhere in New York.

Rubin: So in both cases it's been the fact that you were away from the scene that triggered the reexamination, and then you have kept reexamining it, and it's provided a sort of nourishment, an index of reality if you want to call it that, all the way. You can measure "Who am I?" in terms of the kind of ambiance that you grow up in. What I'm getting at is this: the fact that neither you, Red, nor you, Bill, has been living in the geographical South for a number of years, may make you into a different kind of Southern writer, but nevertheless that very experience itself is a part of the Southern experience—the moving out from and looking back at the past.

Warren: I don't want to talk about myself too much, but something you've said triggers this thought. For ten years I couldn't finish a poem, even a short poem—I have stacks of them unfinished, four lines or six lines or eight lines, and then they go off in a folder somewhere. Now I began writing poems again in Italy, at a ruined castle over the sea. . . . That year I wrote *Promises* and two sonnets, and spent the winter revising them. That book is half Kentucky-Tennessee, and half Italy. There's medieval Italy and boyhood—they make a book. Do you see what I'm getting at? It's the long withdrawal from south Kentucky. But the book is really on that theme as much as any other theme, the other being father-child, father-daughter, father-son, as infants.

Rubin: Don't you think the same thing is true of your most recent novel?

Warren: It's quite deliberately true of it, though it's autobio-graphical only in the deep way that all books are autobio-graphical. I want to come back to one other thing. You said a Southerner asks "Who am I?" but "Who am I?" strikes me as ultimately the question all writers are asking. In the Southern case it's only an especially acute one; it's pointed up more sharply. But "Who am I?" is a basic human question. I just add that as a footnote to what you said.

Rubin: That's quite true. But the extent to which it is a problem is what's involved, and it seems to me that when you look at the great body of nineteenth-century Southern literature, that question could be answered very easily, they thought, and the fact that it was answered so very easily accounts for the fact that the literature has so little tension in it, because the answer is rhetorical. In your generation and Bill's generation this is not a rhetorical question; the indices are all moved around and changed around and mixed up, and therefore you're wrestling with it all the time. You don't wrestle with it literally, in terms of the question "Who am I, Robert Penn Warren?" or "Who am I, William Styron?" but "Who is this person or that person in this dramatic situation?" It comes to the same thing, though.
Warren: Yes, you transfer it.

Styron: You're quite accurate when you point out the huge chasm between nineteenth-century Southern sensibility and twentieth-century. I'm speaking in general. Apart from Edgar Allan Poe and one or two others, don't we tend to localize nineteenth-century Southern writing in sensibilities like Thomas Nelson Page, who were delightfully satisfied with the status quo? And possibly for good reason—the status quo often looked pretty good to them.
Warren: Or their dream of it.

Rubin: That's really more like it. Thomas Nelson Page was writing about the beauties of life on the old plantation, and his best stories are told by the faithful black retainer. Here is a man who is married to the sister of Marshall Field, lives in Washington, D.C., travels abroad all the time, goes up to New England in the summers, serves as the ambassador to Italy during the First World War—a thoroughgoing cosmopolite, and yet when he sits down with a pen and writes there is the dream of the old thing—he's not looking at his own experience.
Warren: It's a pastoral.

Styron: He's not looking, because even at that time the horrors were commencing. To localize history in one single type of event, lynchings were very rare things in the first half of the nineteenth century. It was a post-Civil War phenomenon; it came with Jim Crow. Page was writing during the heyday of lynching. We in the twentieth century, let's face it, have had strange and unearthly experiences that were not dreamed of by and large by our nineteenth-century forebears. The Civil War is an exception to that, but I'm talking about the experience between black and white, the tension—the power and the glory and the horrors and all that reached their crescendo in the twentieth century.

Warren: It's not black or white in the twentieth century, it's everybody.

Styron: It's anybody. You're talking about the whole world.

Warren: About the Dresden fire raid, and a lot of other such things.

Styron: And to me that's another thing that my own imagination has been captured by—a thing that's totally extraneous to my experience, namely, what happened in the Nazi concentration camps, which seems to epitomize humanity at its nadir in all of its history. And I have been able I think to come at it through whatever sensibility I created in myself as a Southerner.

Warren: This is an important point, Bill. It seems to me that the whole problem of modernity, of all modernity, is that of how can the person hang on to the fact that he's a person, and not become simply a thing being shoved here and shoved there, caught in a vast, complicated machine, and depersonalized in the process. The very strong personal sense in the South that makes tales worth telling—sitting around and talking about some*body*, Mr. Smith versus Mr. Jones, or why did this man do this crazy thing, because he's that kind of a person—is involved somehow in the question of how personality is preserved in the face of the more and more mechanized, computerized world of technology.

Rubin: In other words, a gas oven is so much more efficient than a lash, isn't it?

Styron: It's another thing that's just being apprehended, really. It's fascinating to me that a place like Auschwitz is in a curious way an extension of Western chattel slavery. It was of course a place for extermination, but it was equally a place in which slavery was practiced, of a monstrous sort, which was a logical extension of the *relatively* benign slavery practiced in the South—I say "relatively" because slavery in the South was not, inhuman as it was, practiced as a method to extract everything that one could out of a body and then let it perish, whereas Auschwitz was a place in which slavery was practiced with the idea in mind that people were disposable and that after you got the work out of them they died. I don't think it's possible to make any direct comparisons between Southern slavery and Nazi slavery, but the two are somehow linked in what you, Red, were describing as a kind of evolutionary dehumanizing process which is all around us.

Warren: Yes, that's what I'm getting at.

Rubin: The struggle to preserve one's humanity, one's identity, within this—a constant struggle which goes on all the time—in a sense constitutes the burden of a great deal of twentieth-century Southern literature.

Warren: It becomes acute there because the mark of individuality was strong and old-fashioned.

Rubin: It seems to me that your work, and the work of your generation of Southern writers, is a place to look to see this process going on, and continuing, and being imaginatively explored. At least, I know that's where I look.

The Oral Roots of Literature

William C. Forrest and Cornelius Novelli / 1977

From *The Sewanee Review* 89.3 (Summer 1981). © 1981 by William C. Forrest and Cornelius Novelli. Reprinted with the permission of the editor.

William C. Forrest: How important do you believe the sound of poetry is?
Warren: No sound, no poetry. We know the sound works on us; we speak it or we hear it in more than one dimension. We have a whole muscular apparatus working in the mouth, for example.

There is a whole combination of experiences going on at the same time. The semantic content of the words sets off emotional vibrations—their tension or relaxation—in a person's being, whether the speaker or listener. There is also the emotional effect of the imagery that is set off by the words. And the imagery is of two kinds. One is felt imagery, an imagery which is muscular and neural. Another kind of imagery is that of the metaphors and references—this can come from a sensory reference to an object or from a metaphorical use of language. But all of these things combine; they all belong to language. And there is no way to separate these various aspects of the poem from one another—except by rapid reading, which is really a way of not reading except for pure information.

But literature, in contrast to journalism and science, is a use of language in its fullest dimensions. It's experience we're concerned with, and experience is a very complex thing—from what's being said on through all the dimensions of language itself. And the relations established among all the dimensions of language have the most extraordinary power, especially when we are dealing with great art.

Cornelius Novelli: Do you recall, when you were a child, having literature read aloud to you?
Warren: Well, yes, from the very earliest. . . . I learned to read from "Horatius at the Bridge" because there must have been a thousand times my father had read it, and finally he said: "I'm not going to read that poem one more time; you must know that poem by heart; read it yourself." It was my favorite poem

at that time—the age of six. I picked it up and, by God, I was reading. Slow and fumbling—but reading. It was a poem of sound.

My schooling—grade school, I mean—was old-fashioned, too. In some classes we had Friday afternoon recitations in which students memorized poems and said them by heart, badly or well, good poems or bad poems. The same thing was true when I went to Clarksville to high school. I remember "The Skeleton in Armor" to this day. Good or bad the poems may have been, but at least it was recognized that the poem existed as verbal art. It wasn't just something on a page; it was an *action* you took part in, an action that affected you, and affected your hearers. I'm not talking about elocution, about the way to render a poem dramatically in reading, but about simply surrendering yourself to the spoken possibilities of language, something as simple as that.

Let's go one step farther. Most readers of poetry and most poets don't read poetry aloud except off and on. But they have a habit of making the subvocal reading of poetry or prose as full an experience as the actual reading aloud. Their bodies are so trained, their feelings are so adjusted by experience, that they don't need it read aloud. The unspoken reading, the subvocal reading, which has all the physical responses and all the emotional responses, may actually be more effective than any oral reading you can muster.

Novelli: In other words, they're so well trained at reading poetry that, like well-trained musicians, they can hear it under the score.
Warren: They hear it, but as an inner experience rather than as a performance aloud.

Forrest: Do you feel that before a reader gets to the stage in which the sensory qualities come through in a silent reading, a certain amount of learning has to take place by actually reading aloud?
Warren: Yes, it must become a natural process. Even as late as when I was in freshman English at Vanderbilt, one quarter we were supposed to memorize seven hundred to one thousand lines of verse. We were tested on it, with a bonus for anything memorized beyond the assigned minimum. Then, being mad for poetry, I spent all my time memorizing and got a big bonus. Very easy: I liked that system. It wasn't tyranny; you had ordinary college students all memorizing, say, a thousand lines of Tennyson in a quarter. It was natural; that was the whole system. Life has changed; now it's tyranny to memorize a quatrain in a schoolroom.

Forrest: It seems to me that in the fourth edition of *Understanding Poetry* and in the fifth edition of *An Approach to Literature,* you and Mr. Brooks advise students to read poetry aloud more often and perhaps with more detailed advice than you had in the earlier editions.
Warren: In the earlier editions we assumed that this was done. I assumed it because I had always done it myself. But in fact it was a real issue, you see; it was necessary to insist on it.

Forrest: And so you were giving that advice on principle.
Warren: On principle. I guess we were just not previously aware how much the oral reading of poetry had fallen off.

Forrest: Can you spell out some of the advantages for the student of reading poetry aloud?
Warren: Well, first I would say this. Most unpoetical children from, say, six to ten, once they begin to learn poetry, try to act it out. They want to convert poetry to a stance or a position. I've seen this happen over and over again with my own children and with other children too. They recognize immediately that this is a drama, that every poetic form is a drama of some kind. And every form of poetry *is* a drama. A speaker is speaking to some occasion and to some audience. Uncorrupted by bad teaching, the child will, if he has to memorize poetry, almost instinctively move toward the dramatization of it.

Now this is turning your question around. That is, the mere fact of knowing or reading out loud, or knowing the poem and memorizing the poem—and these things are tied together—gives you the sense of the poem as drama. It gives you a role, as it were, to act out, or maybe several roles.

A second advantage that comes to the student who reads poetry aloud, over and above the natural dramatic involvement, arises from the fact that the language of poetry, or to some degree the language of any real piece of literature, is not merely a set of verbal equivalents or equal signs. Literary language is a fundamental experience, a coherent experience; and it affects the body. The body naturally *wants* to participate in this thing and to get its share of the experience. The expression of any piece of good writing, prose or poetry, depends on this capacity of the writer to write in such a way that these natural responses are summoned up and are tied to certain emotional or intellectual effects.

Novelli: You think, then, that a writer should be acutely aware of his language as a physical action and a physical experience?

Warren: All I can do is be personal here. I can't imagine writing a poem without writing it in my head, talking about it. Or, if you can't talk while you are swimming, composing it in your head—what you're hearing in your head while swimming. You would knock off a long thought during a mile of swimming, write the poem. You would combine the two things because the use of the muscles in the regular rhythm of swimming drains away distractions. The mind floats, as it were, feels its own way, leads its own life for a change. The words are coming as heard. Running is another thing you can do, long-distance running, or just sitting in a chair and staring at nothing. You have to somehow detach yourself from the distractions of the physical world. And physical activity can do that; it's rhythmical, even a kind of hypnosis.

Forrest: You have said that literature is a knowledge by enactment.

Warren: I think it is. It's the taking of roles. It's enactment, and part of it is the unconscious. It's natural. It's so natural for you it's unconscious.

Let's compare two lines of poetry in the same meter: Pope's line "And wretches hang that jurymen may dine"; and Shakespeare's line when Antony is coming back from the Battle of Actium, deserted in the battle by Cleopatra, and asks his sword-bearer Eros to kill him: "Unarm, Eros, the long day's task is done." Pope's satiric line is in the front of the mouth; it's a contemptuous act of spitting. It's physically in the mouth. You're enacting this contemptible world; you're spitting on it.

Forrest: And Pope shaped his language in such a way that as you utter it, the language imitates the idea.

Warren: You can't say it any other way: "And wretches hang that jurymen may dine." It's spitting. But in Antony's line there is a total heavy relaxation; it's all played well back in the throat. It's the placement that makes the difference there: "Unarm, Eros, the long day's task is done." It's open-mouthed, not the tight spitting effect in Pope's line. Now in these lines the body is enacting a basic role in the speech. And when you have added this to the whole context of *Antony and Cleopatra* it takes on a massive meaning. The same is true of Pope's line: the body is enacting meaning: the contempt of the world's contempt of justice. Constantly language is demanding, is providing (inviting rather) the enactment of meaning in your physical body. It can be carried farther when a child or a grown man actually has a sense of the drama in poetry. He paces about the room and quotes poetry to himself—a piece of poetry he's trying to write or poetry he is reading. He's a real ham. Language invites it; all language invites it.

Novelli: What has happened, though, is that teachers have somehow found a way to teach poetry without ever getting into the dimensions of voice and physical enactment.

Warren: They have; and what that means is that the teaching of poetry is on the skids. Along with a lot else.

Forrest: How did you become aware, by the time you were doing the fourth edition of *Understanding Poetry*, that it was necessary to recommend the oral reading of poetry?

Warren: I began to be aware that fewer and fewer of my literary students— Yale seniors, say—could quote anything. After long and fancy and expensive educations.

And we had begun to be more and more aware that, in the whole world around us, the notion of language as pure, as a set of mere signs or equivalences, was dominant. Rapid reading, for instance. Rapid reading is the death of literature. It's a useful accomplishment if you can turn it on or off when you want it on or off. But it's the death of literature.

Novelli: Because literature has roots in the spoken word.

Warren: Because it has roots in the spoken word and the echo from the spoken word is important in literature, it gives life to literature. Even with prose the speed is not really the point. I can be a rather fast reader of prose and still get the effect of a decent prose as opposed to a bad prose. I say "I" because I know about myself. I know many people who can do this. It's a sense of awareness which is instinctively cultivated. It's not something to be measured in terms of a watch. It takes education in rapid reading to make a man only half a man.

Forrest: There is an element in your own poetry which is firmly public. It isn't a private or esoteric poetry but a public poetry. Do you feel there is any connection between this quality and your sense of poetry as spoken?

Warren: What do you mean by *public*?

Forrest: By public I have in mind a poetry that is working to be fully communicative with its audience. First of all, by way of example, it strikes me that your openings move to achieve immediate attention. In other words, right from the start, you're already communicating. Does that strike a note with you?

Warren: It does. The great battle of the poem is won or lost in the first line, or the first five lines anyway. If you don't get into motion by then, it's probably going to be dead. You can have a great ending, but you better have a new start.

Forrest: Do you believe, though, that that quality of your openings is connected with your sense of poetry as rooted in speech?

Warren: I couldn't say yes or no to that. I could say yes and no definitely about the question of poetry itself. That is, I want to catch the eye in the opening; I want something to hook there. It's public in that sense. But not yet fulfilled. It's a start. But the word *public* is tricky. The question is always *public* to whom?

Forrest: So that it entices the reader . . .

Warren: It entices because it ends where the reader catches the scent of raw meat. It's like playing a fish. I should *hope* a poem would be public in the sense of establishing a need for communication first. Readers should be asking, "What's next?" Now part of this is a sense of unfulfilled rhythm, an unfulfilled sense of language. The language itself carries a sense of unfulfillment.

Novelli: Then you really have a strong sense that rhythms are not merely metrical phenomena but are living things that you can feel coming to an end or not coming to an end.

Warren: Yes. I think that any poem that's competently done is a closed arch. You start an arch and you come to rest with it. Ideally—and there is no ideal poem written—a poem will lead to the closing of the circuit. And one of the participating factors is the question of the verbal drive rather than merely the rhythm, because rhythm is only one aspect of the verbal drive. I'd say you *could* make it a matter of rhythm and discuss that alone. But this should also be related to the kind of drive the subject has too. Now, if we think of the characteristic rhythm of John Donne as opposed to the characteristic rhythm of Robert Frost, you see right away that we're talking about two kinds of people. The holy sonnets of John Donne against the poetry of Robert Frost: well, it's just like night and day. I don't mean good or bad; I'm just saying they're different. The whole personality is in that one factor, if you want to put it that way.

Novelli: It's ultimately the sound of a particular person talking. You certainly hear Donne arguing with you or talking to some surrogate listener, someone who's out there.

Warren: Yes, well he's talking to himself, really. Of course, in one sense he's always talking to himself. He has to play audience too, as well as speaker. He has to play double.

If you take the opening of Donne's ninth holy sonnet, "If poisonous minerals, and if that tree," that first line is not fulfilled rhythmically. We have a syntactic need: the sense is not completed yet; the rhythm is not completed yet unless we are thinking of rhythm as an abstraction. We want more of this; the line is asking us to push on. "Whose fruit threw death"—it's knotted. Instead of being straight iambic, "Whose fruit threw death" is all spondaic, all accented. Then next comes "on else immortal us." We don't know what the "if" is about yet. But we find a contrast that means something: "Whose fruit threw death" (a moment of human damnation in the garden scene); and then suddenly "on else immortal us" (he is sadly, nostalgically, looking back on what could have been but isn't possible). You see how that line is balanced on that contrast: "Whose fruit threw death on else immortal us."

Then "If lecherous goats, if serpents envious/Cannot be damned; alas, why should I be?" It has fulfilled its movement. "Why should I be?" picks up and echoes that second line beginning "Whose fruit threw death"; it's a spondee that answers it. "Why should I be?"—you can't tell how to accent it even: it's spondaic but not *spondees*; it's hovering. And now your poem has set the question. It's finally put the hook into flesh. It has also put it in by playing with two kinds of rhythm that are involved in this, the rhythm of salvation and the rhythm of damnation. The knotted spondaic rhythms become the rhythms of damnation. And the others, the released iambics, are the rhythms of salvation, the backward look, you see.

You feel it as a going concern; at each stage it's going to another stage. Now, you feel, having gotten this far, then what? It isn't just an episode: it's part of a whole. And when you come to the end, you know you're there.

Forrest: The other founders of analytic criticism, for instance John Crowe Ransom and Allen Tate, were they enthusiastic readers aloud?
Warren: I'm sure they were. Anyone who writes poetry reads it aloud. And having taken classes from Ransom, I know he read a great deal of poetry aloud regularly in class in order to discuss it. He almost never discussed poetry without reading it aloud. His constant effort was to make people hear it, and hear it in relation to the poem as drama, although he didn't use that word, I think.

Novelli: When you're writing fiction, do you have a strong sense of the characters' voices?
Warren: I read it out loud. I always read it out loud; I have to. It's a habit of mine after writing a paragraph silently to read it out loud several times.

Novelli: And this leads to improvements?
Warren: It leads to changes, I hope improvements, but certainly to changes. It's a matter of always reading aloud at some stage. Now in poetry it's usually aloud first. It's talking, or talking in my head—really the same experience if you've sort of sunk yourself into the business as I have. But it has to have its moments of the real voice. I mean the spoken voice.

Novelli: At the beginning of *All the King's Men* you describe that moment when the crowd is in front of the courthouse, and Willie Stark begins talking to the farmers. There's an almost mystical strength of personality being carried here by the voice, the voice itself. I don't know if you've reflected much on the way you talk about . . .
Warren: I don't have reflections on how. If it works I'm glad, but I know such a thing can be *true* because I've seen it work over and over again, on the hustings and in cock-fighting pits and other places. The voice is nothing but a noise in the beginning; bit by bit it *becomes* a voice and is developing in people's ears, in people's beings, as they recognize it as a voice. You can see it happening. Of course the experts at political address and so forth know how to manipulate it.

Forrest: It's been said that the South is an *oral* culture, at least in contrast to the North. Do you believe that the oral nature of southern culture was important in your own development?

Warren: I don't know, I can't be different from what I am, but I do know this: that when I was a child a party would always wind up with tale-telling. But in the 1930's too—in Tennessee. This might be a very decorous party, or might be some men sitting around with bourbon in their hands. Or it might wind up with people acting parts, or playing old-fashioned charades, or one narrator acting all the parts. This was very common, very common indeed. And all classes of people, mind you. It might be tenant farmers, or it might be the man who owned the farm. Or it might even be an eminent professor. It would be the same thing. It was an oral society, and as somebody said, conversation is cheap. It was a long way to the movies, and it cost two bits to get in. In the 1930's this was a characteristic of many parties in Tennessee, including some of the faculty of Vanderbilt University. People like Andrew Lytle, who was a trained actor, on the one hand, and people like myself, certainly not a trained actor, on the other—but people telling tales, acting or half-acting tales. But now *I* haven't heard people sitting around telling tales in many years. They tell *jokes*.

Novelli: It's not the same thing.
Warren: It's not the same thing at all because a joke doesn't require any characterization. A joke is a switch of some kind, and it's usually something you're outside of.

Now it's certainly also true that the sermon-going and political rallies and so forth in the South were very common when I was a boy, even a grown man. The political passion was halfway a passion for rhetoric, for speech. And it was not just a matter of opinions. It was a matter of entertainment, of how good is that man at his job, you know. He ought to be worth listening to, whichever side he was on. But that's going out fast. TV is killing that off.

Forrest: Do you have the feeling that this was also important for other writers from the South?
Warren: I can't say how important it was, but I know it existed. I would say that it was generally important, for the simple reason that the good ones and the bad ones all show some effect of it. I mean of course spoken language that has quotation marks around it but also has sometimes affected general style. It is important, much more important in some cases. There is no reason why it should last any longer because the social habits have disappeared. And we are becoming a more or less homogenized nation. I'm not saying

what's good and what's bad; I'm just saying that there was a difference.
Of course, poverty makes for conversation. It's cheap.

Forrest: In the whole movement of literary analysis, hasn't there been a fairly widespread sense that the results of literary analysis should be constantly tested at least in the inner voice or in an inner-imaginative process of speech? If analysis suggests the possibility of irony in a passage by reason of connotation or allusion, or the slant of the syntax, isn't the tendency to try to verify the hypothesis about the tone of the passage by reading the passage aloud or to the inner ear to see if everything in the language will fit that ironic tone of voice?

Warren: I'd say yes right away. I don't think we need worry over it. It's clear as day to me that you can't analyze without knowing what you're analyzing. If you don't know before you start, what *are* you analyzing? You have to know before you can talk about it at all. And if you're communicating to a class or to a friend, then you may dramatize it. But I don't have any theory about that. I do know that you have to have some conviction about the meaning of a passage before you can talk about it. You have to come to grips with it yourself.

And irony is more than verbal: I mean an irony in events. Even when a man says nothing. There is a book on the silences of Shakespeare, what they mean. Or when somebody might speak but doesn't—that's another case. But it still is associated with the same kind of thing. The nonsaid then becomes the said, and has its own tone of silence as it were. It's a part of the same picture.

Novelli: My students were doing the scene with the rebels in *Henry IV*, Part One, where they quarrel over the map. And I was assigning the parts and suddenly realized that although Worcester says nothing, his silence is the most important thing in that scene. He's watching the whole thing come apart before him.

Warren: In *Richard II* it's the same thing. Richard talks, talks, talks, talks; and Bolingbroke says nothing. But you build a kind of silence in there, and you know what that silence means.

Forrest: Would you say that in giving the self to the reading of literature, what's important is to match yourself with what's there in the literature?

Warren: I think the point is to give yourself to it so you yourself become aware of these things. The matching is in the density of the response, the fullness of the response. The awareness that goes with it is what's important, rather than being able to turn yourself into the perfect performer. You're turning yourself into the perfect *audience*. That's what you really are doing.

Forrest: Do you enjoy reading your poetry to an audience?
Warren: Yes and no. I've never done it systematically except two or three years ago. I went on the road, some weeks reading every night. An agent would have somebody there to get me to the train or plane on time, and so forth for two weeks. I made a business of it, but it's a very tiring business. I'd like to do it four or five times a year, maybe. If you make it a business, it can kill you.

Novelli: Do you find that audience response shapes your own delivery?
Warren: It does indeed. One thing is really important to me. I'd like to sum it up like this: You know the poem—this is *your* poem—and you can tell what's wrong with the poem, what needs a revision, before you get to the line, because of the response. Very often I've done a lot of little revisions on the spot; once the poem is being read I feel that this movement is wrong or that word is wrong. And then I quickly scoot it down on the margin, and it will be corrected when it gets into book form or in the next edition. The *sense* of an audience is very important to a writer—how the response goes. Not how a friend says, "Oh, isn't that nice!" I don't mean that. I mean a real impersonal audience.

Of course, if you have the friendly reader, if you have a friend that you take things to regularly, who'll take the trouble to sit down and write an analysis for you in a letter back. . . . If Ransom would write me a letter, he'd write a page or two, or Tate would, or some other friends. Or John Hollander now, or Cleanth Brooks, and others. People who take it seriously will take the time, if they can give you that time in friendship, and they can help you rewrite a poem. They can explain to you, audibly explain to you, why something doesn't sound right. There's not enough density in that line, or this is wrong or that's wrong.

I was saying at lunch, when we were talking about I. A. Richards, that I sent him the first draft of a little book of mine called *Audubon*. He didn't answer for several weeks. Then I saw him at a cocktail party in Cambridge, and he took me to one side and said: "I haven't answered because I have too much to say. I like what you have, but it's not complete." He said: "It'll be a little book. Now you need some lyric effects here, played against this and this

and this. You've got to find your own *kind* of lyricism for that." And we talked
for half an hour or so about this. He would hum something, giving me a kind
of movement. This had never crossed my mind, and it started the whole
process over again. Three or four days later I began working on it, and the
lyrics are now in the poem, and the poem would be dead without them. Now
Richards had put his mind on it. That's one kind of criticism, but now I'm
talking simply about the spontaneous, even uninstructed, response that you
get in an audience, when you sense the awareness they are getting from something, and you know from the way the thing is going that two lines down
it's got to be a little different, something's got to be changed.

Novelli: This really bears on the poem's integrity, or unity, the way it's going
to take shape.
Warren: Ultimately it will, it should anyway. I think there's no such thing as a
poem's existing without a potential audience. . . . You try to know how it
would affect you if you weren't you. You play a little game with yourself and
read it out loud a lot to yourself. Of course, the real central thing you are trying to do is make an object "right." But the only real test of "rightness" is what
your other self can make of it.

Forrest: Do you feel that in the effort to get a piece of writing right, a poem
or a piece of fiction, part of what you're doing is building stage-directions for
how the reader ought to read it aloud into the language of the poem?
Warren: To use such a metaphor, the stage-directions are, of course, in the
material, the content. But there are other stage-directions too. Now, for
instance, "Whose fruit threw death." You can't *say* those words fast; you get a
block. The language gives you the rhetorical blockage, the dramatic blockage.
    Or you take that wonderful poem of Thomas Hardy's done when he was,
I think, twenty-five years old, "Neutral Tones." The two lovers have met, and
you know that it was their last meeting, and that something irreparable had
happened between them. The sky looked gray, and the sun was fading. The
poem ends:

> . . . keen lessons that love deceives,
> And wrings with wrong, have shaped to me
> Your face, and the God-curst sun, and a tree,
>   And a pond edged with grayish leaves.

You couldn't possibly say those last words fast. The poem *forces* you to read them dwelling on every item as you would something that was loaded with symbolic meaning. That is, those forced pauses where you can't make an elision will force you to read it right.

Only a rapid reader can read it fast, by not *reading* it, just taking the meanings and not taking the words. "Have shaped to me/Your face, and the God-curst sun, and a tree,/And a pond edged with grayish leaves." You *can't* read it fast: it gets slower and *slower*. You're burning the brake bands, you see, and that delay suddenly makes the visualization stronger.

Forrest: When you read Faulkner surely there is some sense of a voice in your own mind as you read it. Is that a very strong experience for you?

Warren: Sure, it's quite definitely one. It's *crowding* to be a-saying, to be said.

Literature wants to be spoken. You fulfill that sometimes by actually reading it; you go along where nobody's going to listen. But if you are an experienced reader, you can get a lot of it without ever making a noise. But any good poem wants to be read, out loud, and any good piece of fiction. One thing that is a little different, it seems to me, is that in prose the rhythm is never as assertive, or rarely as assertive. It's more like a conditioning element rather than something more positive. It's an offstage music. It's affecting you as deeply as the other will affect you, but it is spread out over a long period. You don't dwell on it unless you come to certain special moments, when the author will open the spigot, you know. One instance that just happens to pop into mind is the death of George Osborne, Amelia's husband, in *Vanity Fair*. The account of the Battle of Waterloo ends: "No more firing was heard at Brussels—the pursuit rolled miles away. Darkness came down on the field and city: and Amelia was praying for George, who was lying on his face, dead, with a bullet through his heart."

Now there you have a wondrous sense of panorama, pulling in to this single wound. And the rhythm of the passage enforces that; it gives you that. It's a tricky little piece of narrative prose. A fiction writer is going to make his rhythms mean something, even though they are not very aggressive, even though they may be very, very withdrawn. But they are conditioning the whole response.

Novelli: Novels at that time would often be read aloud.

Warren: That's right, with the family reading.

Forrest: In the present condition in which there *is* a problem about getting a sense of literature as speech, the problem that you addressed in the more recent editions of *Understanding Poetry* with Mr. Brooks, would it be worthwhile to give active training to students in how to read aloud, not with the idea of making them professional readers, of course, but just to give them the sense of how to get their own voices into literature?

Warren: I figure that it should be done not as a thing in itself but as a constant accompaniment. I don't say this as something to be emulated, but, for instance, you can take this passage as opposed to that passage, contrasting them, making students actually say the words and find the experience—usually it's for the first time—of what's happening to the muscles in the vocal cords and the whole muscular feel of the throat and head. That's a great eye-opener sometimes, just a little bit of that. It is combined; it is not a thing by itself, it's a thing that grows out of the simple study of the technical side of poetry. The technical side is not only a technical side; it is an expressive side too; it isn't just a box that you put something into. Make them say something and make them introspect what's happening to them *physically.* Then they know that "technique" and "poem" are identical.

You may not get more than two or three out of a dozen, but you get somebody. . . . Once they are aware of it, those aware of it can pursue it. It isn't something you do just one day in the beginning; but every time something of special interest appears then try it again, keep it alive, taking one thing at a time to get that *felt.* And I think in an informal way; it has to be almost stumbled on at the moment, rather than given as, say, two weeks of this, you know; it has to be a natural part of the experience.

Forrest: Along with other types of analysis.

Warren: Along with other things that you are doing more officially. That is my impulse, the way I've done it, so far as I've done it at all.

Unless we some way recapture in the classroom the physical feel of literature as something spoken, and get beyond the endless abstractions *about* literature and I know not what else, the teaching of literature is just on the skids.

Interview with Eleanor Clark
and Robert Penn Warren
New England Review / 1978

From *The New England Review*, 1.1 (Autumn 1978). © 1978 by *The New England Review*. Reprinted with permission by *The New England Review*.

Interviewer: What is the degree to which you influence one another? When you're working on a piece of writing, is it something that you like to do, so to speak, in a private space, or is it something that you take to your husband from time to time for criticism, and vice versa?

Eleanor Clark: I'm sure that we agree on that: we don't influence each other at all.

Warren: Never. I don't even know what's she's doing now. I hear a remote rumor that she's in the middle of a novel. I have to get my information from other people, or overhear what she says on the telephone. That's about the extent of our cooperation.

Interviewer: Is that true with respect to your own work?

Warren: Almost always.

Interviewer: How about in the penultimate phase . . . ?

Warren: She likes to tell me what she does and does not like when it's finished. I hardly ever show her anything beforehand.

Interviewer: You would see a draft before it went off to the publisher, or not?

Clark: He usually has seen drafts of my things, more than the other way around, because, as you know, he's an extremely prolific fellow, and if I read everything he does in drafts, well, to begin with, I'd get much too involved in it, and get upset and agitated as if it were my own, and secondly, there's such a lot of it that I never would do anything of my own if I . . .

Warren: . . . started to improve things.

Interviewer: So you do need private space?
Clark: Oh, absolutely, we don't work in the house at all, either here or in Connecticut. You just passed his little coop down there by the swimming pond, and my work cabin is way across the road over there, in an old hunters' camp.

Interviewer: So when a book is just beginning, you also need psychological space, because to talk about it would be to ruin the spell.
Clark: We're the opposite that way. Red has always liked to talk about his ideas. To me, that's really appalling. If I talk anything out, I feel it's gone, and I think I'm usually right.
Warren: I wouldn't dare start telling a novel to you, though, darling . . .
Clark: Oh, Red, that sounds so unfriendly.
Warren: Oh no, it's not unfriendly at all. It's just not in the cards. We could talk about *Oedipus Rex* or Shakespeare, but not about each other's work—at least, not in that way.

Interviewer: Won't you ever talk, say, about a novel you're writing on?
Warren: To taxi drivers, and anybody else, I'll tell stories over and over again. It's a way of developing an idea. But never discuss them with my wife. And in late years I find myself talking less and less to anybody, or showing things. That belongs to youth. Eleanor and I have too much to talk about outside of literature, anyway.
Clark: Outside of our *own* literature. Other people's we talk about quite a lot; we talk shop in that sense.

Interviewer: Still, no matter how divergent your individual writings may be from one another, there do seem to be common concerns. One thing that seems to me directly shown in Mr. Warren's work, and implied, at least obliquely, in your work, is a concern—sometimes a dismay—that *historical* awareness seems to be fading from current culture, perhaps especially among young people, even well-educated ones.
Clark: That's a concern, yes, but one, I would say, that is shared by a lot of people, *including* young people. People talk about these jaded times, as opposed to the active sixties, but we see a lot of young people, our children's friends, ex-students of Red's that we're very close to—we see loads of young people all the time, and most seem extraordinarily concerned

with social developments, and so, with what could be called historical development. Not perhaps in sixties fashion, but the concern still goes very deep.

There is one odd similarity between us. Red is, as you know, a Southerner, and I am absolutely a Yankee, but both of us come from backgrounds with a very strong sense of community, he in the rural South and I in a village in Connecticut, a place of small farms at that time. This gives us a highly similar view of a world of non-community, to put it grossly.

Interviewer: I guess that may be what I was getting at. At one point in *Eyes, Etc.*, you write: "Poor doped-up wandering young, who must spit on pity, else would give up altogether, for the first time I think I begin to feel for you in your stinking jeans and sleeping bags. Wild animals have their lairs and rigorous routes to travel. You don't even care if it was Denmark or Afghanistan or the Long Trail you slept on last night. You don't read, so it makes no difference; anywhere is nowhere." And your husband's latest novel is, of course, *A Place to Come To*. You seem to see connections among place, self, and society that those in an a-communal context may miss.

Warren: I think that's just as Eleanor said—that's based on a quest for an old-fashioned American community and a sense of firmly fixed family. By firmly fixed, I mean families that are real families. That makes a vast difference.

Clark: Also, we both came from families with an extraordinarily perceptive sense of the American past. His grandfathers and my grandfathers—for all their great differences of place—had a similar sense of what the whole American experience was, and would talk about in similar ways, as we have found out from each other over the years. His were involved in the Civil War, of course, in a way that mine weren't . . .

Warren: They were bounty-jumpers!

Clark: They were *not*! That's so unfair! They were too young to be involved. Isn't he mean? This is what we call healing the wounds of fratricidal strife . . .

Interviewer: Does that make you have a certain distaste for mass migrations to the cities here in the last fifty years?

Clark: I'd say that whatever distaste *I* have is very mild compared to that of people like Henry Adams and his brother in their time.

Warren: But their time was what it had to be. You don't keep people starving on the farm when factory jobs are waiting somewhere else. In their time, for economic and technological reasons, the growth of the great city was inevitable. Read Hamlin Garland, read Dreiser. . . .

Jacques Ellul, the French philosopher and sociologist, has said what many people—from Kierkegaard at least on—have been saying for a long time, that you find more and more a death of *responsible personality.* Ellul says that it's not a matter of a single massive thing, in a world of technology; if you go to a dentist, you're a tooth; if you work in a factory, you are number so-and-so; and in all your relations you are taken out of human context and put into a mechanical one. . . .

Interviewer: Is there a way in which art—we're talking mostly about literature—can mute this development or forestall it without becoming merely wistful? Isn't that a danger?
Clark: Nostalgia *is* a great sickness now.

Interviewer: Or is art drifting, alternatively, off in the direction of being the possession of a small adversary clique which merely decries dehumanization and technology?
Clark: That would be more or less the end of art, wouldn't it? I mean, art just can't be in that negative a position and continue to be art. I had to make a speech at my old school recently, and I said that we should be optimistic about American education because it's become so absurdly terrible there's no way to go but up. When you raise a couple of generations of ignoramuses by-and-by you're going to get one or two people who want something better, and the same is true in the arts: art cannot get mechanized and contentless beyond a certain point without a reaction setting in. This is partly an inter-ruption of what you're asking, but one of the things that we love about this part of the world, here in Vermont, is that there are still *characters* who are very much that, and we're very devoted to them, to their strong sense of personality.

Interviewer: I'd like to go back to Mrs. Warren's comment that art couldn't continue to be in a merely adversary posture toward the dominant culture.
Clark: Adversary it always is; I mean it couldn't continue to be merely nega-tive. And I can't see it, either, as merely an exploration of the artist's own innards. There has got to be some interplay with all the rest of the show.

Interviewer: Is this in any way at odds with Mr. Warren's thesis in *Democracy and Poetry?*

Clark: Red, would you say that it was?

Warren: My point was that there was a real danger that the "public" could become a great Black Hole, a Nothing which is Everything, the individual dying out. What I would like to see, what I hope for, is enough resistance in the human spirit to maintain the world of personality and the world of art: I equate these two things. But that doesn't mean that I advocate an art of pure self-involvement, any more than I advocate fixity of place or subject matter. You have to try to remain human—that's all—and try to carry your humanity with you. No place has a mystical virtue.

Interviewer: And yet the antidote to dehumanization is not, as Mrs. Warren makes clear, a kind of constant inward exploration. As she says in *Eyes, Etc.*: "Verbally we're allowed two forms of discourse, reporting and arguing. In written fiction the rules are narrowing down to plain and fancy—no brains or nothing but. In the latter it's a point of honor for the reader to pretend to be all agog over the author's next cerebral pinwheel or sparkler: for sustaining interest it's that or nothing."

Clark: One can think of examples. But let's not.

Interviewer: What, then, will return a *healthy* sense of self to us? When I asked whether or not there was conflict between you two on the question of self, I had in mind the phrase from *Democracy and Poetry*: "What poetry most significantly celebrates is the capacity of man to face the deep, dark inwardness of his nature and his fate." How is that capacity to face a dark inwardness to be distinguished from "mere" inwardness and the attendant intellectual pyrotechnics you both may find distasteful?

Warren: Well, I'm talking about *tragic* sense, the sense of human complication and paradox. And a sense not only that the individual faces tragedy but also that the public does. Take the Iphigenia story, which is a tragedy both personal and social; or in English literature, isn't it odd that the age at which England became a world power is also the age of its greatest tragic sense? So Shakespeare lived in a world of mass power, but he didn't retreat into mere solipsism, didn't forget that there were other people in England, too.

Interviewer: So that, as you both imply, the self depends on a sense of community, and what you object to is the self that is purely decommunalized and becomes self-reflexive to a fault.

Clark: Yes, and a self that is in flight. It's a very curious historical fact that the great Greek plays, Euripides, Sophocles, and so on, came at a moment of tragic ending of power in Athens—there couldn't have been a worse time, defeat, plague, the navy at Syracuse, and all that; but drama was at its great height.

Warren: Yes, but Aeschylus was also great, and was a man of the period of the great stand against Persia, and the great *rise* of Athenian power, and Greek power in general.

Interviewer: You never found teaching incompatible with writing?

Warren: I had quite a lot of self-discipline. I shut my door on Friday at noon, fixed a gallon of iced tea, and went to work.

Clark: And all along at Yale, he was only teaching one semester a year.

Interviewer: Teaching full time was pretty demanding?

Warren: Yes, but you were younger then.

Interviewer: Yet you still wrote those novels. You wrote *Night Rider* and *All the King's Men.*

Warren: Yes, and I wrote two novels that were never published when I was teaching. But in '46 I quit full-time academic work.

Interviewer: Were you able by then to be self-sufficient as a writer?

Warren: Well, yes, I guess so. I *always* thought of myself, though, as a writer and not a teacher. I was supposed to leave Oxford and come back to Yale to finish my doctorate on a fellowship there, and I couldn't make up my mind. But in the end it was clear I wanted to write, so I took a vow never to write an article for one of the professional journals. I sent a telegram to New Haven saying I couldn't come back. But I did get to teaching. In those days I was teaching Elizabethan literature, and I could happily have kept on with that. When I got to Minnesota, the Shakespeare spot was filled, though.

Interviewer: Had you done your Oxford B. Litt. on an Elizabethan topic?

Warren: Yes. Elizabethan verse satire. But I spent most of my time reading poetry of that period and the seventeenth century in general.

Warren: I don't know if it's relevant, but I know that I never had any interest in teaching writing as such. The most satisfying courses—for me to give, I mean—were a graduate course in non-dramatic Elizabethan literature, Renaissance, and Shakespeare. I always taught one writing course, but that was not the main thing, that side of it.

Clark: Certainly none of us ever *took* a course in writing.

Warren: Except for the fact that the best writing course is a good one in Shakespeare.

Interviewer: It's interesting that while the Humanities seem to be facing problems of underenrollment and of morale, the so-called Creative Writing programs are growing.

Clark: Yes, but there are so many peculiar courses now. No one would ever, a while back, have taken a course in business administration. Why would they? I just don't get it. Or a course in journalism, getting a degree in it, before going out to work on a small-town newspaper. I find that perfectly ludicrous.

Warren: Yes, I've known stacks of journalists. By and large they wouldn't hire a man from journalism school.

Clark: There are, after all, only two requirements for being a decent writer: one is to have a total passion—meaning a readiness to give up anything for it, rather than expecting to get anything out of it; the other is to spend your life at it, working like hell. I don't know any other way. Of course, behind the passion I'm assuming some native talent, and that's not always so.

Interviewer: How did you manage to write books and raise children, and do all the other things you've done? Did you keep a certain time and place sacrosanct?

Clark: Nothing is "sacrosanct" around small children. You try, but . . .

Warren: You said to me a long while back, "I'm going to enjoy my children; that's what we've got them for. I won't fight them to write."

Clark: We always had a great time with them, never had any inclination, say, to travel to Europe without them. We don't really "travel," anyway. We go to one spot for six months or a year, and stay.

Interviewer: You said that it was becoming fashionable to complain about children and husband. How do you regard yourself with respect to the Women's Movement?

Clark: I suppose that all these things are necessary up to a point, Susan B. Anthony and all the rest. And there have been a lot of situations when women were not getting equal pay for equal work, for instance. If I worked in a factory, or a university, where some male was getting more than I was for the same job with the same or less capacity, I'd be sore as hell. But all this business of just, in principle, wanting to get out of the home, I find "parlous," to use a nice old-fashioned word. I wouldn't have wanted to be out of the home. You can, of course, say that I was lucky: I was a fairly established writer when I began to have children; I had work that didn't require me to be off the premises. However, I do know plenty of younger people who have managed without all the squawks and wails and recriminations. We know a lot of them, young women who've gotten their Ph.D.'s, had children, done their work whatever it was, all at the same time. Sure, it takes character. . . . There's a whole side to this Women's Movement that's neurotic (I don't see why we can't call things what they are). There are certain kinds of suburbs where you'll find droves of women who haven't had the character to do anything, and they are of course delighted to have someone to blame it on.

Unfortunately, any time you get a big movement going, you'll get the lousy with the respectable, and the terms will get confused. God knows they are now. Several of my good friends are women who are real artists; they simply haven't time to be squawking about rights. One's a well-known musician, another's a painter, and so on. If you're really busy doing something, you don't have time to go around complaining about who prevented you from doing it.

Interviewer: I guess it gets back to that business that Mr. Warren mentions in *Democracy and Poetry*, that cant phrase he objects to: "taking time out to find yourself."
Warren: Oh, my God!

Interviewer: A self is not something that you go out and find?
Warren: Of course not.

Interviewer: In order to be a writer, you have to have a self, but that's something, you say, that is made, not found?
Clark: It's not something you have time to worry about. If you're a writer and people come ask you—if you're a woman they do, especially living with

someone like Red . . . "How's your self-image?" It's like a question in the loony-bin. As if you spent hours in front of the mirror, trying to see what developments were taking place. Self is a valid notion, as Red discussed it in *Democracy and Poetry*, but the way it's thrown around in the Women's Movement, it seems more like a term of belligerence.

Interviewer: It's not something that's simply determined for you.
Clark: It's unmeaningful matter for discussion.
Warren: It's not something you go find under a leaf. The self is what you *do*. What you want to do, and what you do do.

Interviewer: I think of the Great Twitch view of history in *All the King's Men*. Are we to dismiss Jack's reverie about history as something that just leaps up at you? Or, say, Dr. Stahlmann in *A Place to Come To*, other figures for whom so much of history—both personal and cultural—seems to be something that comes from without, and that you can't foresee or prevent . . . seems to be a Great Twitch, something determined for you. How does that tally with your sense of self as being what you do, and hence of history as something in which the individual has a hand? Stahlmann, to use a word that has come up a lot, is a man dealing with, or trying to deal with, placelessness. He ends by saying that the *imperium intellectūs*, the sum total of all he has accomplished, is bunk. Are we to take him seriously, or is he merely suffering from the placelessness?
Warren: To speak of Stahlmann is one thing. . . . To speak of that book alone, all the people in it, who are concerned with their relation (or non-relation) to a place—or community—and their relation to self—the book is built around them. The germ is an incident from years ago. I usually carry a book around for eight or ten years before I start it. I know many Southerners who, from babyhood on, hated the South, or felt inferior because of it, and so wanted out. Some are my contemporaries. I know some who have made great successes—heads of corporations, bankers, and so on. And at the same time, they never found a world to live in; they're people without place. They're cut off from one world and never really entered another one. I don't mean a man like Tucker Brook, who was head of the English department when I was at graduate school at Yale. He said, "You know what I'm doing here? I'm spoil-ing the Egyptians!" He wasn't suffering a bit from inferiority. But what I'm

getting at is this: the people who have no sense of human continuity, or community. For example, a man who had been in my freshman class at Vanderbilt—older, or rather, much more mature than the rest of us—didn't come back the next year. He said, "I want to get out of this place. I want to go where the big things are happening." And he went to Chicago. And next thing—more than twenty-five years later—he was on the telephone to me in my hotel, saying "Can I come up?"

I was there alone, and in comes a big wreck of a man. A big powerful fellow, but all bloated with too much food and drink. Richly dressed, a briefcase in his hand. I got him a drink, and we sat down and started old-timing. He said, "I was right to leave college and come up here." Let it be clear that he had made a fortune. Very soon. Then he said, "I want to show you my house." There in his briefcase were photographs of his house, a great rich mansion. "And there's my country place." He showed a sloop moored at a slip, a seventy-footer or so. And "These are my daughters," he said, and showed me his beautiful daughters. "And look at their debutante parties." He had photographs. He wanted to prove his success. He said, "I was right to leave, I knew what I was up to." And then—in the middle of this self-congratulation—he suddenly said, "I'm lonelier than God." People like that were the seed of *A Place to Come To*. But neither in that book nor anywhere else do I attach a mystical significance to a particular place. But I do attach a significance to the way a man deals with the place God drops him in. His reasons for going or staying. And his piety or impiety.

Clark: I think we can get a little too self-congratulatory, though, if we're not careful. We can't help remembering that masses and masses of the world's population don't have the luxury of a place in that sense . . . not only Vietnamese refugees right now; there have been swarms of refugees. People our age knew many, many from Hitler's Germany and Franco's Spain, for example. The world's politics are not always so peaceful. . . .

Warren: I'm being perfectly provincial about this. It's all I can be. I just record what I saw and what I knew. I'm not trying to generalize.

Clark: We can't simply say that a man ripped away from homeland . . .

Warren: I'm not saying that.

Clark: I know *you* aren't, Red. I'm just saying that we are perfectly aware that great things can be done, great thoughts thought, and great art made by people who can't live in their own native place.

Warren: I'm not arguing for regional literature. Not that literature, and fine literature, isn't often provincial; but it's not self-consciously that way. Not *deliberately*—theoretically—provincial.

Clark: Literature suffers more than any other art from displacement; there's no doubt about that. The painters in Paris in the great Fauve and Cubist and Surrealist years, for instance—they were hardly any of them French. They were Spaniards and Germans and everything else.

Warren: But they're not painting in traditional ways. They weren't painting out of nature. Picasso is not so much painting a land as an idea, finally. Modern painting had been moving toward abstraction—denial of nature and place.

Clark: The time and the fact of their immigration coincided happily for that moment. Literature doesn't usually fare that well in displacement. I knew Richard Wright somewhat in Paris in the forties, and it was sad to see him away from his place, because really, France was not material that he could use. He'd been taken up by Sartre and company, and was walking around with great volumes of Heidegger under his arm. Well, I don't think that nourished him in the way that he most needed to be nourished as a writer.

Interviewer: And yet we have the self-conscious exiles of the twenties.

Clark: Well, if you mean the Americans, they weren't, in many cases, exiles for all that long. For some, it was a fling. It wasn't imposed, and they could come back whenever they liked. Of course, the fabulous *Irish* literary picture in the last century, those who stayed home and those who didn't—Shaw, Joyce, Beckett, and so forth—would upset all generalizations. The Irish are like that.

Warren: Let's take Faulkner, with his "postage stamp-sized county." He had a look at Paris and said, "Nothing here for me," and came on back to the U.S. and worked in a bookstore in New York, and Stark Young, who was a very good friend of his, a fellow Mississippian, told me, "You know why Bill came back to Mississippi?" I said, "No." "They charged too much for tail in New York," he said. The point is simple. He was *himself*, carried his world in his being, and knew who he was.

Clark: You know, we all four—our children, of course they're grown—went down to Kentucky recently. We visited Red's brother and his family; they're still there. The children had never been to Papa's home state—a terrific lapse. It had more of an effect on them than many other trips, to Greece or France

or whatever. And on me. This relates in perhaps an oblique way to the sense
of place, but it also relates to the writer's thoughts—"images" is perhaps a
better word—and how they're formed. The three of us got a great wallop out
of it, partly from the association with Red: that is, a lot became clear to us
about his early life that was crucial and dramatic. But along with that, it was
quite a chunk of history, because we stopped a lot along the way, at
Harrodsburg and Cassius M. Clay's house, and so on (not Muhammad Ali,
but the great abolitionist, a friend of Lincoln's, and a very dashing figure). It
was exciting to get under the earth, too, as our daughter Rosanna said: part of
the excitement to her (of course, it was exciting to be in the place of many of
her father's stories and poems) was to go down into Mammoth Cave or a
deep coal mine, to feel the earth that exists under this country. Not to mention the insides of the planet we happen to be on. But there's a matter of
what density—and accuracy—of intimate association one brings to this or
that piece of it. The same with religion: all these little lightweight, skin-deep
Buddhists mouthing around these days—what will they ever know of it? To
know a god, you need a thousand years of nursery rhymes that went with it.
I'm only talking about where one's images and excitements come from, and
why I'd rather not have to be an expatriate.

Warren: It seems to me that all your vital images are ones you get before
you're seven, eight, nine years old. That's true for my life, anyway. What you
learn to look at. I've lived in cities a lot, but I can't work very long in cities.
Oh, perhaps in city libraries. I just have to be able to walk in the woods, to be
outdoors, to be alone.

Interviewer: Is the landscape, then, in the poems and elsewhere, the landscape of the South?

Clark: A lot of his finest poems are set in the Mediterranean . . . and here—
Vermont.

Warren: The things I look for even there, though, are conditioned very early.
You carry some place with you in your head. For example, even a lot of those
late poems are really autobiographical—things that really happened. That
one about the old black man on the mule cart on the wrong side of the
road—well, that happened to me in Louisiana, when I was driving back from
a party, kind of boozy. That belongs to a world I knew very well. I lived there.
A great deal of . . . well, poetry is different from fiction. It's much more
inside: you're reliving your life. For me, anyway. . . . You can absorb a piece of

the Mediterranean, or a piece of Vermont, and *combine* them. My book—
Promises—primarily about the Mediterranean is really half about the
Mediterranean and half about the South. Our small children—babies then—
were living with us in a ruined sixteenth-century fortress in Italy. This tied up
in my mind quite specifically with a recollected Kentucky . . . and my grandfather. They're all one package—contrast and identity in one package—
change and continuity—the human story.

Interviewer: You've recently written, though, a novel. I've often wondered
what the effect of being a novelist has been on your poetry, and vice versa.
Warren: I've often stopped novels and written poems in between. I may
never start another novel. I had one around for about ten years, and when
lately I sat down to write it, this year, I couldn't get off the ground. I ended up
writing a poem every time. I'd write a new poem before the day was over. A
poem's a different thing: it's shorter, after all. And it's a closer thing, a more
intimate thing.

Interviewer: There is a kind of speculative language, which I would associate
rightly or wrongly with the novel, in much of your poetry—and there seems
more of it as you go along in your poetic career. I'm thinking of lines like
"That is a way to love God," or whatever. Some might be construed as
prosy—although I think they work marvelously, as poetry. Is that a borrow-
ing from your training as a novelist, or something independent?
Warren: There's been some kind of cross-fertilization. And more and more
since I quit writing stories. Even in poems as old as those in *Promises,* the
germ is mostly anecdotal. The other way around, the influence of poetry on
prose, is less available . . .
Clark: Nobody wants to write poetic prose.
Warren: The construction of a novel, though, and the construction of a
poem are very close. Even behind a realistic narrative, there is—for me—a
shadow poem. Every novel is probably one big metaphor. Not just mine;
anybody's.

Interviewer: Do you like to read novels?
Warren: I read fiction. I'm reading *Dombey and Son* right now. Haven't looked
at it for twenty years. But I just finished one of the worst novels ever written . . .

Clark: Oh, don't mention that!
Warren: I won't mention it.
Clark: They come in here, you know. In the mail.

Warren: . . . When I was a young poet it was hard for me to tell when an impulse was over. That is, when a book was over. Now I know just when a volume of poems should end—because I've lost the impulse that binds it together. It's time to turn to something else. A thing like *Audubon* was easy. That started in the forties—it took twenty years. It started because in that period I was reading a whole range of subliterary genres—journals, memoirs, and things like that. And it led actually to two other things. One was *World Enough and Time*, a novel, and the other was *Brother to Dragons*. But there was a lot of stuff behind all that besides formal history.

I started a poem on Audubon, but I got stuck in a trap, a narrative trap. There's no narrative there, as such, to work from. You can't carry him that way, because the narrative doesn't have enough bite to it. I wrote a lot about him. I always have a lot of stuff I put in a folder and let lie, then come back to it. I knew when I came back to the Audubon thing that there was something there, a germ. In the sixties I was writing a history of American literature with R. W. B. Lewis and Cleanth Brooks, and I again read a lot of that stuff, not only my own notes, but the texts themselves, and Audubon was included. One morning I was helping to make the bed—which was a moment very rare, something I don't usually do, because I'm not housebroken very well— and one line of that poem came to me. "Was not the lost Dauphin." That line came into my head from twenty years back. It was not a first line of anything, but it stuck. That's when I started composing, by writing at night, going to sleep, and waking up in the morning early—revising by shouting it all out loud in a Land Rover going to Yale. I saw a new way in. Each element in the poem would be a "shot" on Audubon rather than a narrative. It took about six or eight months, but you can see it as a unit. But any poem or book of poems—you can learn to see where a certain kind of emotional motivation is winding up, its curve is coming back.
Clark: I often think of André Gide's phrase, *la part de Dieu*, in this process.

Interviewer: Did that reading in subliterary genres account for the Cass Mastern story in *All the King's Men*?

Warren: Cass Mastern's story had a germ. A lot of the details are historical—it's based on the Jefferson Davis story. His father, Sam, came to Kentucky, to our county, where Jeff was born. Old Sam Davis was so feckless! In our county there's a river valley and rich land to raise horses in. But Sam went up to the northern part of the county, to the Knob section, and tried to raise race horses where the soil is two inches thick over the limestone cap! Instead of five feet thick down our way.

Interviewer: A last question. Time is the great anthologist. When you're a young writer, you may look around and wonder at the shape of things to come. Have you had any surprises?
Clark: There's a fallacy in your question. I don't think, personally, that when you're a young writer you really look ahead in that way. I was looking ahead to see if I had enough in my purse for that night's dinner. Somebody once asked me what I thought about when I was skiing. I told the simple truth: I think about the next turn. And that's what a young writer does. I wasn't thinking about the shape of things to come when I was a young writer . . .
Warren: You were a young skier then, too!
Clark: I was thinking whether this review was going to get me the seven dollars and fifty cents from the *New Republic* that was absolutely necessary to me. I wasn't worried about whether, say, the *New Republic* itself would survive. You don't worry about the shape of things to come; you worry about the shape of *things,* in the sense that you're functioning, and you have to have some sort of outlet, and so on. One does not live in a vague, amorphous, questioning, puzzling Future. There are plenty of questions right now. Of course, one has social convictions too, and they may be passionate ones. I was in the Trotskyite periphery in the late thirties, and I suppose that's reflected in my first novel. In some residual way, it still figures. But I believe that's outside the sense of your question, about the "young writer."
Warren: I'll tell you one thing right now. The people who talked about the future of the world all the time never became writers.

Echoes of a Literary Renaissance

William Ferris / 1979

From Reckon: The Magazine of Southern Culture. 1.1–2 (Premiere 1995): 120, 125–27. Reprinted by permission of William Ferris.

When asked about the death of writer Peter Taylor this past autumn, fellow author Shelby Foote described in a radio interview the great sense of loss he felt. The absence, Foote said in his calm drawl, sprang from missing his friend but it also stretched beyond the personal to the literary landscape, where Taylor's brand of serious and subtle fiction is rare indeed. The moment sounded on the air the faint, gradual passing of an era.

Coupled with the death in late spring 1994 of Cleanth Brooks, a native Kentuckian whose critical brilliance helped revolutionize the reading of literature, Foote's observations invite reflection upon the remarkable assembly of minds at Vanderbilt and Louisiana State during the 1920s and 1930s, a spirited gathering of poetic intensity that bloomed into the full summer of a Southern literary renaissance.

What follows are selected remarks about the unusual confluence of forces during those years in the South, drawn from an interview with Robert Penn Warren (1905–89) conducted by William Ferris in 1979—the year that Fugitive poet Allen Tate died.

My father was full of poetry. In fact, I learned to read from poetry. My favorite was Marshall's "Horatius at the Bridge." When I was five or six I would make my father read it to me over and over again, until finally he lost patience and told me I could learn to read it myself. I looked at it over and over and puzzled it out. That's how I learned to read. The first time I tried writing a poem I was about twelve or eleven. I was ill and in bed. I had a strange feeling that I had to write a poem, and so I dictated it to my father. And my father said, "Well, that's no good. You're not ready for it." I didn't try writing poems again for four or five years.

I didn't have any idea as a boy that I would be a writer. It just wasn't interesting enough. I was more interested in nature and collections of butterflies and stuffed birds. I had no desire to go to college. I was determined to be an admiral for the Pacific fleet. It was a boyhood dream that stuck. I wanted to go to Annapolis and become a naval officer. My father knew our congressman, R. Y. Thomas, and in those days appointments at Annapolis were made primarily on political grounds. My father got an appointment for me from R. Y. Thomas. I was just finishing Clarksville High School [in Tennessee] and I had just turned sixteen. I took the physical examination and so forth, but I hadn't received a letter, although I knew it was coming. Then I had an accident. I was struck in the eye by a stone. I was lying on my back looking up at the sky at the sunset, and my little baby brother was behind a high hedge and threw a rock over the hedge, and it hit me in the face and injured me. Then the formal letter came saying the appointment at Annapolis had been officially accepted, but by that time I couldn't go because of the injury.

So I went to Vanderbilt to be a chemical engineer. Three weeks disillusioned me. Chemistry was badly taught, with no sense of science, just mechanics. But I was in John Ransom's freshman English class and he was fascinating to me. He was a very extraordinary man with a lot of charisma. He wasn't the best teacher in the world, but he'd fire you up. He'd get an idea and just set your mind working.

He then proposed to me that I come into his advanced class in writing. I loathed the man, and we never got along. He later fired me. He was a son of a bitch. But I must say he made you memorize poetry, and I found myself just soaking in poetry. And Ransom was the only live poet I'd ever seen. It was like looking at a camel or something.

The Fugitives became a group long before my time. It was before America got in the war [World War I]. Ransom was a classicist teaching at a prep school in Connecticut and he didn't like it. He was nostalgic for the South and so went back. He got hired by Vanderbilt with [Donald] Davidson. They made friends with businessmen in town and started the group. It wasn't a college organization at all. They met every week or two weeks as a philosophy club. They were centered around a strange Jewish mystic named Sidney Mttron Hirsch, who had no formal education. He had run away from home and joined the Navy and had become a boxing champion in the Pacific fleet. He was terribly handsome and worked in Paris as a male model for various painters. He was a student in a totally scattered and crazy way. He was full of Jewish mysticism and the Cabala and often crazy philological ideas about poetry. I had very little time for him, and Ransom rebuked me for it.

Then the war came along and that changed the Fugitive group. When he came back after the war, Ransom, who had been a lieutenant, published a group of poems. Davidson, who was also in the Army, was full of poetry.

I was reading with Allen Tate, who was then a young man back from the war finishing his degree. He's six years older than I and he had been in and out of college. He was brilliant. I was then writing poetry a lot. They would read the poems and give me lectures and critiques on them. They moved the meeting place to the theological dormitory, a dirty place with half-empty bottles of whiskey and dirty shirts and poems. I made a mural on the wall with crayon of episodes from "The Waste Land" and Sherwood Anderson. The Fugitives then had a poetry contest, and the businessmen put up the money. I entered it, but Hart Crane won the first prize. But they published my poem, a longish, full-bodied poem. They I let them take me to the meeting place as a guest, and just after my sophomore year, they decided to elect me.

We were a great joke over in the theological dormitory. Well, my cup ran over. I didn't think anything else in life could be this good. Ransom was an editor and I was an editor. Ransom and Tate almost came to blows, not literally, but they almost broke up a friendship about the poem "The Waste Land." Ransom was always standoffish about it, and they attacked each other in print over it. The reconciliation took place finally. Ransom since that time has said the person intellectually and critically closest to him was Tate.

But everybody broke up in 1925. Tate went to New York, Greenwich Village, to live, and I went to California at Berkeley on a fellowship.

I'll Take My Stand was written after I left Vanderbilt. It came out in 1930, when I was at Oxford. I was away for five years. I just followed the fellowships for a while after I left Vanderbilt. California gave me a teaching fellowships for seventy-five dollars a month. That was a lot of money then. And I was selling a few poems and making a little bit extra. The level of poetic taste and knowledge in that California community was not far behind Vanderbilt's. It's very funny how a little isolated place like Vanderbilt knew more about modern poetry and art than places like Harvard or Berkeley. I graduated college without knowing about Marx or Freud, but everywhere else those who were advanced on Freud and Marx knew nothing about modernism and the world of poetry. It was strange that this group at Nashville knew about all these things and read everything that was around.

It wasn't conscious in anybody, but some of the Fugitive talk was about Irish writers and their colonial position to England. Yet they were producing great writers, and they were having a vengeance on the English through their literature. Several times the Fugitives talked about the parallels in the South and Ireland. The South felt outside the great industrial establishment of the North, and they felt a parallel with the Irish writer.

The Fugitive boys had no time for the Middle Western renaissance though—[Theodore] Dreiser and Sherwood Anderson. But I was bowled over by Dreiser. I first read *American Tragedy* in the fall of 1925. I remember the exact time I read it and the room I read it in. I began to read all of Dreiser very thoroughly and I wrote a book about him for his centenary. I still think he was one of the two great novelists of this century in America—he and Faulkner.

I met Cleanth Brooks in the fall of 1924. We were at Vanderbilt together. I was a little ahead of him in college, and I didn't know him terribly well then. But then we were at Oxford together and became very close friends. When he was at LSU as an assistant professor, I'm sure he arranged it somehow so that LSU offered me a job. We then found out that we had exactly the same way of teaching poetry or fiction. That's how we got into writing textbooks together.

I met Eudora Welty through the mail when I was working on the *Southern Review*. We published five of her stories one right after another. One of the most delightful evenings I've ever had in my life was with Charlotte Capers and Eudora. We had dinner together and stayed until all hours just talking, drinking, talking. Those two women together are just a circus. They are two great wits, tale-telling.

That's one difference between the South and North. Nobody tells any tales up North. There's gossip, but no one just tells a tale for tale's sake. During my time as a student or teaching in the South, parties were almost always either playing charades or poker or tale-telling. Andrew Lytle, who was a great actor, was a great improviser of tales. He's one of the best raconteurs and conversationalists I had ever known. There are only a few people who can even touch him. Stark Young could and Lyle Saxon in New Orleans could.

I began writing fiction by pure accident. When I was in college I read a lot of fiction, but I didn't have any deep commitment to it. All the talk around me and the people I admired were into poetry, and of course there were extraordinary poets that I was closely associated with, Ransom and Tate. There must have been a dozen students at Vanderbilt who knew "The Waste Land" by heart within two or three months after it came out in 1922. An enormous number of people were interested in it and were writing poetry there. It was a strange disease.

Then I began to meet people like Katherine Anne Porter, whom I knew very well. She was a close, close friend. I knew her in Greenwich Village, before I went to Yale. The Tates were there too. Tate's wife was a novelist, Caroline Gordon. I knew Ford Madox Ford too and talked with him once or twice. There people were talking about fiction from the inside, so that fiction had now a certain kind of insides for me the way poetry had. It made me want to try my hand at it, but I still didn't do it.

My last year at Oxford I was writing a dissertation, a thesis, and in the middle of it I got a cable from Paul Rosenfeld, who was one of the editors of the *American Caravan,* the anthology of new writing, asking me to do a novelette for the *Caravan.* I had never thought of doing such a thing. And I said, "Well, why not? Try." Writing the dissertation bored me. So I wrote a novelette in the evenings. I guess I was nostalgic for home, and the notion of the tobacco war was always very romantic to me, so I made up a story about a Southern farm family like my people ["Prime Leaf," 1931]. I sent it in, and it got good press.

It was the first fiction I ever wrote. I was hooked.

In 1936, I got a telegram from the publishing company Houghton Mifflin. They had a prize out, $1,000 prize, for a novel to be selected. This letter said I could have the reward, but they hadn't seen a novel of mine at all. A friend of mine published at Houghton Mifflin and she had given someone there my novelette to read. They said, "He's got to write a novel out of this," and so they paid me in advance. If she hadn't showed these people the novelette, it wouldn't have happened.

I was then teaching in 1936 at Louisiana State University. I wrote the novel [*Night Rider*] there in the summers. I didn't research it but just went and talked to people. It came out in 1939. And that's the story of how I made my first full step.

A Dialogue with Robert Penn Warren on *Brother to Dragons*

Floyd C. Watkins / 1979

From the *Southern Review*, 16.1 (1980). Reprinted by permission of the Estate of Floyd C. Watkins.

Floyd Watkins: Was the 1953 version of *Brother to Dragons* what you wanted it to be at the time when you published it?

Warren: Well, here Albert Erskine [Warren's editor] and I have a difference in memory. Now at the time when the book was in its last stages, he was coming and spending the weekend with me, the last editorial go-over, the last of the editorial revisions and discussions. My wife and I—my wife was then pregnant with Rosanna—were living on a farm called Paradise Farm, outside of Newport. I guess I felt that, well, I was in a rather excited state of mind anyway. It was about the time of my first child. I had a very happy marriage in process after a period of an unhappy one and the stopgaps between. I probably wasn't as critical of what I had done as I might have been. In style I had wandered into a trap—too often caught in the trap of blank verse—and that had meant some padding. And I published it without enough of the cooling off process—the last hard look.

Watkins: And you think the padding is in the '53 version as it was published?

Warren: Yes, some of the revisions didn't get in. Albert was called back to New York by a telephone call from Bennett Cerf in the middle of Sunday afternoon. Bennett said, "I've got a problem, and I want your help right now. Get the next train out." So we didn't finish the job, you see. Just assumed we had. Albert put the manuscript in his briefcase, and I swept the other stuff into a suitcase and didn't look at it again. And he headed out. When I saw it, it wasn't the text I had thought it was going to be.

Watkins: It was different?

Warren: Quite some severe differences. Now, of people who have gone through the manuscripts at Yale, one of them said, yes, he found the other

170

version. The one I saw. Another said he didn't find it. I've never hunted for it myself. Well, it wasn't worth my time to hunt it. I don't care much about it. At the time Albert said, "Well, when you get the one you want done we'll publish that one." Then it became a matter of trying to make a play. Broadway took it first. There was a whole year they were paying me for it and then with numerous tryouts for actors and things like that. On opening day, the lead actor sent a telegram (I think), withdrawing. It was finally done many times, including New York at the American Palace Theater and then in Providence. The director, Adrian Hall (who was starting out his career then in an adapted church), did a good early production that ran some little time. A year or so later he got hold of a big old Keith theater, remodeled it, and set up the "Trinity Players" in rather splendid surroundings. Meanwhile he had been reworking his *Brother to Dragons* and used that to open his arena theater (there was a proscenium, too). Later he did more work on production and by the time I saw it in Boston after a little tour, a couple of years later, he had it stunningly, imaginatively done. This work on the play also changed my notion of the poem. It still remains a verse play. But when it got on the stage, it changed my sense of the versification and led to a tremendous lot of rewriting and reorganization. There were many changes (bit by bit, mind you) for the twenty-odd years of several versions. But in later years I have taken months of time consecutively and tried to start clean—to leave no old section in if I didn't want it. It must be remembered too that the change of one syllable will sometimes change the rhythm of a whole passage.

Watkins: So it's a basic difference in technique rather than a philosophical difference. But also a difference in organization.
Warren: It is no different philosophically. But it is very different technically—in rhythm (the important thing) and in organization. Also a lot of cutting. The original version had certain sections that were repetitious and wordy. I got rid of those, I think.

Watkins: Do you think it may be less explicit than the first one was? To some extent I thought you interpreted your 1953 version yourself for the critics. Is there less of that?
Warren: Well, I couldn't answer that. I think there's less commentary, yes. Now how much less, I don't know. And also it's vastly improved in general poetic

quality. Now some passages naturally remain the same. Other passages are quite different, and there are many cuts, sometimes very small—but significant.

Watkins: There are already a good many people who say, and I would not contradict them, that *Brother to Dragons* may already be your greatest work, the 1953 version.
Warren: That is wrong.

Watkins: Would it disappoint you greatly if they find the new version not as likable as the 1953 version?
Warren: Oh, I think they'd be wrong.

Watkins: I hope they are.
Warren: I hope they are too. Everybody can be wrong. But I would say they are dead wrong. It is a much more fluid and natural verse movement now than it was before. Of course, I hope I'm not wrong.

Watkins: Is it a matter of technique, or is it something in the meaning of the work that's kept you working at this single thing twenty-five years and more?
Warren: It's not just the idea as bare idea, no, but I wanted . . . I didn't feel right about it. Put it that way. It's as simple as that. I can get more out of it than I got out of it.

Watkins: You can get more out of the same idea with a different technique?
Warren: With a different technique—or even small differences. The change of the weight of one syllable in a line can make a vast difference. I wanted a more natural and fluid thing. I also changed the organization somewhat. Now in the original version Meriwether Lewis doesn't appear until the very end. Now, he appears early in the poem, you see. He is grounded in the poem. And there's a new scene, a scene in the parting of Jefferson when he sends him out. And a lot of reworking toward the "touch" scene toward the end—touching Lilburn.

Watkins: Do you know Caroline Gordon is writing a novel on Meriwether Lewis?
Warren: She is?

Watkins: She is. She is related to him.

Warren: So was John Crowe Ransom. Ransom's mother was the descendant of Meriwether Lewis. When the Meriwether Lewis National Monument was dedicated, she was on the platform. Later, I've had twenty-five letters, at least, from people who are related to the Lewis family and discovered that a close friend of mine at the University of California was a member of the family.

Watkins: When and how did the idea of *Brother to Dragons* first come to you?

Warren: It was back in the forties. I read a great deal of sub-historical material, like letters and journals and things like that, Audubon's journals. I was soaking myself in the period, and Lilburn Lewis and his story were practically unknown. I had known the folk-tale, garbled version in childhood. Then I began serious investigation of the court records and found that specialists knew little about him. I talked to many famous specialists before I wrote the book, the first version. Dumas Malone wrote me. He said, "I know it happened, but that's all I know. I haven't got that far in my researches yet." And various other people. One man finally gave me the records that I wanted. Francis L. Berkeley, Jr.—anyway, the curator of the Lewis-Jefferson Papers at the University of Virginia. And he wrote me something to this effect: that not only did Jefferson have a philosophical shock, he doubted that Jefferson could ever mention the fact. At least, there was no record. Jefferson had sustained a wound too deep to mention. Of course, that is the assumption of my poem. And it doesn't really matter, in one sense, whether it is true or not. Perhaps he did mention it, but I could find no record. But anyway the assumption is that the shock ultimately changed Jefferson's view of the whole nature of man. He who had esteemed man as perfectible, but finds in his own blood the basic horror that raises the question of perfectibility, you see, in a very special kind of way. Of course there is a great deal of unbalance there. Nuttiness lies in the Lewises, in the whole collection of Randolphs. Jefferson's mother was a Randolph, and he had defective siblings and so forth. But my poem is not about pathology as such—only as symbol.

Watkins: You know there is a relatively new book out by the Princeton University Press . . .

Warren: I've read it.

Watkins: I was going to ask you . . .
Warren: I know the man—Boynton Merrill, a delightful man—and a fascinating book.

Watkins: Did that affect your second version?
Warren: No. I had finished mine.

Watkins: You had finished it?
Warren: Before it came out. It wouldn't have affected me anyway. All it did was document the certain divergencies in the family and the intermarriages in the family more than I knew had happened; and also it made old Charles Lewis not a physician, as he was in certain early versions, but a planter. Also it made him a crook.

Watkins: Oh, really?
Warren: A crook. He crooked Jefferson. And Merrill does explain something I hadn't known, the reasons for the Lewis family going west. There were many explanations when I was reading the material. But he was failing, a financial failure. The Lewises were going bust. They had sold what land they could next to them, and bought lots of new land in Kentucky but without enough slaves to exploit the new land when they got there.

Watkins: A lot of people have worried themselves by trying to name the genre of the book. I believe it was Robert Lowell who called it something like this peculiar verse-drama-novel. Do you think of it as having a name?
Warren: I think it's a poem. I don't worry about definitions. A narrative poem—but in dramatic structure.

Watkins: A narrative poem?
Warren: Insofar as it is anything, that is what it is. It is very much to be distinguished from a play. It's not a play.

Watkins: It is the same genre, the same kind of work, in both versions?
Warren: It is the same kind of work. Now Random House is going to publish, they tell me, the play version later on. There is a play version.

Watkins: Is that the one that appeared in *The Georgia Review* or was that . . .
Warren: It appeared in *The Georgia Review*. That is the one that was done by—
the last version—it was done by Adrian Hall with the Provincetown Theater,
the Trinity Square Theater, and ended up in a fine production in Boston.

Watkins: It seems to me that the idea or the fallacy of perfectibility has run
throughout most of your work and that this is one of the best embodiments
of that constant concern that you have. Is that a fair statement?
Warren: I think that is probably a fair statement. I wasn't aware of this until
quite late, you see. The first time I became aware of it as a central question
for me was when I was writing the little book on Coleridge. Now Coleridge
takes that view of perfectibility. I discovered it in "The Ancient Mariner"
itself—that this appeared in the poem. Preceding the book on "The Ancient
Mariner," I had written a poem called "Billie Potts," which was my version of
the same idea. But not derived from Coleridge, God knows. I wrote that
poem in Minnesota, in 1943, before I began my Coleridge piece—which I
worked on at the Library of Congress, in 1944–45, as a lecture for Yale.

Watkins: Oh, yes.
Warren: Where the man comes back to claim his patrimony of the evil
father. And the evil father killed him, you see. He gives him his patrimony, in
other words.

Watkins: Right. Do you think . . .
Warren: That's, I guess, where the puritanism comes in.

Watkins: I see. It seems to me that there is a close tie between what you are
working with here and your theme also in the poem "Homage to Emerson."
Warren: Though I hasten to add I'm not an Emerson man, that could be.

Watkins: In fact, those are so similar it would be harder for me to state the
differences than it would be to state the comparisons.
Warren: Well, it hadn't occurred to me that they were similar until you mentioned it. But that doesn't prove anything now. Things exist in you without
your knowing it. You don't know what comes out of yourself, but it comes. It
is you. But you can't predict always. Sometimes you can plan and predict.
Sometimes you can't. The Emerson poem and "The Ballad of Billie Potts"

and *Brother to Dragons*—they are all of the same cloth, quite clearly—but Emerson is the contrary to the others.

Watkins: Now I can see the connection better between the other two than I can to "Billie Potts."

Warren: Well, "Billie Potts," let me run an exegesis of "Billie Potts" as if you hadn't read the poem. The story is about an outlaw, a wicked old man who runs an inn as an outlaw and spots prey at the inn and then informs some members of his gang to pick up the prospects after they leave the inn. Now his son grows up in this world, and his son is sent out to carry a message ahead about a certain traveler, but decides to prove his manhood by doing it himself. He's nearly a grown man. His family would be proud of him. But he miscarries. The other guy spots him and beats him to the gun and shoots him before he gets a shot off. The traveler has a little derringer in his sleeve and he gives him the derringer. Billie howls, and cries, and runs home. But then his pappy says, "Take this saddle and horse and this fifty dollars in gold and head West, get out of here fast before they are after you." And so the boy goes away. He succeeds out West, and the poem says that in the West every man is a new man, reborn. He is redeemed. Secularly, shall we say. Every man gets a new name in Texas, as the old saying goes.

Watkins: That is the perfectibility.

Warren: The perfectibility. He comes back rich and, to tease his parents, puts up at the inn. Night comes on. And they think now they've got them a fat one. And the father carries him down to the spring to get some fresh water and sets a hatchet in his head. Kills his own son, and they rob and bury him. The wife, the old wicked wife, and the father bury him. But a friend who has met him on the road and recognized him comes to the house and says, "I've come to see Billie tonight. Where's Billie?" And they say, "Billie hasn't been here." He says, "Oh, you wouldn't know him. He was wearing a big black beard and riding a big bay horse and looking fine." The husband and wife look at each other and realize the truth, they exhume the body and they find the mark under his heart, in the shape of a little mole shaped for luck . . .

Watkins: Under his left tit.

Warren: Yeah, under his left tit. And they have killed their son. Well now, this is the question of the man who goes to the West to become a different man—redeemed—prospers and comes back. He must come back. Something calls him back. He doesn't know why he wants to come back. He comes back to his true "human" father—he dies by his own blood—and name. Now when they kill him he accepts from his father's hand the natural gift. He's a sacrifice this time. But he's returned. He's performed the human cycle. He has had the human gift. He receives it from his father's hand.

Watkins: Your aunt told you that story, I believe, in Cerulean.
Warren: She told me that story.

Watkins: Which aunt was that?
Warren: That was my grandfather's sister-in-law, Aunt Anna Mitchell. I knew my grandfather on the Penn side. He was a descendant of Abram Penn, a Revolutionary colonel, etc.—the highway near Roanoke, Virginia, is named for him in the region where he held a Revolutionary grant.

Watkins: Do you remember that there is a very long article in German about the innumerable analogues to "The Ballad of Billie Potts" in European folklore?
Warren: Yes. There are many.

Watkins: Have you read any of those?
Warren: I haven't read any of those. No. I didn't even know about them when I started the poem. The poem had its origin originally in hearsay. The old lady was chatting along, telling about things that happened, that she had heard about when she was a young girl. Then I read about it. I read the story in some publication, I think, of the historical society of Louisville.

Watkins: Filson. The Filson Club.
Warren: It was primarily the tale she told me that I was telling. The outlaws lived up in the cave-in rock section, I think. I put it down between the rivers in Kentucky, a very wild country at one time.

Watkins: Don't you think that the perfectibility of *Brother to Dragons*, though it came from the eighteenth century, may have attached itself peculiarly to America?
Warren: It came out of the Enlightenment. It started in the Enlightenment. Man can be made a different creature—by rediscovering his "natural" innocence, Rousseauism.

Watkins: Don't you think even our thinking about penal institutions and the correctibility or perfectibility or sinlessness of man still shows the influence of that kind of Jeffersonian thinking?

Warren: Absolutely. Sure it does. The whole notion of America, we find in the penitentiary. The penitentiary is an American institution, and was based on the idea that a man could be reformed, and of course the penitentiary backfired on us. It didn't reform anybody. Of course, this isn't final evidence on the point. But go look at a penitentiary.

Watkins: And still is backfiring?

Warren: Still is backfiring. But it is a product of the Enlightenment and was based on the notion that man can be remade.

Watkins: Is Jefferson's thinking almost the opposite of the thinking of writers like you and Herman Melville?

Warren: Melville was absolutely opposite. He says the eternal *No*. Life is basically that, and he capitalized the *No*'s. Face the eternal *No*. That is the essence of life. He is exactly the opposite. Also, Melville was obsessed, you might almost say, with the notion of the difficulty of finding good and evil. The paradox of life was what Melville saw primarily, the paradox of life. He would say, the Civil War is where it comes out most vividly; he was swept off his feet by the heroic figure of Ahab, you see, and that sort of thing. And the Civil War comes along and becomes personal. Your own country is involved in it. He was an emancipationist, but he also saw the war as a crime against humanity. Now in a poem of his on Charleston—"The Swamp Angel"—with Charleston being bombarded, he sees this as a crime, too, and in another poem, earlier, he had said, however the war comes out, it will show the "slimed foundations" of the world. That's his phrase, the "slimed foundations" of the world. And the war, being fought for good, will show the "slimed foundations" of the world, as the good cause does not change the nature of the face of the world. Many things may nest under the shelter of a good cause.

Watkins: So you could see yourself not in Melville's position, but somewhere between Melville and Jefferson.

Warren: Well, I believe we are stuck with trying to improve the world. Put it that way. We are stuck with it; we have to live with nature, so we have to try to improve it. But I have no romantic dreams about quick improvements, no romantic dreams about quick improvements of human nature or of human society.

Watkins: Jefferson's idea, was that Lilburn's idea also?

Warren: Lilburn was a madman, really; what his idea was doesn't really matter. It simply is not relevant to Lilburn. Now what I put in the story and what is in the history of the thing—I use things there, but I'm using them for my own purposes. That is, after all, the mother was not buried on Lilburn's place. She was buried on the estate of the older brother. I put the grave on Lilburn's place so that the brothers could shoot themselves, each other, across the mother's grave, and I put the mother there to give her significance in the story, not in history. Lilburn hates the father because the mother—he brought his mother to Kentucky—the mother, who presumably loved Virginia, the old ties, the blood ties. The mother couldn't see her youngest son becoming a frontiersman, a ruffian, you see. Isham, he was a bum; the real Isham was a bum. The beautiful aspect is not in the historical records; I put that in. I did certain things to the story, a lot of changes. The wife was pregnant, historically speaking, the new wife. Lilburn had been married before and had children in the house. Well, you can't clutter a house up in a poem with children. I changed this with materials for a poem. I'm not trying to write a history. I stay as close to history as humanly possible, but there are certain irrelevant things like children. I put Aunt Cat in. She isn't even mentioned in the record—and the name was the name of my grandfather's nurse, whom I knew, and he was born in 1838. But I needed Aunt Cat, and certainly there was an Aunt Cat around of some kind, you know. I made changes, historical changes, but none that are important.

Watkins: You also changed the moral stature of Isham, if he was a bum, didn't you?

Warren: I put Isham not as a bum but as a pawn for Lilburn; the younger brother, rather dumb, a dumb younger brother, you see, worshipping him, and deprived (as the historical Isham was) of education. He crossed the line, to become an almost illiterate frontiersman, you see. The wilderness calls him, you see. These men—the Lewises—are men who are supposed to bring light to the dark wilderness, even civilize it. And as a parenthesis, I'll say that Meriwether Lewis is a true "lightbringer," in contrast. The wilderness, however, gets the other Lewises; they become brutes. But Lilburn keeps the surface of a gentleman. Isham does not. Isham is rather thin-witted anyway. He is younger; he is made more childish in my treatment of him. Actually Jefferson took Isham for a time and tried to teach him surveying. And he got him a job with the government down in Mississippi. But then nobody knows what happened to Isham during this period. He was only periodically at Rocky Hill. But he was present when the Negro was murdered.

Watkins: And Lilburn was the mutilator?
Warren: He was the mutilator. Isham was much less intelligent, and he had also lost much of his sense of gentility, you see. The frontier was absorbing the brothers. Now in the present poem I have Madeira in the beginning of the poem and corn whiskey in the end. Now the gentlemen in Virginia didn't drink corn whiskey. They drank Madeira. They drank port, as a great eighteenth-century gentleman would. Now it is said in the poem that the decanter of Madeira has long since been replaced by the jug. And I made that change and tried to indicate other small things like that, and the speech of Isham as contrasted with Lilburn's. But, of course, the frontier brutality entered the soul of Lilburn too, even though he, at one level, hated it and looked back to Virginia. He blamed his father for killing his mother by bringing her to the wilderness.

Watkins: Now in the '53 version you describe two trips that you made to Smithland.
Warren: Yes, I did make two trips to Smithland. I may have made another one, I've forgotten.

Watkins: You make those trips in the '79 version too?
Warren: I keep them.

Watkins: And your father went with you?
Warren: Both trips. Or three trips, I forget which it was.

Watkins: Is it a fair question to ask you what the purpose of the father is in the poem?
Warren: Yes, it is a fair question. I want to set the poem in the modern world. I don't want to set it as a historical poem, put it that way. I want a modern

man, myself, you see, and my father. I want such a relation too, myself, in time, with my old father there, and older than he are these other people, back there. I want a sense of a historical sweep, you see. And one of these is a modern man, RPW, who talks back to these other people. He has things to say about them that are more modern than they have ever thought of. I want RPW to make some commentary; he's supposed to make commentary to these people. And this is all a fantasy, you see, a kind of dream situation. And my father, I don't know, the special relation with my father that I had is also tied in the poem. He had some relation in his boyhood with that world, some tie to that world. I don't want to get you off on autobiography at this point. I am perfectly willing to discuss it now or later, but I have it in there my father telling of his boyhood and of his own father, who died when he was quite young, when he was about sixteen. The burden of the family on him. And his older brother ran away to Mexico and made a success as a mining engineer. But Father took the responsibility, even as little more than a boy, to raise the family (and take care of a stepmother little older than he and his half brothers and a sister), and struggle for his education and at his writing. In my study there're two or three of my father's old Greek books I want to show you.

Watkins: I want to see those. You mention them in your poems.
Warren: He was studying; he hired a tutor at the university to tutor him in Greek, and he learned French from an Alsatian clerk in a boot or shoe store. He was French Alsatian. My father took me to see this old man once. He had given my father lessons for a long time. The other day I found another of the Greek books. There was a dictionary with his name on it and a date on it. Battered. The backs torn off. His books had been thrown around by his stepmother, who was a woman of very little education. And I found the books when I was a boy—in a closet or an attic, a lumber room of some sort. When I was a little boy, I had to spend my yearly, annual day with her, you see, because my father said, "She is a good woman, and she had done the best she could. Because you find her dull and stupid is no reason why you shouldn't spend a day there as a matter of decency, you see."

Watkins: And that's where you found Dante?
Warren: That's where I found the Dante and other books like that. I don't understand; it is a mystery to me here. I don't understand how this

farmer—my father's father—in the 1850's or '60's. . . . He was rather a young man so he probably got married at twenty or twenty-one, as they did in those days. Where he got all these books now, where would he come in contact with the sources of the books? Of course these small sorts of log colleges, they called them, usually Presbyterian ministers, from, say, Princeton, wandering around and setting up a little school. It must have been that. By the way, it's easy to misunderstand that semifrontier world. When I worked with the Melville papers at Yale and Harvard, I found a letter to Melville from the Clarksville, Tennessee, Literary Society; in 1857, I think it was dated. After Melville had come back from the Holy Land and his trip to Europe, which was (he said) for curative purposes (he was about to lose his mind). This was a very formal letter, signed by so and so, secretary of the Clarksville Literary Society and signed by the president, other officials, saying, "Dear Mr. Melville, The members of our society have read all of your works and discussed them in great detail." Now this was in a town of about three or four hundred people—maybe more—in Tennessee, you see, in the 1850's. I recognized the names as old settlers—names still carried on in the neighborhood. Now, 150 years later, I'm sure you wouldn't find four leading citizens of a thriving city like Clarksville who read Melville.

Watkins: That's unusual.
Warren: "We have read all of your works as part of our general interest in literature. We are great admirers. We hear that you are going to give a series of lectures this coming fall, and we have no concern with your fee. We have no concern with your fee if we can have your presence, can see the man, and shake the hand of the man whose work we admire so much; we would consider it an inestimable privilege. If you would let us know on what terms we could persuade you to come to Clarksville."

Watkins: Did he ever come?
Warren: So far as I know, he never came—in fact, no biography ever says he did—and there is nothing else in the file in the library. It is strange, these backwoods contacts, you see. Things like that. It is a strange floating culture that was mixed up with all of the frontier. Brutality and ignorance.
This grasping for something else going on in many places. And on the frontier, you could usually find adventurers or pioneers of culture, or cultural yearnings.

Watkins: I believe that probably happened more around Guthrie than it would have in my hill country. No one where my father grew up and his family in South Carolina did that.

Warren: But Guthrie had not then been founded. It was a railroad town, not like the native settlements. Guthrie was founded as a railroad junction, in '79, after the Civil War. It has no relation and very little to do with the ordinary Southern settlement. It is a different kind of town, a real-estate venture where two railroads make a crossing.

Watkins: I meant that general area of Clarksville. When you went to Smithland, what did you hope to find in the place that would have a connection to your poem?

Warren: I just wanted to see it and see what it's like. Concreteness.

Watkins: Well, I've been there myself.

Warren: You've been to Smithland?

Watkins: I have.

Warren: And did you go up to the top of the hill?

Watkins: I was older than you were when you went, and it was the hottest day of the hottest summer; so the man who was there told me he didn't have much sense but he had too much sense to try to climb it.

Warren: He had been up it.

Watkins: Yes. But today I didn't climb.

Warren: Uh huh.

Watkins: Do you think there is, well, we both went for curiosity, but I have a feeling—I don't know whether it came from your poem or from history—but I still feel that there is something there between the crime and the place. Is that absurd?

Warren: I wouldn't want it absurd. Of course it's gone back to wilderness and the carriage road built up there to the place is in ruins and rubble now. You can see the old stone work bracing the road—the retaining walls up to the big house.

Watkins: It is overgrown in trees entirely now.
Warren: It's all gone?

Watkins: Overgrown entirely in trees.
Warren: But on the top, as I remember it, there was a kind of a tree-grown meadow. There were grazing cattle back in there and big trees with open grazing space between them, but the snake is true.

Watkins: You saw the snake?
Warren: I saw the snake. It was staring at me on a pile of stone work of a ruined chimney, a big old central chimney. And this snake, an *elaphe obsoleta obsoleta*, is big, you know. That is, it wasn't a black racer, but the other kind, bigger. I've checked on this. They grow as long as eight feet, but five and a half to six is the usual length. This thing rolls up [*Gesture; laughter*] about three feet and a half from my face, looking down at me like that. And this was a find, the very spirit of the demon of the place. And that the thing happened, actually happened, was too good to be true because you would have to put it in if it didn't happen.

Watkins: Yes.
Warren: You would have to put it in there anyway. And the little town was just about like Hannibal, Missouri, in Mark Twain's time, a little river town, defunct. And a little brick jail on the green, and a man in jail hanging on the bars, and a little girl.

Watkins: You saw the man and the girl?
Warren: And the girl and a tin cup, and she'd play with acorns or dolls or something under the window of the jail. Then the man would yell, "Daughter!" And the daughter'd go and she'd get the cup and go pump him some fresh water, and he'd take a drink. The town drunk, you know, sobering up, no harm in him, just a drunkard. And the little girl, six or seven, five maybe, taking care of her drunk Pappy in jail. When I first went there in those days, there was little paved road, gravel, and it was wild. The last time I was there they had good signs, traffic lights, and they had some pavement, and the Korean War had made them prosperous.

Watkins: They have rebuilt two or three of those old homes now.
Warren: They have?

Watkins: So that they look beautiful. Did you see the inn there where Lafayette and Charles Dickens stopped on their journeys . . . ?
Warren: In Smithland?

Watkins: Yes.
Warren: I saw it, but it didn't mean anything to me at the time.

Watkins: It is still very much falling down.
Warren: It is?

Watkins: Yes.
Warren: The oldest inn in Kentucky in continuous use is in Bardstown, which used to be beautiful and had marvelous food. It had a clock, about four feet square in the face, on a short stubby bottom, keeping time. I was interested in it, and I began to inquire about it, and the proprietor (this was Nelson County, in the thirties, in Bardstown) told me that a pioneer (way in the backwoods) family had taken a wandering preacher for some days, and the preacher had a watch. The fourteen- or fifteen-year-old boy had never seen a watch. He would look at it and look at it and try to see what made it work, and the preacher would try to explain it to him, and the boy would draw pictures of it as best he could, and after about a year or two of struggle, he made a clock that would keep time. All carved with a hunting knife from hardwood. Now that boy had the mind of an Einstein.

Watkins: He did.
Warren: With that much of a start, to build a timepiece which was there in the inn, I'm trying to trace the thing now. I've got a man trying to trace the thing in Kentucky—who's got it. Of course, the old inn folded. They've got a little junk eatery, you know, in that beautiful building. But I'm trying to trace that pioneer boy's clock.

Watkins: This is old territory that we don't need to rehash, but what right does the artist have to make a change in, say, the character of Jefferson?

Jefferson in your poem I believe has already at the beginning of the poem completely changed his idea about perfectibility . . .
Warren: He's dead. He's dead. He now wants no part of . . .

Watkins: So you're not changing the living Jefferson?
Warren: No, not changing the living Jefferson. He's dead. He's a spook. He speaks of much later events in American history. They're all spooks. It's said in the poem. This is no place and no time—this dialogue has no place and no time—a meeting of spooks, as it were. A real person like myself may step in and talk too. But I'll add this: nobody knows what effect the terrible crime in his own blood had on Jefferson.

Watkins: I see.
Warren: But the poem is a fantasy. It is all one large metaphor. Put it that way. It is thought of as one large metaphor. I see no obligation when you put a historical character into a poem or a novel to be bound by any fact. You say, I'm doing this my way. Now there's a bargain that goes on from very close to the reality or to the actuality or as close as you want to get it, to a pure fantasy. But I see no principle involved there. If the reader knows what you're doing. If I put Lucy's grave on Lilburn's farm or Lilburn's plantation, instead of on his brother's plantation up the river, I don't feel bad about it. I don't feel I'm lying. I want the relation to the mother, because the mother's pitcher is the cause of the killing of the Negro, you see. The mother's pitcher, a gift from Jefferson.

Watkins: Yes.
Warren: And I want Lilburn to go out and look at the mother's grave and to hate the grass because the grass will grow back and cover it up. Robbing him again of his mother by covering up the grave. And I want those things more than I want accuracy with where she's buried. His first wife was actually buried out there. I just transferred the graves.

Watkins: I taught this work especially in the sixties to my classes in Southern literature, and once I asked the class after I had taught it, "What would you think about my leaving out *Brother to Dragons*?" I was met with a howl of protest because they felt, surprisingly to me, a very strange and strong affinity with the work's definition of the possibility of the evil of man. I found that rather surprising in college students. And maybe this is too much outside the work, but I believe the current generation may be renouncing perfectibility more than my generation did. Or perhaps yours.

Warren: I think that is probably true, though you have in modern education the great drift toward "let's improve it," you know. "Let's improve man. Let's make man different." I say "improve" too, but I know that it's slow and hard. And you have the other old-fashioned view that man could make himself better with institutions and so forth, with some organized approaches very different from the old-fashioned notion of facing the self (a conscience, or God).

Watkins: You read Meriwether Lewis's speech at the Fugitives' Reunion.
Warren: I had forgotten that.

Watkins: Is that speech preserved pretty much intact in the new version?
Warren: Yes. That's preserved. I've done some changing in versification and I've done some cutting in that, the Meriwether Lewis speech. It is substantially the same. I have done some cutting and some changes in rhythm and some other things.

Watkins: The work must exist in dozens of versions by this time.
Warren: It does indeed. There's some samples. Just opening at random, some sample pages. I tried to cut. I tried to change rhythms, and I tried to cut. Those are very slight cuts. There's sometimes one little thing, one little thing like that will change the rhythm of a passage, you see [*Turning the thick manuscript*]. Those are—every—page—those are—there's nothing on those pages. There's a whole section cut there, you see. These are additional pages that have had to be added. And whole sections like that. It's a reworking; it's a thorough reworking over many years. Sometimes one word gets changed. Sometimes a whole page.

Watkins: Have you thought of the similarities in technique between *Brother to Dragons* and Faulkner's *Absalom, Absalom!*?
Warren: It never crossed my mind.

Watkins: That wouldn't negate the similarities.
Warren: It wouldn't negate the similarities. It never crossed my mind, is what I'm saying. That's not saying it is not true.

Watkins: It seems to me that it's an unusual likeness in Quentin's and Shreve's and the other narrators' of *Absalom, Absalom!* searching for the truth of the past and their knowledge of their region and man in those long discussions in a way that is certainly not unlike the search for the truth in *Brother to Dragons*.

Warren: What you are saying makes sense to me, but I would also say that these are not the only two examples of this in literature. You see, it isn't just A and B only; it's A to Z. In any case, it never crossed my mind. Not that I'd care if it had.

Watkins: Well, I think it is a mark of the greatness of the two works—they may be two of the best examples of their . . .

Warren: Of their time? But I'm saying it didn't cross my mind. Let me say one more thing. There can be all sorts of influences, all sorts of suggestions from other works that you are never aware of.

Watkins: Oh, surely.

Warren: And then life itself. Life itself.

Watkins: Even a spirit like mine which is not creative like yours can certainly see that.

Warren: You can't say yea or no to certain questions because you don't know. What I do know is that it never crossed my mind.

Poetry as a Way of Life:
An Interview with Robert
Penn Warren
David Farrell / 1981

From *The Georgia Review*, 36.2 (Summer 1982). © 1982 by The University of Georgia / © 1982 by David Farrell. Reprinted by permission of David Farrell and *The Georgia Review*.

David Farrell: Did your parents or family encourage any artistic interests in you?

Warren: I started out to be a painter as a twelve-year-old. One summer my father tried to get me a teacher, and the only teacher he could locate (though she wasn't very good) was Sister Mary Luke, a nun at St. Cecilia's Academy in Nashville. So I stayed with a family who knew my mother, and I went out to St. Cecilia's every morning on the 8 o'clock bus and painted all day with Sister Mary Luke. I was mad to paint animals; this is what coincided with my interest in the woods—the boy naturalist, you see. You know, many boys have that phase.

Farrell: Were you particularly fond of birds?

Warren: Well, I was very keen about birds, but animals even more so, even snakes which I captured and kept around.

Farrell: A sort of boy Audubon? Did you capture animals to paint from life?

Warren: Sometimes I did, but most of the animals I did that summer with Sister Mary Luke (when I began to get a little technique—God knows I was no good, as I quickly discovered) were animals in Glendale Park Zoo. She would go with me and, poor old lady, she'd lie on her back and snore like an elephant in her robes—you know, with her little black kid shoes pointed skyward—while I would paint a lion or something. I painted the whole damned zoo, practically. And she'd snore and then wake up, then we'd eat all this great delicious feast that the nuns had sent out with us. They all took an interest in me: I was the only male in the whole academy. I came only in the morning and went back out at night. I painted in the studio with her sometimes, too. Sweet old thing; I called on her years later when she was a very old lady still in the nunnery, and we talked over old times.

Farrell: Was she a trained artist?

Warren: She had taken first prize in watercolor at the Chicago World's Fair. She had that much of a reputation, whatever that means; I don't know. She had some talent; she knew a lot of technical things.

Farrell: You worked primarily in watercolor?

Warren: Yes. And she knew a lot about watercolor, about the application of watercolor. I didn't. That's the last I ever painted except when I went to California. Every time I got to California I'd want to paint.

Farrell: Why?

Warren: It's such a paintable land out there. I was there in graduate school and during the summers in the thirties. And one summer I spent painting, partly with the wife of a couple who were visiting us up in deep, wild country. She was a rather good painter, in fact, but somehow it didn't seem quite appropriate to my then-wife when I'd go off to the mountains with another painter, so it sort of broke down.

Farrell: This was in northern California?

Warren: Yes, where there are the great yellow hills and mountains, wonderful yellow hills and live oak, and the sky—all full of colors. But I never pursued painting elsewhere. I haven't touched a brush in years and I never will again. I know I'm no painter, but I had the impulse to get the images of landscape down whenever I was in California. I can understand what's behind the landscape painter's impulse—the link with nature, I mean.

Farrell: I heard that you made some paintings inspired by *The Waste Land* when you were an undergraduate at Vanderbilt.

Warren: Well, "paintings" is not the word for it.

Farrell: What were they?

Warren: Well, this goes back to the little room in Wesley Hall, the Divinity School at Vanderbilt, which I shared my sophomore year with Allen Tate, William Cobb (a graduate student who later became a textbook editor at Houghton Mifflin), and Ridley Wills. Wills had fought in World War I and published a novel before I knew him. Now, while finishing college, he was also an editorial writer on a local paper. Wills asked me to come room with him, and I was greatly flattered; he was a most amusing man, wonderfully witty and friendly, and he knew a lot and read a lot.

So there were four of us in two double-deckers in a tiny room. The room was filled with dirty shirts, cigarette butts, filth to the waist, and empty bottles. Gangs of people would come there to argue poetry and read aloud. Tate would hold forth and Wills would hold forth on some poet, and so I contributed by decorating the walls with episodes from *The Waste Land* and *The Triumph of an Egg* and God knows what else.

Farrell: What did you draw with?

Warren: Well, the walls were so dirty I simply drew on them with art gum. They were comic representations. I discovered that by using an eraser you'd get back to a pale yellow, a perfect line. Then the University wanted to make me pay for the damage, and I said, "Well, if you'd clean the walls properly you wouldn't have any damage. I was simply getting part of the dirt from your walls; it's your job to do the rest." And I got by with that.

The only thing approaching "creative writing" was this three months, one term, course in advanced writing; thank God there was no other creative writing course. I studied literature the rest of my time there, and philosophy.

. . . There was the miracle of people like Donald Davidson, who in sophomore English would allow you to write imitations instead of the biweekly critique. You could write a new episode for *Beowulf*, keeping all the form—not in Old English, of course, but keeping all the alliterative form. Or Chaucer: we could write a new Chaucerian episode. Every two weeks I always chose, or nearly always chose, to do an imitation, unless it was somebody like Lamb whom I wouldn't be caught dead imitating.

Farrell: So you began by writing imitations.

Warren: Well, it was not a deliberate intention, but the thing was there, I can see now, looking back on it. And there were poetry societies; there were formal ones and there was an informal one. And one friend somewhat older, who was expert in French, gave what amounted to a seminar many a night from about 9 o'clock until 4 in the morning on Baudelaire or Rimbaud; he had a big collection already of such things and later had one of the great Baudelaire collections, which is now in the Vanderbilt library.

Farrell: How did this influence your writing at the time?
Warren: Well, I just know it did. Rimbaud—how much? I don't know. It was, you know, some booze (in reasonable quantities) and Baudelaire; this fellow, W. T. Bandy, started Tate on Baudelaire translations. Bandy created a one-man Left Bank on West Side Row. And then there was the new type of poetry. Ransom was never very hot on Hart Crane or on T. S. Eliot, but I was deeply impressed by them both and by Ezra Pound.

Then in junior year I had a brilliant teacher of Shakespeare, Walter Clyde Curry, and then I salted away the Elizabethans as well as I could to go with the Shakespeare—here Tate and other friends being guides. . . . And the imitations of the poetry later wound up in poems of mine like "Bearded Oaks," which has a touch of the Marvellian, or "The Garden," which is definitely a Marvell imitation.

Under a maple tree on a blanket, on a weekend visit to Guthrie, John Ransom read some Hardy to some other guests and me one afternoon, and I was never the same. I thought, this is the real thing, and I still think it is. He's the greatest poet after Wordsworth up to . . . I don't know who or where you should stop. I used to say, to Eliot, and I still think Eliot's a very great poet. But somehow I like Hardy more; he was somehow a writer I felt closer to. And I first saw in Ransom's poetry—the first book, *Poems About God*—a world I could feel some recognition of. You see, I could feel *his* experience, not mine; I could feel experience, human experience, through his work. Ransom made me see poetry in the common light I saw around me every day, in the country. Hardy did the same thing for me. Of course, he's a very massive, much more massive, poet than Ransom; a much bigger poet. Ransom was more polished, more classical and literary, less ambitious, a more nearly "perfect" poet. Ransom was mad for Hardy, as a matter of fact.

Farrell: Was Whitman in Ransom's pantheon?
Warren: No, I don't think he ever mentioned Whitman. But, mentioning pantheons, don't let's make Ransom's taste the point here. "Ransom and his

disciples"—that phrase would have appalled him. There were people with violent divisions in the Fugitive Group; I mean, Tate and Ransom almost had a breaking of friendship over *The Waste Land*. And there was no church, as it were, of principle. They had a common passion in poetry and a common background in the world and a mutual respect; but there was usually a finger-shaking quality as much as a *bruderschaft*.

Farrell: Like many families, a range of tastes?
Warren: Yes, like a family. You can't make any school out of their poetry, you see; many had totally different views, violently different views. They hung together because they were all crazy about poetry.

Farrell: Whom did you know at Vanderbilt besides members of the Fugitives?
Warren: Well, I had another set of friends who were different people entirely.

Farrell: At the same time you were learning about literature?
Warren: At the same time. They didn't even know each other. The last three years at Vanderbilt I was rooming with poets but I had other friends, too. Some were journalists; some were ruffians.

Farrell: Students?
Warren: Graduate students, mostly.

Farrell: Were they of a more scholarly bent than the creative ones you knew?
Warren: They weren't scholarly at all; they were able to do their work, but none too seriously. Most of them never amounted to anything as far as I know. The ones I was closest to who *did* amount to something were Charles Moss (a young poet who later, however, was editor of the *Nashville Banner*); Ralph McGill, who started out as a sportswriter (out of Vanderbilt) for the *Atlanta Constitution* and wound up as an editor and then publisher with a national column; and Brainard Cheney, who knows more about Tennessee politics than any living man, still a close friend, wonderful company. He helped me a great deal when I was writing *All the King's Men*. These three were a constant source of information, pornography, and friendship. We remained friends all our lives. Only Cheney still lives. Ralph was a man of great wit and courage who helped me when I was writing *Who Speaks for the Negro?*

You know, it almost dropped out of my mind until now, the memory of that first period of poetry. It was so different from what I had set my life up to be; I mean, being a naval officer and all of that. But the poetry became so extraordinarily important to me. The reading of it and the trying to write it became simply matters of life and death to me.

Farrell: During the Vanderbilt years?
Warren: Yes. And part of it was the influence of the people I knew and the Fugitive group. I absorbed so much from them. But there was something else, too, involved in it, I think—now that I look back on it. This real sort of passion I got for poetry may have been due in large part to my fear of going blind at that time. I had been told that the injury to the first eye some-how would affect the other eye, you see; nobody understood why, so far as I know.

Farrell: Your physicians thought that the injury to the first eye might transfer to the second eye?
Warren: That's right; you could get sympathetic blindness. So I was watching for this and for a while using glasses on the other eye to protect it. And I got fits of depression during that period. I felt myself going blind. I was sort of, you know, watching, watching, watching . . . always aware of it. And my refuge became in a way the study of poetry and the writing of poetry.

Farrell: So you had all the pleasure and excitement of new friends and the discovery of poetry, but at the same time you were terribly anxious about your physical handicap?
Warren: That's right. I was sometimes—God knows, not always—in a state of depression, and I'd fight it by work and by the passion I had for poetry and by the natural pursuits of youth. I don't mean anything ever was said, but the fact is that certain friends, a few of them, took a real interest in helping me. I didn't realize it at the time, no, but I must have sensed it.

And this was a great support to me, though I loathe the word "support." I had these fits of depression, one of which actually led to a suicide attempt. I would never do that again; I would never *have* done it because it was so   ·
wicked, as the results would have been for other people.

Farrell: Did your friends know about your depression or your suicide attempt?
Warren: I never talked about it. They were bound to know about the attempt, yes. That was bound to be known, and for a while it was misinterpreted by various people. I never tried to explain it to anyone.

Farrell: How could it have been misinterpreted?
Warren: I mean the reason for it, which was that I was quite sure at that time—I had talked myself into the notion—that I really was going blind. I was watching every day, you see, and it was a constant obsession.

Farrell: Did you consult doctors to get a medical opinion?
Warren: No, I didn't. I was afraid to face it. I just worried about it; I never discussed it with anybody.

Farrell: When did the fear finally leave you?
Warren: Well, it remained a long time, but I never got that down again with it, you see. Later on, the doctors began to get certain of the effect on the other eye, so they removed the bad eye (which by then was completely blind). This was in 1932 or 1933 when I was teaching at Vanderbilt.

Farrell: What were your feelings about the handicap itself?
Warren: Well, I felt maimed. One thing was the purely psychological effect of *feeling* maimed.

Farrell: Even though it wasn't apparent?
Warren: Even though it wasn't; still, it gave a sense of somehow feeling disqualified . . . or maimed, you know. It's something that one sensible talk with one sensible person might have changed; but I never had a sensible talk with a sensible person about it.

Farrell: You had sensible people around you.
Warren: But we never discussed it. It was never mentioned.

Farrell: Not even to your parents? Or to Ransom?
Warren: No, I never talked about anything with my parents, not seriously. I mean, I was totally aware of their affection and concern for me, but we never had any talks. Meanwhile I was leading a perfectly normal college-boy life;

I mean, going to parties and dances, and had girl friends and all the rest of it, you know. And in the summers I'd get jobs of hard physical work. When seventeen I toted a Springfield rifle around Fort Knox in the ROTC camp. The next summer, to stay in Nashville where I had friends and a girl, I drove a truck for American Express. And I once worked on the highway; pick and shovel work. I liked that. But it was all a façade.

Farrell: Consciously a façade?

Warren: Yes. Well, no—only at times. This life had its real interest. But it was a way of trying to distract myself, you see, and the poetry was the thing that was a real, passionate concern with me. It was a way of talking to somebody or of talking to yourself; it was kind of like taking dope.

Farrell: Do you think this anxiety came out in those early poems?

Warren: I don't know; I never thought of that. That's the natural thing to think about but I never did. Now I see that wanting to be a poet gave some direction to my life which was lacking in the first year or so in college.

Farrell: Did it make you feel special; I mean, other than feeling maimed? Did you feel your injury gave you a special outlook?

Warren: No, I've never had that sense about it at all. I don't have any sense of the poet as a special person in any sense at all. He's a man who has a special interest in life, yes—but no more than a lot of other people do, no more than a man in the Pacific fleet might have.

Farrell: But there are, obviously, differences between the poet's outlook and the sailor's.

Warren: Obvious differences yes, but none that mattered for me at that point. Poetry then was a refuge, it was something to do, it was (and is) simply something I got a great emotional bang out of. And fear of blindness was a chief factor in those years, but it's so far away I had almost forgotten it. I think of those times now without even thinking of that.

Farrell: Since Vanderbilt, your professions have been writing and teaching, and you've seen a lot of the world. I wonder about your life in Italy—just to pick more or less randomly among experiences that have greatly influenced you. Why did you go to Italy?

Warren: Well, I've always been interested in the Elizabethans; I took my graduate work chiefly in Elizabethan literature. And I had an interest in Italian history from that; a lot of things take one back to Italy. For instance, you can't understand Thomas Wyatt without knowing what he did with Petrarch. I once did a complete comparison of Wyatt and Petrarch—line by line—but got no impulse to publish it. And of Aretino, too.

So I got to reading Italian, and later all those things flowed into the novel *All the King's Men*. Machiavelli and Italian history flowed into that, too; the whole case of the man of power, the man of virtue and the world about him, flowed into the novel (along with William James and American history). They all tied back to my learning to read Italian and then coming to Italy as some sort of vague . . . what? You can't explain these things.

Farrell: You taught Elizabethan literature, didn't you?
Warren: I taught Shakespeare, and for years I taught a graduate course in nondramatic Elizabethan literature. I was soaked in Shakespeare from the years I'd taught it. In fact, I had always planned in old age to write a book on Shakespeare as poet, a very special kind of book. There isn't one like it even yet. I don't mean just the sonnets and lyrics; I mean the plays, too.

Farrell: When did you first go to Italy?
Warren: I was there in Perugia and Umbria in the summer of '38. Then at Sirmione. In fact, I began writing the verse play *All the King's Men* there, in a wheat field near Perugia, sitting under an olive tree. And I wound up towards Christmas in Rome, in '39, hearing the boot heels of the Fascist troops on the cobblestones.

Farrell: Did you see Mussolini?
Warren: Oh, yes, speaking in front of the Palazzo Venezia.

Farrell: Did you meet Pound in Rome?
Warren: No; I had known Pound slightly in Paris in 1928 or 1929 when I was an Oxford graduate student. But I didn't look him up in Italy. By that time I was thinking he was a crazy man—though a great poet, which I still think.

That same year I was writing a great deal of poetry, and I finished the basic version of *All the King's Men* at Christmas. Then I went back to *At Heaven's Gate* during the winter of 1939–1940. At one point I became stuck.

Then I had typhus with a good deal of fever. In a delirium one night my problem was suddenly solved. I had the most vivid dreams during this fever and went through the whole story of the mountaineer coming down the river and into Nashville and his torch blowing the thing up. That all began with a dream.

Farrell: A dream, or a series of dreams?
Warren: I'm not sure; it seemed continuous. The fever had breaks and would begin again and break and begin again, you see. The fever was up to a hundred and four or five.

Farrell: Were you in a hospital?
Warren: I was at home with a nurse, and the nurse would put her feet on the pillow by my face at night and she would snore. God, what a nurse! She knew nothing about nursing, for sure, but those feet and that snoring! Anyway, that was a dream; but the typhus and the feet weren't dreams. And, God, the fool Fascist doctor! He didn't even know it was typhus. I got that diagnosis back home from a record of the symptoms. And when I got well enough to write I had the novel practically written.

Farrell: Dreams come up a lot in your work, especially in recent poems.
Warren: Well, I dream a lot. I love dreams, especially funny dreams, funny, elaborate dreams. I'll tell you one. I'm in a barroom that somehow is like a fake barroom scene in the Far West; but clearly fake—as if it had canvas walls or something. There's a big bar, a lot of high-heeled gunmen around with Stetsons—ranchers and cowhands and so forth—and everybody's drinking. A man leaps on the bar. He's a man of some importance, a rancher, and he has a gun in each hand, and he says, "Everybody knows I know how to use a pistol." He waves them around and he says, "Somebody here's betrayed my daughter. Now, I never shot a man down without warning. I'm going to give him the count of ten to declare himself." And he begins, "One . . ." and he shoots out a light. But it doesn't make a boom; it makes a "ping"! Then, "Two . . . three . . ." He got to nine and then, "Ha, ha, ha!"—a burst of laughter comes in sudden blackness and a big explosion, and offstage a voice says, "And he fell with sixty bullet holes in his body!"

Farrell: What was your role in this dream?
Warren: I'm an observer.

Farrell: Not the man who's betrayed the daughter?
Warren: No. I wish I had been, but I can't say that I was.

Farrell: Is this a recurring dream?
Warren: No; it just happened once. And I often dream poems.

Farrell: Whole poems? And you wake up and write them down?
Warren: No, I've never done that in my life except once: a short poem. The dream may come back when I'm writing later, or it may not. But mostly my dreams are comic; I often awaken laughing. But I have to say, I've sort of had my quota of vague anxiety dreams, too—nagging anxiety dreams. I don't remember those very well. I'm a pretty heavy sleeper, and I don't awaken much unless my wife kicks me for snoring. Then I go in the next room and sulk.

Farrell: What took you both back to Italy in the 1950's when you were writing *Promises*?
Warren: I had spent a year there just after the war, on a second Guggenheim. But in 1954, when I went back, the summer I began *Promises,* I had recently married Eleanor, and we had a baby. Italy meant a lot to my wife and to me. She had spent a lot of time there in childhood. Several years before, one Sunday, we had once gone to Cosa on the Tuscan coast, where Frank Brown, who was a Yale professor, was supervising a dig. Eleanor pointed to a castle on a hill across the bay and said, "I'm going over there tomorrow, and I'm going to live there." And she worked it out. She found the old lady who owned the fortress, and she got a big section of it.

Farrell: Did you move in then?
Warren: No, *she* moved in; we weren't married yet. Much later we got better acquainted. Anyway, that's the reason we were there in Italy; but there were so many factors. . . . It was a new life with wonderful swimming, and so forth. And Italian friends. . . . In this great fortress by the sea—in Argentario, which had been the Borgias' hunting ground at one time. But the fortress was not begun until 1559, by Philip II of Spain. It's a blood-drenched place and an incredible, beautiful place as well. And we had a pretty, yellow-haired baby girl, a baby of a year, and next door was an idiot child and a saintly older sister of twelve or so who kept trying to teach the child to say one thing, to say "Ciao," the Italian greeting.

Farrell: What was your apartment like?

Warren: Well, we rented a big quadrangle of the fortress. The apartment had a tremendous living room about seventy feet long—it had been a stable when the Spanish were there—a big stone room with a stone floor and beamed ceiling and a built-in stove at one end. We had a marvelous cook and oleanders blooming around and dust and storms and sea in every direction. Across the quadrangle there were some regular rooms which we used as bedrooms, and we had a sort of reception room close to the big room where we occasionally entertained guests while the cooking was going on.

Then we had, way high up, the *vedetta*, a lookout house. It had two rooms and a hall between and a toilet to share; so Eleanor had one room for her study and I had the other for my study. But I worked outdoors chiefly. And there were moats seventy feet deep on each side of the castle—all a most elaborate piece of Renaissance military architecture, extraordinarily elaborate. And beautiful. . . . So, every time Eleanor and I went to Italy, it was poems, poems, poems. It's a magic country; crazy, crazy, crazy. It was magic.

And the poems that resulted were a combination of my childhood and my early world and the country and the European world. They played back and forth, intermingled. Not autobiography—that would have been too easy—but a psychological penetration. From that time on, poetry never ceased again. That book, *Promises*, came out; it took all the prizes; was a fresh start.

Farrell: While we're on the subject of writing a successful collection of poems, what would you say the profession of poet means to you?

Warren: Well, there's something I can say about it. I would say poetry is a way of life, ultimately—not a kind of performance, not something you do on Saturday or Easter morning or Christmas morning or something like that. It's a way of being open to the world, a way of being open to experience. I would say, open to *your* experience, insofar as you can see it or at least feel it as a unit with all its contradictions and confusions. Poetry, for me, is not something you do after you get it fixed in your mind. Poetry is a way of thinking or a way of feeling; a way of exploring.

Farrell: Can it be summed up in your phrase, one that goes something like "[It's] a way to love God"?

Warren: Well, yes, I think so. It's a way to accept, to deal with the world. A way to love God?—yes, I think it is. If you want to put it that way. The only way some people can live is by assuming that life is worth being interested in. It's worth giving yourself to; and giving the best you can. I would also say that poetry is not like a profession, but a way of life. These are two quite different things.

Farrell: A profession isn't a way of life?
Warren: Not often; not usually; not necessarily. Very infrequently you find a devoted family doctor or somebody to whom his profession is a way of life. It can be a way of life, but I'm saying that poetry damn well *better* be a way of life, because it's something quite different. It's a way of existing meaningfully as much of your time as possible. And that's never much.

Farrell: Are you distinguishing between poetry and prose?
Warren: No. I wouldn't set poetry apart from prose here. I think this would be perfectly true of a novelist or a dramatist. I'm really talking about literary art—or any art. But since we were talking about poetry I kept it to poetry.

Farrell: Are you still writing prose?
Warren: I've sworn off all expository prose. I'm not going to write any more lectures and I'm not going to write explanations or criticism.

Farrell: Short stories?
Warren: Short stories kill poems.

Farrell: How about novels?
Warren: I started to write a novel a summer or two ago; I owe Random House a novel. And for a week or ten days—or more, a month—I started every morning at 9:30 and put a pad on my knees and picked up my pen and started to write a novel. And after an hour or so, I had not written a line of a novel, but way down in the corner I had started a poem. So, despite my good intentions, I gave it up. I felt very good about the novel, and I wanted to write it, but the poetry was just too demanding.

Farrell: It seems like you feel almost in harness, almost gripped, by the poetic urge.
Warren: For now, yes. The future will take care of itself, and I'll write the novel if I can. I just don't believe in making something a job that doesn't have to be a job.

Farrell: You're enjoying good fortune with poetry now; you're writing more than ever.

Warren: Well, I've got more time than ever before. I do a lot of gardening, and I do a lot of extra things, but I stay home a lot.

Farrell: Would you have written much more in the past if you'd had more free time?

Warren: I would have put time into poetry, if I'd been freer; but, you see, I enjoyed teaching so much. . . . I liked it, knowing the young. They're stimulating; they have ideas; they are a different world, and your own children don't make up for it. In one way you know more about other people's children than you know about your own. My own I know in a different and deeper way.

Farrell: Some readers of your work have remarked that you're drawing more, and more consciously, on memory now, late in life.

Warren: Yes; I'm drawing more and more on memory. Memory reinterpreted, of course; not memory taken literally. It has a strange liability; I feel like I'm using up stock, capital. You know, there are so many things that happen that you don't know the meaning of at the time; they acquire meaning only after a long time. They *may* acquire meaning after a time. I'd have to say there's an apprehension, too, at this late stage. One thinks about the day when it won't come.

Farrell: Of course, that's always been true. One day it won't come.

Warren: Sure, it's always been true, but nobody ever liked it!

Farrell: You feel a lot closer, then? It's around the corner . . .

Warren: Right; not ten miles down the pike, you see.

Farrell: Do you feel pressure about that, a sense of urgency?

Warren: No, I don't feel that way at all. I feel more leisurely, in fact; I can take all day with a line, then throw it away. That's how I live—with that limitation. And one thing one has to realize is that there's no virtue in writing a poem if it isn't good. Just writing a poem doesn't mean a goddam thing. Anybody can write a sort of poem.

Farrell: Well, your poems are finding publication readily in a variety of journals; critics like them; people think they're very good.
Warren: That's something you can't know, really. Let's hope so . . . but, you know the breaking point's approaching—you're bound to know that. The thing to know is to know when you've hit that line and try not to force it.

Farrell: How are you going to know?
Warren: God's got to tell you. Just trust God—whatever God is.

Farrell: So, for the present, you're writing and you're pleased enough with what you're writing. Do you think your writing is as good as it's ever been?
Warren: I've done some of my best poems in the last few years, and I've thrown away a lot of poems I didn't think were. Quite a few I've thrown away. I'll just say that it's the best I can do. Ultimate judgments are just not to be had, you know. The whole history of literature or art shows us that painting something to one generation means nothing to another generation.

Farrell: Are you working every day?
Warren: Not every day. I've been doing a lot of hot, physical work for the past month. I haven't written a poem in a month. I've been using a pick and shovel in the yard!

Farrell: That's another kind of vigor remarkable for a seventy-five-year-old . . .
Warren: Yes, six hours a day of it. If you don't believe it, look around the place.

Of Bookish Men and
the Fugitives
Thomas L. Connelly / 1982

From *A Southern Renascence Man: Views of Robert Penn Warren*, edited by
Walter B. Edgar (Baton Rouge: Louisiana State University Press, 1984).
© 1984 by Louisiana State University Press. Reprinted by permission.

Warren was the focus of an Institute for Southern Studies program at the
University of South Carolina in 1982. When he was unable to attend, Thomas
L. Connelly went to New Haven and interviewed him on camera. The following is
an edited transcription of the videotaped interview made February 10, 1982, and
first published in *A Southern Renascence Man: Views of Robert Penn Warren (1984)*.

Connelly: Mr. Warren, we're sorry you can't be with us at the Southern
Studies Institute program in South Carolina.
Warren: I'm very sorry for more reasons than that of climate—humanly
sorry but I must say that our luncheon conversation was some compensation
for the fact that I couldn't come.

Connelly: Well, we'll miss having you there. I would like to ask you first some
things about your background as a writer. We're both from the same area of
the country; I grew up in middle Tennessee and you grew up in Todd
County, Kentucky, which is really a cultural satellite, I suppose, of Nashville.
Warren: Well, a hundred yards from the state line, whatever you want to
call that.

Connelly: As a matter of fact, you went to high school in Montgomery
County, Tennessee, in Clarksville.
Warren: Well, one year. I went the first three years in Guthrie, and being
young to graduate from Guthrie was no great feat, I must say. And I couldn't
get in Vanderbilt because I was not old enough, so I had the good sense—or
the good luck—to go to a very good high school in Clarksville the next year
while waiting for my sixteenth year to go to Vanderbilt. Autobiographically,

my family was so bookish. My father read to the children before dinner, or after dinner, poems or history before we had to do our lessons. . . .

Connelly: You said you had to memorize a lot.
Warren: That was in school; but of course we know education is in terrible condition. Don't deny that! One thing to be said for the schools in Guthrie, Kentucky, is that you had to memorize poems, good or bad. It's hard to believe it, but in a school of six rooms, twelve grades, and six teachers, I . . . and others . . . read *The White Devil* by John Webster. There was still some contact with literature. It was possible there, in a town like that. And men, the older men, you might say, the better farmers, many of them were men of bookishness.

Connelly: Do you think being a Kentuckian has had something to do with your approach to the difference between reality and myth? Louis Rubin said something in an essay about you, that more than most writers in Vanderbilt's group in the twenties you had more of a double vision, that you had more of a border-state way of thinking than Faulkner or Eudora Welty, that you never as much subscribed to the myths of the lower South as they did.
Warren: I just don't know . . . I haven't thought about that. I always felt myself more of a Tennesseean than a Kentuckian because . . . only a hundred yards from the state line. . . . And then I lived in Tennessee a lot. I went to college in Tennessee and taught there later on. So I always felt Tennessee . . . I knew it better as a state. I felt it much more my own country than Kentucky. I began to systematically investigate Kentucky later on.

Connelly: A lot of your work is Kentucky-oriented.
Warren: Yes, but that was just my wanderings in Kentucky. . . . The time I've been wandering in Kentucky, learned Kentucky.

Connelly: I think another part of that strikes me, another part of that Kentucky or Tennessee influence on you . . . that border-state influence is that you were really in the last Confederate generation, weren't you, the last generation of Confederate veterans, people who knew veterans, who heard their tales?
Warren: Well, I spent every summer from age six to fourteen with a grandfather who had fought in the war. He was also a very intelligent man, and a

bookish man; and he, like my father, quoted a lot of poetry at the drop of a
hat. And he had me read to him from an old book called *Napoleon and His
Marshals*—or he, on the ground, scratched the Battle of Fort Pillow or Brice's
Crossroads or other adventures and explained the tactics thereof. So I felt
quite Confederate in that sense. It was purely a literary sense; I felt that that
was the way God had made it.

Connelly: My great-grandfather rode with Forrest, too; he's the one I told
you deserted after the Battle of Chickamauga. One thing that strikes me
again about that border-state area, Tennessee and Kentucky, and growing up
there, is that even the Confederate army there never indulged in that mythol-
ogy of the army of planters' sons, such as the Army of Northern Virginia has
for an image today. It was the rather hard-core western approach, people very
much into evangelical religion—quite a different image from that of Robert E.
Lee's army, wouldn't you say?
Warren: That picture in general, I think, is right. But also, let's not forget
what was made of the Confederacy by the Civil War writers who created a
mythological Confederacy which has gained much popularity in the North.

Connelly: Sometimes it was more popular in the North than in the South.
You went to Vanderbilt when you were sixteen. You left Guthrie and
Clarksville. Was it purely by accident that Vanderbilt flourished at this time
as a cultural center? Wasn't 1914 the big date when the university won
control of the school from the Methodist bishops?
Warren: Sometime along there, before I can remember, anyway.

Connelly: Then right after that the Fugitive movement started, right before
World War I. . . .
Warren: Well, the Fugitive movement had so little to do with Vanderbilt. Certain
members of the faculty thought it was rather a shame to be associated with the
Fugitive group. It didn't seem good enough academically or something . . . but
it started long before my days there. . . . It was before the war, before America
got into the war anyway. Some were young businessmen: one was a young
banker, one was a merchant . . . young men who were interested in philosophy
rather than in poetry who met together because they liked each other, because
they all had common interests. That's long before my time. They had all been
fighting in the war and then going off to places like Oxford and the Sorbonne

. . . as some of these young men did in that period. They got more interested in poetry and Ransom published his first book of poems, just after the war was over. I ran into a man in California, an editor out there, who said: "I know a friend of yours, I have a book of his. . . . He gave it to me the day the first two copies reached him in France." And he had the second copy. So this book came out during or just after the war when Ransom was still in uniform.

Connelly: Was that *Poems About God?*
Warren: That's right. Ransom, as I remember, was an officer of regulars— Davidson of volunteers. They had very different attitudes toward the war. Ransom rarely mentioned it and certainly had no romantic view of war. He was the old twenty-year man, you know. He was in artillery. But there was something of a romantic spirit of war about Davidson. I once started out to be a naval officer. I had an appointment to Annapolis and couldn't go because of an accident. But my desire was to be admiral of the Pacific Fleet of course. . . . Who wouldn't want to be admiral of the Pacific Fleet? I could clearly tell there was going to be a war with Japan—but I was saved from the burning.

Connelly: After World War I, you were sixteen when you entered Vanderbilt in 1921 and became a member of the Fugitive group.
Warren: I entered college in '21 so it must have been '23. I'm guessing now. I can't be sure. . . .

Connelly: My impression is the Fugitives had really kind of divided into two groups: those who took it seriously as a poetic exercise, like yourself and Ransom or Allen Tate, and some local businessmen whom you could almost call dilettantes.
Warren: Well, they were serious in their thinking about it. Some of those men were clearly not poets . . . were not talented the way Ransom was, but they were serious about their interest and they would talk seriously. They could understand what was going on; they had opinions that were argued. I remember that quite well.

Connelly: You roomed with Allen Tate at the old Theological School.
Warren: Well, when I was a freshman, the only undergraduate was a man named Ridley Wills who had been in the army in the Tennessee regiment that Luke Lea commanded.

Connelly: The one that tried to capture the Kaiser.
Warren: Tried to capture the Kaiser. Ridley had come back to finish his degree . . . and I was seeing a young man, an undergraduate who had written a real book published by a real New York publishing house. I thought that was quite wonderful, and it *is* quite wonderful when you are sixteen to have a friend like that. And he asked me to come room with him and he was rather a wag . . . a very funny man . . . a very great wit and so he said: "I'm getting a room over in the Theological Dormitory," which was a piece of early Methodist Gothic, about five stories high. And so we got a room over there among the theologs, as a kind of joke we were playing on ourselves. And then, the next thing he brought in Allen. It was a little bitty room and two double-decker beds. Allen took one of the double-decker beds. And then another came in and there were four of us. In the evenings among the dirty sheets and cigarette butts and not-quite-dry bottles in the corners, poetry was discussed and argued and so was modern philosophy. Tate and Wills were much older than the others and dominated. This became a kind of nameless club. Most people were undergraduates, but they led a very active undergraduate literary life . . . had the last of an old-fashioned kind of teaching in some of the classes. In freshman English you had to memorize at least nine hundred lines of Tennyson before Christmas and be tested on it. You had to memorize things.

Connelly: Did you memorize Coleridge?
Warren: Not then, no. I found I could memorize poetry very easily because I had been living with it all my life with my father and my grandfather and so I enjoyed doing it. Many students would line up just to buy the latest *New Republic* to see the latest poem by Yeats or Frost that might be in there. There was a large, a big interest among the undergraduates. It is very hard to understand now in my later years of teaching, the lack of that, by and large, in the undergraduate body.

Connelly: So you say, Mr. Warren, that there were really two poetry groups at Vanderbilt?
Warren: Two, quite different. One was undergraduate and this poetry club met regularly, wrote a great deal, published a book, a hard cover book of their own, before *The Fugitive*—or just after *The Fugitive* began to come out. Just after, I guess. The poetry of Eliot, particularly *The Waste Land*, had a

tremendous impact. You could probably find twenty people who could quote it in the freshman and sophomore classes. This sounds romantic but it wasn't. There was a sense that this was new; something was happening or was felt to be happening. And there was! An interpenetration of the young students and people like Wills and Tate who were older, who were members of the Fugitive group through this room that I mentioned where Tate and I lived. You see, it was kind of an interrelationship and this was something I haven't seen duplicated—this passionate interest in an art or in certain ideas that occurred then. And later on, being personal: when I was struggling with my poems, Wills and Tate would come in; and I might be asleep; and they would sit down and start revising them or talk to me the next day about them . . . or criticize. So I was getting a kind of tutorial free during that period. But I was not alone. There were a lot of young men in the same situation, only I was more privileged by having these guardians, as it were, at hand.

Connelly: A lot of people who have written on you—as you well know there's a book of 275 pages which is nothing more than a bibliography of writing that you have done and a bibliography of things people have written about you. And a lot of people have commented on John Crowe Ransom's influence on you at this time—that there was a tremendous influence in two respects: one was in the nature of a poem. . . . Did he teach you something about what a poem was supposed to be?
Warren: He taught it to everybody who would listen! In his class he always brought a new angle, a new view to the question of a poem and explained its especial qualities. Never, ever as a job, but always as a kind of running comment. And his influence on a lot of people—and many people have said this—was highly personal. That is, it was not the question of what he had to say or what he had in his head, but a kind of personal dignity and personal self-control that was felt by almost everybody around him; and he was a man who was greatly full of fun and loved poker and loved athletic activity.

Connelly: He almost believed that a poem was a miniature world, didn't he, an entity of interplay complete with a backdrop and landscape?
Warren: I remember one thing when I saw his first book when I was a freshman. There's a man who's written a book. That was a great shock. There stands that little man who has written that book. And I read the book; and the book was mostly about the background that I knew. It was about the

background of Tennessee, Kentucky, and north Mississippi, you see. And he somehow brought poetry into your world, my world. You felt it was a world that you inhabited. Now that book is not anything like his real books that came later, but it did bring the sense of poetry belonging to life, poetry being connected with life—with your life, your place. I remember that very strongly and the effect it had on me. . . . Later on I heard him say, "I want to be a domestic poet. I want to write about the small things of life as I live it." And you can see that in his poetry. Well, I must say that wasn't exactly my ambition . . . or the ambition of say, Allen Tate, but the perfection of Ransom, he was a perfectionist. His small poems are perfectly done . . . perfectly done, and of deep feeling. . . .

Connelly: Did he influence you a lot in your later approach to the New Criticism, and attention to text, to images?
Warren: He always did. Later on it became more formalized. But he was constantly, from the time of the freshman class on. Mimms taught the poetry one day a week. Two days a week Ransom taught the writing; and the writing meant all sort of stylistic problems brought to the level that a freshman could understand. After the first term (I boast now a little bit), he said, "I'm taking you out of my class, I'm taking you to another class I have which is more concerned with the problems I'm now dealing with." And this was the greatest day of my life. That he would then give *me* some personal attention in another class of older people.

Connelly: I believe, in 1930, came *God Without Thunder* in which Ransom defended belief in religion; and he said in effect that religion was almost a metaphysical myth established in order to understand nature. One thing I've noticed about those of you gathered at Vanderbilt in that day is that most of you came out of that common heritage of middle Tennessee, southern Kentucky evangelical religion: Methodist/Baptist. . . .
Warren: I came out of it with no religion at all. My father was called an old-fashioned free thinker who gave me Darwin to read when I was fourteen. He also made me read the Bible. . . . He played fair.

Connelly: But, don't you think as a group that religion, that Southern religion in the upper South did affect their whole view of being somewhere between the Old South, the agrarian South that had passed and the industrial New South?

Warren: I think it may have had. Now let me tell you one thing about Ransom in *God Without Thunder*. In the end, that book is not a book about religion at all. It is a philosophical work. Because, really, it just dawned on me that that's what the book's about, not a theological book at all. Way back in 1931, standing in a kitchen, with a bottle of bourbon in hand, pouring me a drink, he said: "I find it very odd that I who am not a religious man, should write such a book; but I had to write it for the truth that's in it." Now he said that to me in '31 and it clarified something in my mind about it, myself being a very nonreligious man . . . not antireligious; that is, I have the deepest awareness of its importance. But I'm a yearner. I mean I wish I were religious. Ransom certainly said that religion is a necessary myth; a necessary myth is what he was saying—to paraphrase him. You see what I'm trying to say? I'm bumbling it I'm sure.

Connelly: In one form or another did not a lot of people in the Vanderbilt group in the twenties, some of whom were later in the Agrarian group, cope with religion? Allen Tate, for example, coped with religion in a different way.
Warren: He was deeply concerned. He was a Catholic twice! And buried a Catholic.

Connelly: Your own approach wasn't a total rejection was it? You talked sometimes of what you said was a "religious sense" in your work. You've mentioned that several times.
Warren: I think it is. It's about the quest for religion.

Connelly: After graduating you went to California and then went to graduate school and became in a sense, a non-Southerner. How important do you think it is in your own writing that you had a quality of what you would call alienation, being out of the South?
Warren: May I interrupt just a second? I think I became a Southerner by going to California and to Connecticut and New England. When I was at Vanderbilt, I couldn't have been paid to go to the Scopes trial. I was right there by it. I was not concerned with it, at all. My Civil War was primarily anecdotal from my acquaintance with old soldiers. They were my old soldiers all right. When I went west I began to read, much more than in some of the graduate courses I had, Southern history and American history. That continued. I really became a Southerner by not being there.

Connelly: Do you think Southerners sometimes have a love/hate relationship with the South?

Warren: Well, I think that is necessary, there's so much wrong with it and there's so much right with it. You have to have it divided. I was always not at ease with the whole race question and I wrote two books about it.

Connelly: *Segregation. . . .*

Warren: . . . and then the other one [*Who Speaks for the Negro?*] Previously, the Agrarian thing was an essay about it. . . . It was a constant nag to me.

Connelly: In your book *Segregation,* which is subtitled *The Inner Conflict in the South,* you talk about the race problem as being one you called "self-division," not just division of a society between a Southerner and society but the self-division within a man.

Warren: One woman, an extremely intelligent woman and a thoughtful woman, a well-educated woman, talking about this to me during the period that I was writing that book, said (she was a religious woman, too, in a very intelligent way, not just automatically so), "I pray to God to change some of my feelings about this question." Now she was really divided.

Connelly: As long as we're on this subject, may I ask you this? When the Agrarian movement came along—and I know that your relationship to the Vanderbilt Agrarians is quite different from many of them—that you were far less into the economic and political interests. But you received some criticism for your essay "The Briar Patch."

Warren: Are you referring to criticism from my friends or others? I got both kinds!

Connelly: I was referring to criticism from others, that from a position standpoint they felt that your essay was attempting to defend a racial status quo.

Warren: I was just very uncomfortable with the piece, but it was this. My position was exactly that of the Supreme Court. Equal, you see; "different but equal" was the view of the Supreme Court and of 99 percent of the white people in the country.

Connelly: You feel very strongly about that criticism of the thirties.

Warren: Well, I think that point is quite clear. Unless I misremember the book entirely—and I haven't read it in a thousand years and don't intend to read it again—that was the basic legal view of the world and that was the one I took. Now that doesn't cover the whole case. There are all sorts of things gone and done and there was unevenness of all kinds. But I remember this quite distinctly that my father, who was a very remarkable man in many ways, saying to me when I made some slurring remark about a Negro, he said: "I have never found a man whom I have treated like a decent human being that has not treated me like one." Another time, using the word "nigger" in his presence. . . . "Never let me hear that word come out of your lips again!" These things I just told you occurred when I was ten or twelve, something like that. But the other part . . . equal pay/equal work, that's clear enough in there. And the Supreme Court view of equal schools and equality . . . but a social difference . . . a social distinction between them . . . a separation. And that's about all of that! Now the way I came back after many years away from the South . . . to live in the South in 1930. . . .

Connelly: When you came back to Vanderbilt?
Warren: I came back to Memphis first, to Southwestern College. I was then struck by the quite undefinable pressures that were there. It didn't come under the picture I had remembered. I felt quite differently and bit by bit it crept into my poetry. Vinegar Hill was the name of a Negro graveyard in Todd County. And some others. There's something about a lynching in "Pondy Woods." It is something that has always been on my mind in some way or another. There was some sort of confusion of mind about it. Then in novels later on, it began to enter in. *Band of Angels* is such a book, a novel about that question primarily and what it means to be free. You can be enslaved in many ways, the book says. What does it mean to be free . . . the book's about that. Then there are the two books directly on the subject which I did first for *Life* magazine and the second for *Look* magazine. *Segregation* was done originally for *Life*. The other was done originally as an option for parts of it for *Look*. I had to have somebody to pay the bills. I was taking two years off, you see, to make a living. They would pick up the bills.

Connelly: I think one of the ironies of the criticism you received for "The Briar Patch" is that it was almost your only effort for the Agrarians. And yet, so many times people have identified you with the Vanderbilt Agrarians, but weren't you really a lot different?

Warren: "Agrarianism" is just a word. It did not describe in any basic fashion to my mind what the thing was about. It was like a tent with a menagerie, with fifty kinds of animals under it. Disagreement was more important than agreement. Now for instance, in the industrialized, mechanized world, a man like Ransom would feel, I think, primarily that other things, too, are involved here, not only economic problems, but would also feel that this is a misunderstanding of man's relationship to nature . . . using nature as a thing to be exploited, as a tool of man and not as man having a relationship to nature which is both aesthetic and spiritual. See what I'm driving at? I think his emphasis was going somewhere in that direction and mine would have gone somewhere in that direction, too.

Connelly: But not Donald Davidson?
Warren: Not Donald Davidson! In many ways, he was like those people who see the violation of nature as a way to commit suicide, for society to commit suicide. Then there are the people who really took it as a way to go live, like Andrew Lytle's buying a farm, and running a farm and trying to be a writer at the same time! Well, you can be a writer at the same time if you don't write very much! I know enough about farming to know it takes time. I would never have tried . . . I like to live in the country. I do live in the country. I have a place in the country in Vermont and I have a place in the country in Connecticut.

Connelly: The land was more of a metaphor for you wasn't it?
Warren: That was the place to be alone. A year's time in the city is enough for me. I have been in many cities but that's enough. I want to see myself in relation to the natural objects. That is an important point in my life and I basically live in the country. I go to the city and I've lived in many cities. I've lived in San Francisco a long time and then New York and Rome and other cities . . . Paris, and London . . . but I don't stay there.

Connelly: One thing I've noticed . . . one difference between you and the other Agrarians is the way you deal with history. That you were never that concerned with the events, rather what you called the historical sense, the meaning of the event, the philosophy of the event. I've seen that even in your poetry. I brought one of your poems which I wish you would read for the audience. It's from "Kentucky Mountain Farm." It's "History Among the Rocks."

Warren: This is so long ago. I'm turning now back to my twenties. I'm glad it's not a mirror. This is also a poem that involves, you might say, the divided world of the Confederacy, of the Civil War. And I was thinking specifically here of a division of the hill sections of Kentucky—which these sections of Kentucky were, then completely unknown to me firsthand. This was purely just fact I knew from other sources. I had never been in the Kentucky mountains until I was a grown man, quite grown.

History Among the Rocks

There are many ways to die
Here among the rocks in any weather;
Wind down the eastern gap, will lie
Level along the snow, beating the cedar,
And lull the drowsy head that it blows over
To startle a cold and crystalline dream forever.

The hound's black paw will print the grass in May,
And sycamores rise down a dark ravine,
Where a creek in flood, sucking the rock and clay,
Will tumble the laurel, the sycamore away.
Think how a body, naked and lean
And white as the splintered sycamore, would go
Tumbling and turning, hushed in the end,
With hair afloat in waters that gently bend
To ocean where the blind tides flow.

Under the shadow of ripe wheat,
By flat limestone, will coil the copperhead,
Fanged as the sunlight, hearing the reaper's feet.
But there are other ways, the lean men said:
In these autumn orchards once young men lay dead—
Gray coats, blue coats. Young men on the mountainside
Clambered, fought. Heels muddied the rocky spring.
Their reason is hard to guess, remembering
Blood on their black mustaches in moonlight.
Their reason is hard to guess and a long time past:
The apple falls, falling in the quiet night.

Connelly: Someone said about you that you are not a historical poet, histori-cal novelist, but that you are a philosophical poet and novelist who uses his-tory for understanding. History permeates so much of your poetry . . . and your fiction, of course.

Warren: I don't see a sharp division between the use of history in the two things. I can see what they meant by saying that. Looking back on the origins of one thing, a poem, another thing a novel, I see something very similar, not basically different. Now the poetry tends to be more philosophical because it's less narrative. It has only an echo of narrative in it. Most poetry does.

Connelly: Your use of history is not just facts; it's symbols, really.

Warren: It is the significance of those facts.

Connelly: Do you think a poet or a novelist, I always thought so, in some ways can be a better historian than a historian? That he can generalize about. . . .

Warren: Well, he might be. . . . Which historian?

Connelly: This idea of tension in history, of tension between the past and the present certainly permeates at least the first five of your novels.

Warren: Novel after novel that I have written, and poem after poem, have had some germ in historical reality. I mean it had some germ in it. It's inter-preting that not as mere history, but as history moralized, to use a more obvious word.

Connelly: I know in your first five novels you had this common theme of a search for understanding and this kind of tension between the ideal and the practical—of a self-division within a person as he gropes for understanding in reaching back to the past. I got the impression when I read *The Legacy of the Civil War* that you were taking the same structure and applying it to the nation as a whole.

Warren: Well, I wouldn't deny that. I wouldn't know how to deny that, really. I think I see what you mean more clearly now.

Connelly: Do you think the Civil War was the great Southern experience, the great catalyst?

Warren: Well, it's the thing that we most violently lived through as a nation. It also produced our power. And I'm glad of our power, but I think there is also a great danger in the kind of victory that was had. We have been lulled into the assumption that the mechanical expert and the advertising man can control all the values of life. I can't quite bring myself to believe that.

Connelly: And I think in sixty years of writing, in your poems and your criticism and your fiction, that you never have believed that.
Warren: I never have.

Connelly: Mr. Warren, I want to thank you for giving us this interview and again we regret that you can't be with us at the Institute for Southern Studies at the University of South Carolina.
Warren: I regret it deeply for personal reasons, not that I regret I can't bring the wisdom fresh off the griddle, but I regret not seeing your human presences before me.

A Conversation with Robert Penn Warren

Tom Vitale / 1985

From *Ontario Review* (Fall 1986/Winter 1987). © Tom Vitale. Reprinted by permission.

Tom Vitale: Many of your poems are filled with images of memory and mortality and references to time. Do you think it's fair to say that you're obsessed with time?

Warren: I can only answer by saying that I was born of human flesh.

Vitale: But after you say that, what can you say about time? You have a reference to knowing time, but we can't really know time, can we?

Warren: An old question I encountered first in conversation with a professor of medieval literature. He said, "What is 'now'? What does 'now' mean? 'Now' is all that is passing. Have you felt a 'now'? He was quoting a passage from St. Augustine, from *The Confessions*. The question of how man lives in time: he's constantly aware of it, or should be. He's always dating himself in one way or another—tomorrow, yesterday. He's trying to find a place in time. And I don't think it's morbid at all—it's only natural. We're consigned to that. And you think of the past, you think of parents and grandparents and you feel your way back, back to what? You have children: you think forward. To what? You're in a flow, and it's only natural to swim, if you can.

Vitale: Many images in your poetry show careful observation of nature. Would you consider your work to be in the Romantic tradition?

Warren: I don't think that way. I know perfectly well how it began, because a boy a couple of years older than I was, when I was seven, was a real woodsman. . . . He'd go to the woods, and take me with him. He was two years older than I, and a hundred years older in experience. Going to the woods was a great escape, because I spent all my summers at my grandfather's farm. Nobody ever came there; he didn't want to see people. He said, "Any man here who opens his mouth, I know every word he's going to say. Why talk to

218

him?" And he lived with his books and so forth, and talked about his adventures in life. I'd go to the woods, or the cane brakes, or swimming holes all summer, and I got the habit of observation. And I continue with my wife. We'll go to the mountains of Vermont, at every opportunity, where we have a place.

Vitale: You were born in Kentucky. Your roots are in the South, in the rural South. As a young man, you were associated with Southern intellectuals, the Fugitives and the Agrarians.
Warren: Well, the Fugitive group, . . . that was my university, . . . grown men with books and things like that, discussing high matters—it was wonderful! That's what a real university should be like. That was my "Classics."

Vitale: And those groups took a stand against industrialization and urbanization?
Warren: Well, the poets weren't much concerned about that. Some of the people there got involved in something else later on, of their own manufacture. They were opposed, I think quite justly, to the excesses and confusions of the modern, mechanized world. Now people who were born into that world and don't know anything else, don't understand that.

Vitale: And how did you feel at that time?
Warren: I was a boy. I wasn't even there at the time that was going on. But they asked me to write an essay on the race question. I was in England then, doing graduate work at Oxford. And I tried to say what I thought. And my view was simply this: that (this was in 1928 or '9, a long time ago)—and this was perfectly legalistic, mind you—that as far as prejudice, the Supreme Court's decision on race at that time, follow it honestly. Separate but equal: I wanted equal, that's all.

Vitale: What was the reaction to that?
Warren: Well, some didn't agree, and some did. Those I was closest to, agreed. The South has always been a very mixed package. When I was a boy, I used the word "nigger" once at home. My father said, "If you go on living under this roof, you're never to use that word again in my presence." And he said, "I don't know a man black or white who, I treated him decently, did not try to treat me decently." My grandfather, who was an officer of the cavalry

under Forrest, said, "I didn't join the Army when it was first talked about, because I didn't want to see the country Balkanized." I never heard the word before, or since. He said, "My folks helped found the country," and they did. And he said, "I didn't want it Balkanized." And he said, "Slavery? Anybody could see that slavery was an outmoded mode of labor." "But," he said, "when they put their feet on Virginia soil, I joined, as a private."

Vitale: So you had a real personal sense of American history.
Warren: Well, I knew something about family, I did, and it was a bookish family. . . . But then I came back to the South in '31, and I was then twenty-five years old. I got the notion that "separate but equal" had proved itself ineffective. Because nowhere was "equal" taken seriously. Anyway, I was in California; I lived there for a couple of years. Orientals were treated like dogs. The Californians would say, "How are the Negroes treated in the South?" Same thing. Another race. And I lost faith in the "equal" business, bit by bit. And then I got very much concerned with the race question later on. I spent several years over this; I wrote two books about it, one called *Segregation*, which is a trip, just a trip I had taken privately here and there in the South, talking to people. This became an article in *Life* magazine.

It wasn't big enough because I got too interested in the question. So I went, or my agent went, to *Look* and made a contract with them. They would pay all expenses for two years or so of travel, and all the expenses of interviewing, and so forth, if I would devote my time to it and mix in some poems, and I was in Mississippi and all over the place and talked to everybody. You can't call Martin Luther King and say, "Let's talk sometime." You say to his secretary, "Look I'm doing a piece for *Look* and I have a contract for a book to come out thereafter." You know what he thought: "Oh, yes!" You couldn't get anyone who wouldn't fall for it, except Malcolm X. But he I got in the end. He was one of the smartest men I ever knew in my life. He sat there with two of his goons, one on each side of him. And he said, "I'll give you ten minutes. You newspapermen are all liars." I said, "I never worked on a newspaper in my life." We stayed there for three hours. He had a real boxer's mentality. He came out always from his corner. He was powerful, you know. And when it got to be three hours, I said, "I got to go now. I'm sorry." And he said, "Come back tomorrow. I got the day off." I was going to Italy the next day. I couldn't go. Too bad. He was killed five months later, in February.

Vitale: Are you still interested in race relations? How do you feel now?
Warren: Well, I see it's a different story now. Now, Malcolm X was partly to blame for that, but not entirely. He had changed his mind in the end, definitely. He said to me, "Muslims"—he was a Black Muslim—"I went to Mecca, as a Muslim you see, and I said, My God, there were people there that had blue eyes and yellow hair!" And so he recanted on the black nationalism. That's why he got killed. Anyway, I just watch things, now. It's just curiosity. It was a sideline; it wasn't my profession. I wanted to be a writer. But meanwhile, poetry had taken over entirely for me. I had been writing mostly fiction, or reading American history. I love American history. But poetry became more and more important.

Vitale: Since the 1950's you've been primarily writing poetry.
Warren: Yes. I had been writing a lot of poetry before, since I was sixteen or seventeen, and took it seriously, or tried to, and had it published a lot by that time. But that last period in the late forties, most short poems would die on me. . . . But it was in the early sixties when my poems first began again. We were living in Italy, Eleanor and I; I got married sometime in the early fifties, and we went to live at a place where she had lived—a fortress on the Mediterranean, ninety miles north of Rome on a seacliff, the sea on three sides and a mountain beyond, and a tremendous view of a Renaissance fortress. . . . And we had a little baby, and the sight of this little baby—a beautiful little yellow-headed kid—I finally wrote a poem about that baby ["Sirocco"] and started all over again. Poems came, and they kept on coming. The next little boy came along the year after, and then the book *Promises* in '56, a book of those poems, was laid in that place; and recollections of my own childhood, and my own world as a child, were in the same book, *Promises*. And the book had success—a Pulitzer Prize, among other things.

Vitale: For many people, you're best known for *All the King's Men*, your novel.
Warren: Oh, that was '45, '46.

Vitale: Yes, I know. You've been writing primarily poetry, and you've written a lot of criticism. How would you evaluate those separate facets of your writing?
Warren: I don't. They're things I wanted to do, that's all. I got interested in them. There was no plan to it. How the interest took hold—how does anyone

know? The poetry was always primary for me, from the start, from fifteen, sixteen, seventeen on. There were things I was interested in and went off and pursued.

Vitale: And you've said elsewhere the idea you want to get across is primary and not the form, that you're fluid. If an idea started out as a poem, you could also express it in fiction.
Warren: Sometimes you start, that's all. *All the King's Men* started out as a verse play. I began under an olive tree, by the side of a wheat field, in Umbria. . . . I finished it by a lake in northern Italy, and in Rome. I sent it to Kenneth Burke and two or three other friends whose opinions I valued, a few days before Christmastime that year, '39. The war had already started by early fall. I got permission to stay in Italy, and I stayed on until they let the refugees out at the end of the war.

But back to *All the King's Men*. . . . Years later (I had discarded it—it didn't succeed), I took it out of a drawer and looked at it again, at the writing. And I thought, "No, this couldn't be a play. That's too cramping." It has to be a novel, because the vague notion in the play was that a man of power isn't a man who has the power to dominate other people, though he has something of that, but he feels some need to have it. They feel in him a frustration to help them. So the play then—the novel then—became something else. You had to populate this whole world to get a sense of him. You couldn't do it in a verse play: that was too tight to read. See what I mean? So, well, Adam: he does things for many people, but what he does for them is always very different. For Jack Burden, a man with no sense of direction—brilliant, but with no sense of direction—he gives him something to *do*. Which he does cynically. It's a form of life for him. He had no ambition, no direction. . . .

Well, it just goes on and, finally, the woman, the other woman, Stark's sister, he seduces her. He gives her something she couldn't have before, some sense, as with her brother, some meaning to life: he brings her that. And all the people around him have the same sense. That's what makes power. It's not being strong; it's knowing instinctively how to use other people, without thinking about it.

Vitale: And how did you get interested in the question of power?
Warren: Well, I had been interested in that before. I had written one novel about it already; it's just been republished. That novel [*At Heaven's Gate*] was

also about politics in another state: Tennessee. But I wasn't writing about Long: I didn't know anything about him. I never saw him in my life—and I never tried to talk to him. I was interested in the myth of Long, not Long himself: I couldn't have cared less.

Vitale: You talked before about nature, about writing what you see. But with politics, that's something else, unless you're observing very carefully.
Warren: Well, I couldn't have cared less about what any individual politician *did*. I was interested in a notion that seemed to be borne out by history, from Caesar on—before that too, really.

Vitale: Did you find that certain forms are better for certain subjects? You talked about *All the King's Men* starting as a verse play and then becoming a novel, because of the situation. But are novels better for writing about power, and poems better for writing about mortality?
Warren: Well, it depends upon what kind of form it is. Now, I wouldn't off-hand make it general like that. It depends on who's doing it, and what. For me, it had to be that way. Now, I don't think I could have written Shakespeare's *Julius Caesar*, for instance. I don't think I'd have been up to it. But in my little play, that later on became a better play and was published and acted several times, were the seeds of the novel that grew slowly out of an idea that I had long before I saw Louisiana. But Long was an example of it, that was the thing: what he meant to people, not what he was. I had no idea what he was like. I'm sure he was a son-of-a-bitch, in many ways.

Vitale: What about literary influences? You've said that you were steeped in Shakespeare when you were young.
Warren: I taught the senior Shakespeare course for seven or eight years in the university. If you want to write, immerse yourself as best you can in the best stuff that's been written.

Vitale: What other writers had powerful influences on your ideas and your own writing?
Warren: Well, it's hard to pick and choose, but I can tell you, all kinds of writers. Folk balladry became very important to me. And at the same time, in the old days, in the country school, some old warhorse of a teacher would make you memorize a poem a week, and stand there and recite it. The poetry

wasn't very good, some of it, sure—Longfellow was one of them; some of them were—but you had to memorize the whole poem—you had to, god-dammit, to pass! And then in college, in freshman English, one day a week—one class a week was taught by somebody else (not the regular teacher, a Brahmin, you know)—you had to memorize that term nothing but Tennyson. You studied Tennyson all term. You had to soak in one man a term of freshman English year. You had to memorize a minimum of 700 lines and prove it. And they had a very tricky way of finding out, too. They gave a bonus for every fifty lines above that. Having been to a country school, I had no trouble memorizing. You get soaked in the poetry of a poem. And then as you get older, you get interested in it. Blake I got soaked in, and Keats, and Donne, the Elizabethans and the Metaphysical poets of that period. Plus the Shakespeare poems. And so, if you liked it you'd go into it—just as simple as that. So your head is full of it. Whether you know it, you find you've picked it up, things you never even knew you picked up.

And now I've tried in classes in universities, advanced students, every year, "Who can quote a poem?" And only one time has anyone ever said, "I can!" and quoted one—a good one—by William Butler Yeats. And this has just drifted out of the world. Except for the poets, I guess. They naturally do it because they want to.

Vitale: Should teachers today encourage learning poetry through recitation?
Warren: Well, I think so. If they're going to teach it at all—go ahead and teach it! You know, a kid doesn't know whether he likes it or not or whether it's interesting or not. My children have been to school in France and every week they had to learn a poem by a good French poet. And I've seen kids catch fire that way. My son did. And I sent him to a French school and he didn't know French—a little bit, maybe. He was only about nine or ten. And he was angry for several months, and then suddenly he loved it; he'd go about and quote poems with me. You get hooked.

Vitale: Is there any particular direction that very recently you find your poetry moving in?
Warren: I can't say that. For one reason, it hasn't crossed my mind to be curious about it, except in individual cases. There are some poems I'm no longer interested in, that I was once mad for. That's bound to happen. And I

certainly wouldn't want to write the same way anymore. I have a new batch of poems—they're too much like the ones here [*New and Selected Poems*]. I'm not going to publish them in a book. You find that self-imitation you've got to guard against all the time, because you've done something that seems to work a little bit, and then you do another just like it. Uh-uh—that's a bad sign. Stop! Start over again! Retool! Give yourself a chance to retool. And you go through that many times. And if you just take a book that's a long time-period collection like this, you can see it. . . . Some poems I have written are in magazines, but I wouldn't put them in a book. They lack a new impulse. You can tell phases. You go through a certain phase and you realize when it's done, as quick as you can. You're just imitating yourself. You can do that trick over and over again, if you want to. Some poets do their whole lives. That's death. Now growth is another thing. You can have the same thing continuing in terms of development; that's one thing. But to repeat yourself in the same old way: that's death. And you have to fight it, all the time.

Vitale: Your work is unique and distinctive. Do you feel allied with any of your contemporaries among the poets?
Warren: Well, I admire a great many of them. It's been a very rich century. There are many fine poets in it. But, again, you have to try to be yourself in some way, and you can say this of all poetry, probably: any poet's work is a long attempt to define himself.

Vitale: Are you satisfied with the definition you've come to?
Warren: Satisfied isn't the word. You do the best you can, period.

Vitale: Do you feel you've got it?
Warren: When you feel you've got it, you're through.

Vitale: You've grown up with the century.
Warren: Well, I was born in 1905, so my awareness didn't begin until 1920, say.

Vitale: But as you say, there's been a lot of fine literature created in your lifetime.
Warren: In my lifetime—I remember when *The Waste Land* was first published. I was a sophomore in college. And there must have been twelve boys in my class who could quote the whole damned thing. . . . And it was unbelievable. None of us, I'm sure, could have written an essay, when it came out,

or analyzed it. But it hit you. This last summer, I read the whole of Eliot's work again, just to be sure how I felt about it. *The Waste Land* still works. Even with all the nonsense and dissemblance about it, it still works. Even though it's a false picture of the universe we live in, that's not the point. He's writing in his own times.

Vitale: And at this point, in the mid-1980s, are you optimistic about the future of English literature and American letters?

Warren: Well, I cross my fingers. We'll see. There are certainly some damned good poets around, right now. I had dinner with two of them in Boston last week; they're quite remarkable. They're both non-Americans—Seamus Heaney and Derek Walcott. Our daughter teaches in Boston, and in fact she's a poet, and she's a friend of theirs, and she had a little dinner when we were there and they were among the guests. And I know their works pretty well and they're both fine poets, very fine poets. I got a lot out of them, personally, too. What an evening! And Richard Eberhart is a poet who's never had his due. He's published so much. And you can't tell one poem from another, in a way, but you don't have to. He's a good poet, marvelous. I hate to say this—on this thing [tape], anyway—because I like him, but I won't take it back—but he is a marvelous poet. I've read his poems since way, way back— my God, fifty-nine years.

Vitale: Well, what do you like in a poem? What's your criteria for what's good in a line when you read it?

Warren: Well, I don't know. Any word I use would be wrong. If I had a line before me, I could say something about any poem, but not a line. You have to have more of a context. But the line itself must fully be what it means. And I'll give you an example. When Antony comes back from the battle after Cleopatra has fled in her own ship—she's just trying to see if he'll follow her. What a witch! And he does. And the battle's gone. The world is gone from his hands, at that moment. Now, in Shakespeare's play, Antony says, "Unarm, Eros, the long day's task is done and we must sleep." Listen how it goes: the line gives the emotion of what is said, in words: "And we must sleep." See how the line flattens out? It says what it means: it *is* what it means. The isness of meaning is what the purpose of a line of a poem should be.

Index